# HOGAN

Other books by the author:

*Texas Golf Legends*

*The Eternal Summer: Palmer, Hogan, and Nicklaus in 1960, Golf's Golden Year*

*Full Court Pressure*

# HOGAN

## CURT SAMPSON

BROADWAY BOOKS / NEW YORK

**BROADWAY**

This book was originally published in 1996 by Rutledge Hill Press. It is here reprinted by arrangement with Rutledge Hill Press.

Broadway Books titles may be purchased for business or promotional use or for special sales. For information, please write to: Special Markets Department, Bantam Doubleday Dell Publishing Group, Inc., 1540 Broadway, New York, NY 10036.

BROADWAY BOOKS and its logo, a letter B bisected on the diagonal, are trademarks of Broadway Books, a division of Bantam Doubleday Dell Publishing Group, Inc.

*First Broadway Books trade paperback edition published 1997.*

ISBN 0-553-06194-1

97  98  99  00  01  10  9  8  7  6  5  4  3  2  1

*To caddies*

# CONTENTS

# ACKNOWLEDGMENTS

A small army of people helped with this book. The generals in the army were Jim Donovan, president of Jim Donovan Literary in Dallas; Mike Towle and Lawrence Stone of Rutledge Hill Press; and my family—Cheryl, Clay, and John.

Author John Strawn, Texas Golf Hall of Fame curator Frances Trimble, and historians Peter Bown, Dan Greenwood, and Mike Brown dropped whatever they were doing when I called for help and advice, and I am extremely grateful to them.

Invaluable medical insights were provided by Dr. Fran Pirozzolo, Dr. Cheryl Sampson, Dr. Craig Farnsworth, Dr. Rob Hillery, Dr. Greg Pearl, Dr. Rob Rutledge, and Sylvia Foladare.

Among the golf professionals whose help and insight I depended on were Byron Nelson, Jack Nicklaus, Jay Hebert, Herman Keiser, Jackson Bradley, Henry Picard, Jack Burke Jr., Sam Snead, Jack Fleck, Don January, Ken Venturi, Freddie Hawkins, Frank Wharton, Hal Underwood, Tod Menefee, Shawn Humphries, Gilbert Freeman, Jimmy Gauntt, Larry Box, Mike Morrow, and Dan Strimple.

David Hueber, Gene Sheeley, Elgin Berry, Jerry Austry, and Charles Harris of the Ben Hogan Company explained Hogan the businessman, eloquently and affectionately.

Guy Yocom of *Golf Digest*, whose knowledge of Hogan is unsurpassed, was wonderfully open with his opinions and information. Jim Frank and Mike Purkey of *Golf* magazine helped get me started—and finished. Herbert Warren Wind, the Shakespeare of golf writers, was kind and helpful as usual. Jim Apfelbaum, the Sam Levenson of golf writers, spent an entire day finding and reading *Follow the Sun* star Glenn Ford's autobiography. It turned out to be about gardening. Rare golf book dealer Dick Donovan ferreted out facts I would never have found on my own.

I also appreciate the help of Robert Atkinson Jr., Marte Bassi, Troy Baxter, Tom W. Blake, Jon Bradley, Hal Brewer, Walter Buenger, John Capers, Nancy Castiglione, Bill Cowan, Mike Daniels, Burt Darden, John David, John Derr, Lester Epps, Bill Gray, Gaylen and Sally Groce, Merle Hancock, Johnny Henry, Francisca Hernandez, Frances Hirsh, Blake Hodges, Carolyn Holden, Clem Jensen, David Johnson, Julie Ketterer, Joy Lynn King, Chuck Kocsis, Mike Kondrat, Mary Margaret Lashbrook Kowalski, Christy Krames, Bo Links, Mike and Mary Long, Margaret Maves, Janet Maynard, Chris Millard, Ed Moughon, Tim Murphy, Barbara K. Ordway, Tom Otteson, David Parker, Russ Pate, James Peebles, Ann Peeler, Steve Pike, Jim Reed, Matty Reed, Bob Rickey, Dennis Roberson, Judy Ross, John H. Sampson, Robert and Ann Sampson, Bill Sebelin, Tom Steinhardt, Carlton Stowers, Jerre Todd, Peter Walsh, and Bob William.

Ladies and gentlemen, thank you.

# INTRODUCTION

Ben Hogan hit golf balls until his hands bled. How many hundreds of times did I hear that when I was a kid?

The first time I heard it must have been at the overgrazed public course a few miles from our house. One of the regulars, Ed Romito or Bernie Washko or Jim Lacina, or the pro, Bill Shoaf, would spot me as I walked from the rock-strewn practice range to the putting green, a putter in one hand, a Mr. Frosty root beer in the other, and three or four of my best balls in my back pocket. They knew I was mesmerized by golf.

They all smoked. "You know," Ed or Bernie or Jim or Bill would say, exhaling blue clouds, "Hogan used to hit balls until his hands bled."

The Christlike image of bleeding hands on a golf club hit me and stuck, a fly on the mental flypaper of a fourteen-year-old boy. What manner of man or madman or masochist or golf messiah would torture himself like that? Should golf be practiced until it hurt? I began to believe it should. Blood seeped from my knuckles as I hit more and more balls—not really such a big deal, as I bleed easily. But I got the attitude, too. I became (I thought) cold, implacable, unflappable, a golf-ball-hitting machine. "Hogan still hits the ball better than anyone else in the world," the four wise men told me, clicking shut their Zippos, blowing their smoke. "But he can't putt." I couldn't either.

Yesterday, twenty-nine years later, I hit balls with Ben Hogan's clubs. It felt like clacking out a paragraph on Hemingway's typewriter—a delicious, guilty, and totally unauthorized pleasure. Strange sticks, too. The rough-textured cord grips are significantly oversized and turned slightly counterclockwise. The heads are very heavy, with two-degree flat lies that remind you of hockey sticks. The twelve custom-made putters he was trying the last time he played or practiced all have the length, lie, and grip of his six-iron, and all have lead tape, for added weight, under the grips. The most unusual of the putters has little sighting devices epoxied to the top of the offset brass blade, like the eye pods on a hammerhead shark. From the crest of the hill on the eighth fairway at Shady Oaks Country Club in Fort Worth, I hit Ben Hogan's one-iron and his black, wooden three-wood, trying to imitate his flat, ferocious slash and the gentle left-to-right curvature of his shots. Then I stabbed a few putts with one of his weird putters. Seven hundred yards away, Hogan sat in his customary chair by the window in the Men's Grill, a cold, implacable, unflappable old man eating lunch.

Purists, the golf world's most influential subset, have long regarded Hogan with an almost religious awe. Here was a man who let his clubs do his talking. His clothes and equipment were uncluttered by logos, his swing a work of art. Check the office walls of Ben Crenshaw, Jack Burke Jr., or any of a thousand other defenders of the traditional game of golf, and you will find the same photograph: Hogan in a mythic pose, following through after drilling a one-iron shot to the final green at the 1950 U.S. Open at Merion. He was in terrific pain at that moment, and you can almost make out the bandages on his legs. Some visitors to Shady Oaks watch him eat while pretending not to, like lonely boys in the high school cafeteria, stealing glances while the homecoming queen nibbles her baloney and cheese. But that's as close as you get because the first rule for a guest at Shady Oaks is to leave Mr. Hogan the hell alone.

Few sports figures have engendered this reverential awe, a respect so heightened we call it "the Hogan mystique." His myth derives from far more than mere popularity. The milestones in his life—his failure, his triumph, the accident that nearly killed him, the comeback, and his Secret—resonate like the stations of the cross. Hogan's fierceness overlaid a great dignity and an instinctive nobility, similar to an unlikely near-contemporary, Indian religious leader Mahatma Gandhi. Before he made the movie of Gandhi's life, Sir Richard Attenborough was asked to consider using a point of light instead of an actor to represent Gandhi. That's the way Hogan's devotees think of him, as a symbol of perfection rather than a man, his commitment to golf pure and undefiled. And to hell with any of that feet of clay stuff.

Yet those whose interest wants more depth and less adulation feel unrequited and slightly troubled by the standard Hogan epic. Anyone who has thought at all about Hogan knows something is missing. While some things about him are known absolutely—he hit balls until his hands bled—so little is really comprehended. The standard golf library won't solve the mystery. There are thirty-six titles by or about Hogan's contemporary, Sam Snead, and thirty on Bobby Jones, who retired from competition in 1930, but there are just five Hogan-related books, and two of them are instructionals written by the man himself: *Power Golf* (1948) and *Five Lessons: The Modern Fundamentals of Golf* (1957). The Jack Nicklaus section contains forty-five volumes and the Arnold Palmer shelf bears forty-six. Hogan's life is memorialized in two protective, sketchy biographies, the more recent written almost twenty years ago. A later coffee table book, *The Hogan Mystique*, polishes the myth rather than looking at the man.

Some of the men who presumably knew him best remain baffled by him to this day. Henry Picard, a contemporary on the tour, was puzzled when Hogan dedicated his first book to him. "Picard is one of my best friends in professional golf," Hogan wrote. "We weren't at all close then or now," Picard says. "Ben and I hardly know each other, even today." Writer and golf historian Herbert Warren Wind worked with Hogan extensively on *Five Lessons*, which was an immediate and enduring bestseller. But he claims no insights into his collaborator, other than to observe, "He was a very odd man." Gene Gregston, author of *Hogan: The Man Who Played for Glory* (1978), says that, as the golf writer for the *Fort Worth Star-Telegram* from 1948 to 1958, he knew Hogan "very well," but the biographer and his subject had not spoken for years before the book was published, did not do so during the writing of it, nor have they since. "No, Hogan didn't cooperate," Gregston says tightly. "No, don't tell him hello for me."

Hogan picked apart everything that was written about him and found almost all of it inaccurate. For a time he took a perverse pleasure in telling writers in blunt terms how stupidly wrong they were. Later he wouldn't bother to correct the mistakes, even the basic and often-repeated ones such as where he was born, his middle name, and who his friends were. "I can't say anything," he complained privately. "Everything I say gets blown up." He spoke so infrequently with writers or for the camera that an interview with him became an event. There was the *Time* magazine cover in 1949, the *Golf Digest* feature in 1970, Ken Venturi throwing home run pitches in a CBS interview in 1983, the *Golf* magazine Q and A in 1987, and the truncated chat with ESPN in 1991. "He would answer questions carefully, politely, and quietly," wrote Pat Ward-Thomas of the *London Guardian* of a talk they had in 1965, "but always with a full stop at the end, as if wary of the ebb and flow of ordinary conversation."

He was as mysterious to his colleagues on the tour as he was to the press. "Hogan and I played lots of practice rounds together," says Freddie Hawkins, a pro from Illinois who joined the tour in 1947. "I knew him as well as anyone. But I didn't really know him." Sam Snead, Byron Nelson, Shelley Mayfield, Gus Moreland, and practically everyone else he competed with tells you the same thing: "Knew him. Didn't really know him."

But what Hogan might anyone claim to know? From a distance his life looks like a patchwork quilt, with some matching or complementary squares and others that clash and contradict. In one patch he is a bewildered nine-year-old boy standing nearby as his father shoots and kills himself. In another he is a kid with a downturned mouth looking for an excuse to punch another paperboy or caddie or schoolmate. In a third he rides down Broadway in flurries of ticker tape, perched above the back seat of a big black Chrysler convertible, America's conquering hero. "That little bastard," was about the nicest thing a lot of people had to say about him. "Finest gentleman I ever knew," said others. Hollywood made a movie of his life, a compliment not bestowed on Churchill, Eisenhower, or Arnold Palmer. But the movie and the parade were expressions of admiration and respect, not of love and affection. How could you love a man who made it plain he didn't give a shit what you thought of him?

"I could [*sic*] care less," he said in 1970 about his reputation as a cold, machinelike person. "I get along with everybody I know. . . . Life's too short for me to go around explaining myself. A lot of people don't understand modesty. Not everybody wants publicity, you know." But by daring to become great at a game, Hogan exchanged his natural right to privacy for a certain amount of wealth and notoriety, a deal with the devil he struggled with all his life.

He had always been secretive. Nelson, who practically grew up with him, didn't know the tragic circumstances of the death of Hogan's father until he read about it in a book in 1992. Hogan sometimes intentionally misled writers and the curious, and made a fetish of his secrets and a publicity bonanza out of his secret—"the Secret"—the key to perfect ball-striking.

"I've always had the feeling he was laughing at us," *Golf* magazine editor Jim Frank says.

"I think he secretly enjoyed exploiting his legend," agrees Guy Yocom of *Golf Digest*. " '*I try to hit it on the third groove.*' He couldn't have been serious."

The widely held presumption that he was infallible on anything related to golf brought out an amused cynicism in him. An example of what former Hogan Company president David Hueber calls "managing the mystique" occurred when then-PGA tour commissioner Deane Beman sat in the visitor's chair in front of Hogan's desk, and the talk turned to how much farther the modern golf ball flies compared to the old one. Hogan's lower lip came up. "You know, if I were playing today, I'd play Surlyn."

Beman's mouth opened. Surlyn is a hard plastic golf-ball-cover material. Virtually all serious players use balata, a softer, rubberlike compound.

"Why, Mr. Hogan, why would you use Surlyn?" Beman asked.

Pause.

"Because it's better."

"But why is it better?" Beman pleaded.

Longer pause.

"I'm not telling."

Obfuscation in all things, even trivial ones. "Many golf fans are surprised to learn that I learned to play golf left-handed when I first took up the game," Hogan wrote in 1948 in *Power Golf*. "I changed over when I was a small boy. The only clubs I could get were right-handed. Moreover, most of the fellows I played with then were very convincing in telling me that left-handers never made good golfers. At that age I was gullible enough to believe them and to make the change, but I wouldn't now."

"So," an interviewer asked him in 1987, "you were left-handed?"

Hogan replied, "No, that's one of those things that's always been written, but it's an absolute myth. The truth is, the first golf club I owned was an old left-handed, wooden-shafted, rib-faced mashie." His explanations were often meant to mystify.

Myths and undenied misinformation were accepted as fact. He didn't care. And he didn't turn pro when he was nineteen, as he had always allowed us to believe. He was seventeen. The middle name is Ben, not Benjamin, and he was born in Stephenville, Texas, not Dublin, Texas. He was an excellent amateur golfer and at least pretty good as a young pro, not the duck-hooking dud as he was usually portrayed. He did not adore his British Open experience or Augusta National. Jimmy Demaret was supposed to be his great friend; he wasn't.

If you don't mind waiting, you can get his autograph, although he might require the obviously mercenary to make a donation to the SPCA in lieu of payment. Although he seemed incredibly stoic, when under stress he showed a bizarre nervous habit: repeated grunting, as if he couldn't get his throat cleared. He didn't react to poorly hit shots, but mis-clubs made him furious. He never walked off yardages and didn't care where the 150-yard markers were.

He never fully recovered from the accident that almost killed him in 1949. Pain enveloped him like a second skin for more than half his life. He abhorred cheapening his name, but he didn't blow off every endorsement opportunity. He pitched Pabst Blue Ribbon beer, coffee (for the Pan

American Coffee Bureau), Toro lawn mowers, Timex watches, MacGregor clubs, Slazenger balls, and, appropriately for one of the world's foremost chain smokers, cigarettes: "I've been a Chesterfield smoker for seven years. I know they're best for me. Try them yourself, " said a 1953 print ad, quoting "Ben Hogan, World's Greatest Golfer."

Opposites attracted him. The grim, gray man's partner in team competitions was golf's most garishly dressed extrovert, "Sunny" Jim Demaret. His favorite writer was a frequently hilarious smart aleck and Fort Worth homeboy named Dan Jenkins. He liked a fistfight and he liked to dance. He attended church for much of his life, but what Ben Hogan believed in most was Ben Hogan. He swore like a marine—or like a typical golf pro—and in his later years drank like a sailor, yet he never gave offense and was in fact obsessed with correctness in comportment, clothing, and speech. At times Hogan was the most polite man you ever met, but at others one of the world's greatest putdown artists.

"You might as well be doing calisthenics," he told a competitor who bragged about how hard he had been practicing.

Nick Faldo asked him for the secret to winning the U.S. Open. "Shoot the lowest score," Hogan said.

"Hi, Mr. Hogan! I read your book—but it didn't help me much," a smiling stranger said in the dining room at Colonial, his right hand extended. "Better read it again," Hogan said, ignoring the hand and continuing his slow, limping walk to his table.

Opposites: He was both rude and polite, desperately poor and quite wealthy, and prouder of having been poor than of his money. His beautiful, ten-tooth smile helped make him the most photogenic athlete around, but a look into his opaque gray blue eyes made even the strongest men uneasy. He failed miserably and repeatedly, then succeeded beyond imagining. No public person since Greta Garbo was more private. That of course only increased the clamor for his time, his attention, or his autograph. He was short with fans and the press—especially anyone with a camera—yet late in life he had become quite affable. After decades of hearing our questions and not answering them, he knew us better than we knew him.

If getting a handle on how the various Hogans were stitched together is a puzzle, the immediate problem is in finding someone to solve the mystery. Hogan will not explain himself and never has, as the paucity of books about him and interviews with him prove. And now it is too late. Age has caused the memories to fly away one at a time or in little groups, like birds leaving a power line. "I don't remember, I don't remember," he says when cornered by the inquisitive.

Perhaps psychology provides the common thread. "Losing his father like he did must have had a tremendous impact," says Dallas-based counselor Sylvia Foladare, who often treats the survivors of suicide. "[In general] If the child doesn't have a support system, there's a loss of the capacity for intimacy and trust. There's increased detachment and bitterness. The child often becomes a loner. A lot of them I see become workaholics, much like the overachieving children of alcoholics. There's usually a lot of guilt, too, especially for children. . . . And when the means of accomplishment goes away, the survivors of suicide often turn to drugs or alcohol."

All of this might apply in Hogan's case in varying degrees, but a single event does not explain a life, certainly not Hogan's. A single psychologist may be inadequate to explain the complex web of his mind and emotions. Like Ted Williams, the moody, perfectionistic baseball player to whom he was often compared, Hogan had an active relationship with an alter ego. Williams had silent conversations with an invisible friend named Teddy Ballgame. Hogan often referred unashamedly to the little man on his shoulder he called Hennie Bogan. Both were lonely boys with weak or absent fathers. The boys' imaginary playmates nagged them to work harder, accomplish more, practice longer. Both turned pro before they were old enough to vote. Neither could abide a stupid question from a writer. And each worked harder at his respective sport than anyone else before or since.

Batting practice was nothing new in baseball, of course, but Hogan virtually invented practice in golf. Was his incessant drilling a symptom of something else? Maybe. In his book *Obsessive Compulsive Disorders*, Steven Levenkron writes, "These repeated activities, or rituals, are actually self-soothing devices used to fill an emotional emptiness caused by underparenting or impaired receptivity to parenting in early childhood. What is the magic of repetition? Repetition brings familiarity, and familiarity is the opposite of the unknown."

Hogan seems to fill the obsessive thinking and compulsive behavior bill in a variety of ways, especially in his disconnection from others and his preoccupation with his rituals. As for the cause, no one is sure if nature or nurture is to blame.

Another aspect of Hogan's behavior might take it *out* of the realm of OCD. The actions of the compulsive hand washer or dieter or worker or shopper or underwear changer are ultimately pointless, but Hogan's behavior was anything but that. His main rituals were purposeful. No indecisive wretch in the throes of a disorder ever had Hogan's bulletproof confidence. His perfection of the world's least perfectible game was not a disease; it was a triumph. His single-mindedness turned the negatives of his past into a future filled with glory. Inquiry into how he did it has been a cottage industry for years, but unfortunately, it leads right back to where you started.

"Why did you practice so much?" he was asked in his TV interviews in '83 and '91.

"I had to. My swing was so bad."

"Is that all?"

"No," he allowed. "I loved it."

*Why* he loved the brain- and back-numbing torture of nonstop drill he does not say. Was practice a shield against his fear of failure that was the same as his fear of the past? If he hit five hundred balls, was he five hundred steps closer to a future faultlessness? Was the practice tee an oasis of control in a world of chaos? Hogan does not say.

"I have baseball players come up to me in the middle of a game and tell me about the anger they have toward their fathers," says neurologist and sports psychologist Dr. Fran Pirozzolo, who has devoted a good chunk of his life to the study of the Hogan psyche. "I think Hogan felt the same way. Everything he did was a response to the loss of his father: his mistrust of any male; his need to achieve; his becoming this distrustful, cynical semanticizer. I think you could give him *ten* U.S. Open trophies and he would be the same way.

"On the other hand, his story was tremendously positive. He was a survivor. The adversity he faced led directly to his achievement. And he always took the high road."

Perhaps no one aspect of his life or personality illuminates all the others. Maybe those in search of Hogan should recall a couple of those cryptic remarks for which he was so famous. "I dug it out of the ground," he said when he was asked how he developed his golf game. On another occasion he grew weary of the postround questioning from a semicircle of sportswriters. "Someday a deaf-mute will win a golf tournament and you guys won't be able to write a story," he announced.

These two quotations might be Hogan's advice for those who seek his life story. Because he never bared his soul to anyone, especially not to anyone with a notebook or a tape recorder, inquiring minds will have to figure out Hogan for themselves. He won't do your work for you and his private life is none of your damn business anyway. So if you must know Ben Hogan, you have to get your knowledge the way he got his—dig it out of the ground.

# HOGAN

# CHAPTER 1

# BLACKSMITH'S BOY

I FEEL SORRY FOR RICH KIDS NOW. I REALLY DO. BECAUSE THEY'RE
NEVER GOING TO HAVE THE OPPORTUNITY I HAD. BECAUSE I KNEW
TOUGH THINGS. AND I HAD A TOUGH DAY *ALL MY LIFE* AND I CAN
HANDLE TOUGH THINGS. THEY CAN'T. AND EVERY DAY THAT I PRO-
GRESSED WAS A JOY TO ME AND I RECOGNIZED IT EVERY DAY. I
DON'T THINK I COULD HAVE DONE WHAT I'VE DONE IF I HADN'T
HAD THE TOUGH DAYS TO BEGIN WITH.
—BEN HOGAN

THOSE HOGANS ARE FUNNIER THAN HELL.
—DAN GREENWOOD

Two huge oaks spread their limbs over the tiny
gravel-strewn lot in Dublin, Texas, that once held William
Alexander Hogan's blacksmith shop. Now it's as blank as the
look on a cow's face, but back then it was noisy, dirty, and ex-
citing. A little corral contained newly shoed or waiting-to-
be-shod horses, and the grandchildren learned to ride. The
father and son worked next to the pen, inside a long, narrow,
wooden building with big doors, like those on a barn. In it
were pyramids of coal on a dirt floor, black clouds of coal

1

smoke, the hiss of hot metal in a cooling tank, muscular men in leather aprons clanging sledgehammers on metal, and heat—preposterous heat—billowing out from the forge and down from the God-awful Texas summer sun.

Dublin is a simple, peaceful town of three to four thousand near the geographical center of Texas, about eighty miles southwest of Fort Worth. It sits on the scenic northern edge of the Balcones Escarpment, a geological oddity of limestone outcroppings and hills that runs all the way to Mexico. *Old Yeller*, the book by Fred Gipson later made into a movie by Walt Disney, was set in Mason, which is one hundred miles farther southwest, although Dublin would have worked as a setting just as well. It was still relatively wild and new when the Hogans settled there after the Civil War. At least it was new for white men and women, because Comanche, Kiowa, and Lipan Indians had lived in the area for untold centuries. "Double in the wagons! Indians a-comin'!" is supposed to be the phrase that gave the town its name. On the other hand, one of the founding fathers was G. W. O'Neal, who might have been honoring the capital city of his native Ireland when he named the place around 1858.

The Hogans were Irish, too. After Europe, most of Ben Hogan's forebears lived in the American South. His father's father, the blacksmith William Alexander Hogan, was born in Choctaw County, Mississippi, in 1847. When William was sixteen, soldiers from the Seventh Illinois Cavalry riding south from Tennessee passed within a few miles of his home. Those who were "wiry and active enough," as one Confederate general put it, were deemed good candidates to chase and fight the invaders on horseback. Young William fit the description, so he enlisted in the First Mississippi Cavalry Reserves on September 30, 1863. During the first two years of the conflict, the Southern cavalry had fought the North to a draw. "War suits them," wrote Union Maj. Gen. William Tecumseh Sherman in reluctant admiration of the Mississippi

2

cavalrymen. "The rascals are brave, fine riders, bold to rash-
ness and dangerous in every sense." Vicksburg fell on July 4,
1863, and the war's hot spots moved east. William Hogan left
the Confederate army on June 18, 1864, as he had entered it,
a private and unhurt.

William married after the war. Cinthia J. Hogan, born
in 1843 in Alabama, was an older woman—twenty-two to her
husband's eighteen—at the time of their marriage. They remained in Choctaw County in Mississippi's north-central hills
to raise cotton on rented land. Tenant cotton farmers such as
the Hogans lived a miserable life. Regardless of family size,
shelter was a three- or four-room wooden box owned, naturally, by the landlord. And because food crops mature during
the same season as cotton, and because the owners didn't
want their land planted with anything that didn't earn cash,
growing corn or cabbage to eat was virtually impossible. So
the tenant farmers lived on canned goods bought at fancy
prices at the commissary. In effect, they were white slaves.

Even more damaging to the spirit than the work, the
heat, or the inadequate food and shelter was the paltry financial reward for all the suffering. Choctaw County was not the
greatest place for cotton. They had planted it in every other
part of the state—except in the malaria- and flood-filled
Delta—before farmers moved into the hills in and around
Choctaw County in the 1830s. The poor upland soil there
was soon exhausted by the land-deteriorating crop, and erosion finally melted the ground away. Add to this the postwar
economic depression and the necessity of paying the landlord
his one-quarter or one-third cut of the crop, and the picture
becomes even more bleak. In 1870, William Hogan estimated
his net worth at five hundred dollars. His real estate holdings
were zero.

Not surprisingly, the Hogans left Mississippi some
time after 1870, part of a significant westward migration from
the former slave states. "GTT"—Gone to Texas—was

scrawled on countless abandoned dwellings throughout the Southeast. William and Cinthia led their four children on the five-hundred-mile trek to Dublin. The Hogan children had started to arrive in 1867. By 1870 there were four: William, Josephine, Martha, and Mary had been born within three years of each other, all in Mississippi. The fifth, and last, child was born in Dublin on February 2, 1885, when Cinthia was forty-two. They named the boy Chester C., perhaps after the outgoing president of the United States, jowly, mutton-chopped Chester A. Arthur.

In Texas, William Alexander Hogan gave up farming for the blacksmith trade, which he had been exposed to during his cavalry days. He taught the skill to Chester, who joined him in the business. The bulk of the Hogans' work came from the cotton industry, which had moved west along with all those people from the Old South. Over time Dublin had grown to where it had five gins, a large compress, a cottonseed mill, and a cotton futures exchange. Cotton and cattle had been the area's economic mainstay since the Indians left in 1870. But in 1891 Dublin grabbed an identity quite distinct from Duffau, Blanket, and a hundred other Central Texas cow towns. That was when Sam Houston Prim, a former bookstore owner from Sulphur Springs, Texas, moved to town. Bookstores sold fountain drinks back then, and Prim had noticed that a new concoction made in Waco was winning converts. So he seized the opportunity to start the world's first Dr Pepper bottling plant, using an L-shaped stucco building in Dublin's star-shaped downtown. Prim's plant was just a block down Elm Street from the blacksmith shop. Once the enterprise got a little momentum, Mr. Prim went out and hired Chester Hogan.

Chester and the other two members of the production staff—Prim's brother and a nephew—rinsed out the empties with cold water; refilled them using hoses through which flowed a mixture of pure cane sugar, carbonated water, and

Chester Hogan, Ben Hogan's father, is pictured in the foreground working at a Dr Pepper plant in Dublin, Texas. The resemblance between father and son is striking. (Photo courtesy of Bill Kloster)

Dr Pepper syrup; and stuck in wire corks that went "pop" when extracted. About twelve hundred bottles a day was the maximum output. Chester Hogan bottled Dr Pepper for a brief time, probably less than two years, before he returned to the family blacksmith business.

Many years later, in 1955, the *Dublin Progress* found a photograph of this turn-of-the-century bottling operation and ran it on the front page of its July 8 edition. Chester Hogan, then about twenty, stood in the foreground, straight-backed and unsmiling. Except for around the eyes, he looked identical to his second son, yet unborn. Ben Hogan had never seen the picture before, so he wrote two of his typically careful and correct letters to the newspaper:

> I would be most appreciative if you would furnish me, at my expense, a glossy print of the original of this picture at your earliest possible convenience.
>> Thanking you for your cooperation, I am
>> Sincerely
>> Ben Hogan

Then:

> I would like to express my appreciation to you for your time and effort in getting this for me. Incidentally, you failed to advise the expense incurred.
>> I must admit my memory of those days [in Dublin] is very vague.
>> With all good wishes and personal regards,
> I am
>> Sincerely
>> Ben Hogan

In neither letter did he identify himself as the son of the man in the picture. With one exception, in 1949, this was the only correspondence Hogan had with the city of his birth after he left it in 1921.

"He severed all ties with this town," says Carolyn Holden, Dublin's librarian. "He even buried his mother up in Fort Worth. I guess it [Dublin] held such bad memories for him." Actually, Hogan kept one connection with Dublin: He and his brother still own the little lot where the blacksmith shop once stood.

His mother's maiden name was Clara Williams. Her family had also followed the slave-state migration west. Clara's paternal grandfather had been born in North Carolina and her grandmother in Mississippi. The couple moved west to Louisiana and in November 1855 gave birth to their son, Ben H. Williams. Ben H. was married in 1886 at age thirty or thirty-one, which was considered late in life to be jumping the broom in a culture where teenagers routinely married and when the average American lived only into his midforties. Ben and his wife had five children: Willie, Sam, Clara (born in August 1890, in Dublin), Thomas, and May.

Clara's father was a cotton buyer, a middleman between the growers and the thread or clothing factories. He bought the dirty white bales by the hundreds as summer turned to fall, when random bits of cotton filled the air like snow flurries. The Williams family lived in town in a rented house on Grafton Street, just a few blocks away from the blacksmith shop.

Despite standing only about five-foot-three, Clara was substantial, almost imposing. Her fastidiousness about her appearance, combined with her coal black hair, a beaklike nose, and the blue gray mirrors of her eyes, hinted at her strength. Clara was a laugher and a talker; thin, handsome Chester was quiet. Neither Dublin, nor Erath County, nor neighboring Comanche County has a record of their marriage, a curiosity which leads to the intriguing possibility that the couple had eloped.

Clara was eighteen and Chester twenty-three when they began to have babies. Royal Dean, a son, was born in 1908. He looked like his father and was relaxed around people, just as his mother was. Chester Princess, a girl, came along two years later. Their third and last child, another boy, was delivered by Dr. J. J. Mulloy on August 13, 1912, at the hospital in nearby Stephenville. That was slightly unusual as most children in those days were born at home. The baby had his mother's nose and her striking blue gray eyes. They didn't name him right away, for where do you go after Royal and Chester Princess? Finally, they named the boy for his grandfathers—William Ben Hogan.

"I knew all three of the Hogan kids," says Troy Baxter, a lifelong Dublin resident. "I was between Royal and Ben in age. . . . We played baseball together at the school. Royal was the pitcher, I was the catcher. Bennie was our pigtail [he chased down the balls the catcher missed], which I guess he didn't like too much. We never played any golf. There were no golf courses around here.

"Princess was very talented in singing. We had a vaudeville place above Novit's Department Store and she sang there and was in some plays, too. Touring companies would come here and perform two or three nights, and they'd get local people to perform with them. I saw Royal downtown once while I was at TCU [Texas Christian University in Fort Worth] between 1928 and 1932, but I never did run into Ben. He was likable. I never had no problems with him."

Retired Dublin postal employee William Cowan sounds a similar defensive note: "Lots of people here think he snubbed his hometown. I never thought that." As postmaster and president of the chamber of commerce, Cowan tried hard to preserve and commemorate Hogan's birthplace with either a brass plaque by the front door or a sign on the highway. The owner of the house was happy to oblige, but no one else, including Hogan, was interested. The frame house was subsequently razed for a brick one. No one in town today can pinpoint exactly where the Hogans lived. "Over on Post Oak or Camden," the old-timers say vaguely, "close to the high school, maybe a little north of it." At last there is Merle Landers Hancock, who now resides in the Dublin Nursing

Center but who long ago lived down the street from the Hogans. "Their house was at the corner of Camden and East Harris," she says confidently. "Just a little square bungalow."

Clayton Barbee lives there now, at 503 North Camden, in a brick house under a green umbrella of huge pecan trees. He had had another passing connection with the Hogans back before 1920. A farm boy, Barbee occasionally brought broken plow tools on a horse-drawn wagon to Hogan's blacksmith shop. Several times he saw young Ben in there conversing with his father. One day Chester introduced the two boys, but they did not become friends, Barbee says, because he was several years older than Ben.

Dublin was a shady oasis amid the cotton fields. The neighborhood hangout was a water well in the back yard of the big house across the street from the Hogans. Another magnet was the open-air movie theater downtown, where twenty-five cents bought a bag or two of popcorn and a ticket to sit on a wooden bench to watch silent film stars such as Chaplin, Keaton, and Valentino. On weekends, townspeople rode out to the country to buy fresh eggs and butter.

"I'll tell you a funny story," Cowan says. "After Chester died, a Mr. Holland bought the blacksmith business and decided to move it to another location. The building started to lean when he'd moved everything out except the forge. While he was trying to move it, the building fell on him and killed him. This was in 1927 or 1928."

After forty years in Dublin, the Hogans left the town in June 1921 for Fort Worth. It is uncertain if the Hogan children had ever been to the big city before, although Cowtown had a new attraction that was drawing people from many miles away—the Leonard Brothers Department Store. The Leonard brothers, Marvin and Obie, had invented the superstore—everything for the home, farm, or ranch under one roof. Fort Worth also had indoor movie theaters, of course, an electric train between Fort Worth and Dallas called the

Interurban, and a thousand other things you couldn't find in
Dublin. But the Hogans did not leave the rural life for the
shopping and the excitement in the city. They moved because
Chester suffered from an illness no country doctor was
equipped to handle. He was so mentally ill that Clara felt forced
to put him in a sanatorium. The closest one was in Fort Worth.

Those few people in Dublin who remember Chester
Hogan do not recall him acting crazily, but they were just
children when Chester became noticeably ill around January 1921. He was quiet, they say, a man of good character,
but they never saw him much. Doctors hate to diagnose
from a distance, but those who have examined the record
say with certainty that Chester suffered from depression.
He endured it in hopeless silence, and when in its black grip
he found no joy in his job, his family, or himself. He
thought about death, and at times he was unable to work.
He drank.

Two scraps of evidence suggest that Chester's sickness
was not the unipolar disorder depression but the two-sided
disease known as manic depression. Friends of his in Dublin
commented on his "unusually good spirits" just two days before he died, and the impulsive way he took his life was typical of the recklessness and grandiosity of mania.

Mental illnesses are often as biologically and chemi-
cally based as heart disease or the mumps, but the enduring
misconception is that mental disease is as inexplicable and
shameful as suicide. Demaret mentioned neither in his book:
"On a bleak February day," he wrote, "Ben and his mother
had to drive Chester Hogan to Fort Worth and put him in a
hospital, where he died shortly afterward." What really happened was a good deal darker.

Valentine's Day 1922 was cold and cloudy and a slow
news day—"Shoe Dealers Begin Annual Meeting Here" was
the lead headline in the *Fort Worth Record*. "Babe Ruth
Holding out for $75,000" was the big story in the sports

section. But in the center of the bottom third of the front page was a shocking headline: "Child of 6 Sees His Father Shot." The *Record* article said:

> No one was in the room with Hogan at the time, excepting his six-year-old son, who was playing on the floor. His wife and two other children were in an adjoining room when they heard the shot, and rushing in, they found Hogan on the floor with a smoking revolver by his side. . . . The bullet, fired from a .38-caliber revolver, entered Hogan's body just above the heart and passed through, coming out below the left shoulder blade. It was stated by physicians at the hospital that while his condition is critical he has good chances for recovery.

But Chester Hogan was already dead when the paper hit the street, twelve days after his thirty-seventh birthday, eleven and a half hours after his final act.

The account of the tragedy in the Dublin paper undoubtedly came from Clara and is misleading. Who was in the room when her husband fired the gun? Was it Bennie, age nine, or Royal, age fourteen?

DEATH OF CHESTER HOGAN
*The Dublin Progress,* February 17, 1922

Chester Hogan, thirty-seven and well-known resident of Dublin for many years, came to death by his own hand at Fort Worth last Monday evening at 6:30.

11

The family had moved to Fort Worth in August of last year, expecting to make their home there, but Mr. Hogan returned to Dublin a month ago and reopened a blacksmith shop, in which business he has been successfully engaged in practically all his life. Saturday he returned to Fort Worth to induce Mrs. Hogan to return to Dublin, but she objected at this time on the grounds the children, three in number, should remain in Fort Worth until the end of the [school] term. When he left Dublin, he was in unusually good spirits according to local parties who saw him at the train and to whom he told how satisfactory his business was at this place and had always been.

The family home was at 305 Hemphill Street, Fort Worth. Late Monday, Hogan was in a room at this place aside from the rest of the family at the time. The twelve-year-old son Royal entered the room and seeing his father searching in a grip before him asked, "Daddy, what are you going to do?" Hogan drew a .38-caliber revolver from the grip and shot himself just over the heart, the missile passing through the body and coming out below the left shoulder blade. He was taken to Protestant Hospital in Fort Worth, where he died twelve hours later after declaring, "I wish I hadn't done it."

Mr. Hogan had been in bad health more than a year and had been from time to time under medical treatment in a Fort Worth sanatorium. It is believed this ailment from which he could secure no relief, was one of

12

the contributing, if not the prime cause of his rash act.

The body was brought to Dublin over the Frisco train arriving at Dublin at noon Wednesday, February 15. It was taken to the home of Willie Williams, where funeral services were held and interment took place immediately following at the Old Dublin Cemetery.

Mr. Hogan was born in Dublin February 2, 1885. He attended school in this city, was married here, and his three children were born here.

He was an industrious man and had many friends.

A .38 is a heavy weapon. When fired in an enclosed space such as the Hogans' little house, the roar would have been deafening, and the air in the connecting rooms would have been filled with the acrid smell of gunsmoke. The source for the *Fort Worth Record* story—which put the youngest child in the room with Chester—was either the Spelman ambulance driver or one of the attending physicians. The *Dublin Progress* account might have represented Clara's futile attempt to shelter little Ben in a small way. No one in the house could have missed the shock of the weapon's discharge, so it really didn't matter who was in the room when Chester pulled the trigger. Everyone in the family shared the horror of the moment equally.

At the age of nine, Bennie Hogan's childhood was shot through the heart. Richard Rhodes, author of *A Hole in the World*, endured a similar loss—his mother, from suicide—at about the same age. Rhodes later wrote of his "deep sense of vulnerability . . . one parent lost and only one parent left, like one kidney left or one lung, between me and the void."

AT THE AGE OF NINE,

BENNIE HOGAN'S

CHILDHOOD WAS SHOT

THROUGH THE HEART.

As his life took a Dickensian turn, Bennie's childhood came to resemble no one's more than that of Charles Dickens himself. The great English novelist, born a hundred years and six months before Hogan (February 6, 1812), was also a young boy who helplessly watched his family crumble. Hogan likely visited his father in the sanatorium just as Dickens visited his father and the rest of his family—in debtors prison. Both were forced to work. For both, the heartbreak of their early years led directly to an unshakable determination to succeed.

"No words could express the secret agony of my soul," Dickens wrote. "My whole nature was so penetrated with the grief and humiliation of such considerations that even now, famous and caressed and happy, I often forget in my dreams that I have a dear wife and children; even that I am a man; and wander desolately back to that time in my life."

Dickens purged his despair directly by writing about it in *David Copperfield* and *Oliver Twist*. But Bennie Hogan hadn't the words. He would have to find another way to express his grief and rage and loneliness, another way to fill the hole in his world.

Hogan's instinctive reaction was to attach himself fiercely and protectively to his mother, his lifeline. His mission in life, he later said, lay in not being a burden to her. He mothered his mother and was furious many years later when a writer interviewed Clara without his knowledge or permission.

Reporters were hardly the Hogans' problem in 1922. In addition to dealing with the devastating psychic wounds from Chester's death, there was the more immediate problem of money. They had some cash from the sale of their home back in Dublin, but neither Clara's family nor Chester's could

This is a contemporary view of the house on Fort Worth's Allen Street where the Hogan family moved in 1921, following Chester's suicide. (Photo by Gaylen Groce)

offer the widow much additional help. Few women worked outside the home in 1922, and those who did had to take the most menial and low-paying jobs. The typewriter had not yet liberated large numbers of women for better-paying office work. Clara couldn't type, anyway. She could sew quite well, however, so she took a job as a seamstress at Cheney's, a small, relatively expensive dress shop on Main Street. But it wasn't enough. The children would have to work.

Fourteen-year-old Royal quit school to deliver office supplies by bicycle. Little Bennie sold newspapers after school in or around the Texas and Pacific Railroad Station. The Hogan boys probably would have sold papers or shined shoes regardless of their father's death; kids worked a lot more in those days than they do now. Besides, the Hogans' little house at 305 Hemphill in downtown Fort Worth—it's now a parking lot between a barbecue joint and the Justin Boot factory—was just several hundred yards from the railroad station, an excellent place for free enterprise. (Soon after the suicide, the family moved into a house at 1316 East Allen Avenue, in what is now a poor and dangerous neighborhood.) The train station was a huge, echoing brick box, a beehive of people and trains, with blue, black, and brown tiles inlaid in a thin ring around the pale exterior brick. Bennie would stake out a nearby street corner or busy doorway, or walk through the arriving trains holding a *Star-Telegram* over his head, yelling out a headline, such as, "Coolidge Sees More War in Europe." With his profits, he would treat himself to a nickel hamburger, sometimes two. The rest of the money went to Mama. Several times it took Bennie almost all night to sell all his copies. Royal would go down to the station in the wee hours to find his little brother asleep on a waiting room bench, his head resting on a pillow of newspapers.

Bennie resented the "rich kids" who had a monopoly on the best train station doorways and corners, which the paperboys called their "beats." Lots of times, you had to fight for your beat. So Bennie fought. He found that he liked fighting.

The image of two red-faced kids brawling on a street corner is an apt symbol for Fort Worth in the twenties. It had been a border town once and in a way it still was, with some of the "anything goes" feeling of Laredo, Tijuana, or Juarez. Fort Worth perched on the edge of Indian territory when it was founded in 1849. A few generations later, the city was the last major outpost before arid, empty West Texas. The town "Where the West Begins" got a major boost after the Civil War when Thomas Scott of the Pennsylvania Railroad proposed to route a new line, the Texas and Pacific, through town. Congress quickly voted to give him eighteen million acres. Scott had greased the wheels by giving the legislators shares of stock in the new company, or cash. Then came 1901 and oil—lots of it.

Fort Worth was the first large town back east for the newly oil rich, the West Texas intermediate crude gentlemen from Burkburnett, Electra, or one of the other boomtowns. It was, in short, a place to raise hell. Prohibition was given a tip of the hat and a wink. You bought your whiskey at a garage on Eighth Avenue, anything you wanted and as much as you wanted. A local sheriff was always nearby, like a partner in the business. After Repeal in 1933, the garage became the Eighth Avenue Club. Gambling was also technically illegal but widespread. You could roll dice or turn cards in the plush surroundings of the Petroleum Club, in a dingy hotel basement, or in scores of curtained back rooms. The police would stage a "raid" from time to time, just for appearances, and everyone arrested would give his name as Smith. Cardsharps, con men, lowlifes, and whores gravitated to Fort Worth. Wildcatters, entrepreneurs, and boastful, Stetsoned oil millionaires were their customers, or victims. Cops were on the take; law and order were somewhat improvisational. But Fort Worth and Dallas were also centers for the no-drink, no-dance Baptist Church, which added a certain tension to the atmosphere.

Crime can seem colorful and romantic, almost fun, provided it was long enough ago and no one in your family got shot or went to jail. But as anyone who has seen *The Godfather* knows, twentieth-century American bad guys became increasingly organized, an ominous and ugly trend. Organized crime reached Fort Worth in the thirties, and it touched the life of Ben Hogan.

The blacksmith's boy gradually quit selling newspapers. A friend had told him he could make real money—

between fifty and sixty-five cents—for carrying a golf bag around eighteen holes. "So one day [probably in the summer of 1924, when he was eleven going on twelve] I walked the seven miles from my home to Glen Garden Country Club to see what it was about," Hogan told *Golf* magazine in 1975. "The established caddies at Glen Garden ran a sort of kangaroo court. For a new caddie to break in, he had to win a fist-fight with one of the older, bigger caddies. So they threw me against one of those fellas and I got the better of him."

It wasn't that simple. Bennie was belligerent, small, and had an amusing tendency to fight back, so he got picked on a lot. He wouldn't cry. The big kids stuffed him in a barrel (blindfolded in at least one account) and rolled it down the hill behind the club, down toward Mitchell Boulevard and Glen Garden Drive, a thirty- or forty-yard roll with a twenty-foot drop. The barrel broke at the bottom and Bennie thought he had broken some ribs. He climbed back up the hill, humiliated, while his tormentors jeered. According to legend, he was then forced by the boss caddie to fight one of the other kids. Newcomers were also periodically made to run between two lines of boys who whacked them with their belts as they scurried by. Meanness wasn't the only motivation for the hazing. There were usually more caddies than bags, so organized cruelty to newcomers was a way to reduce competition. "It's hard in the yard" is the old saying about the caddie pen. Years before *Lord of the Flies* was written, the Glen Garden caddies lived out William Golding's novel, in which a society of unsupervised adolescent boys descends into taunting, fighting, gambling, and swearing. Little Bennie got into all of it. He also lit the first of the approximately one million cigarettes he has burned in his life, averaging two packs a day for seventy years.

Yet the positives of the caddie experience far outweighed the drawbacks. Before the scourge of power carts robbed American golfers of exercise and young boys of employment, thousands of caddies benefited from exposure to successful adults and to the game they loved.

"During the mornings we would bang the ball up and down the practice field until the members arrived and it was time to go to work," Hogan recalled. "It was through the caddie experience that I got the golf bug." He also liked the money, of course. Sometimes he slept in a sand bunker at the course so he could be first in line for a bag in the morning.

But why golf and not another game, such as the Texas state religion, football? The sixty-five cents was part of it. More important was the absolutely thorough way his and golf's personalities meshed. Insular types such as Bennie Hogan have always been drawn to golf, a sport requiring an ability to concentrate for long periods of time but with no mandate for cooperation or closeness with a teammate. He also enjoyed the utter fairness of the game, the way it compelled him to accept all the credit or all the blame. He loved its solitude, the way it absorbed him, and the opportunity it gave to hit something. The rituals of the game soothed him like soft music. His anxiety quieted with each repetition of hit it, find it, hit it, find it. . . . And he made the wonderful discovery that the rituals built on themselves. The more he practiced, the more his shots and swings acquired the calming reiteration he craved.

Best of all, golf provided competition without end, which made the rituals doubly absorbing. It's possible that no one walking around felt more inferior than Bennie Hogan, so it's conceivable that no one felt a greater need to prove himself. His father hadn't just died, he had chosen to leave, and he had died with the names of his children on his lips. So like nearly all survivors of suicide, Bennie probably felt some irrational complicity. Did something he did or something he didn't do cause his father's death? A round of golf might have been a three- or four-hour vacation from such feelings. And when he won, it stood to reason that he was validated, he was worthwhile. At least for a little while.

Even a caddie could feel the thrilling escape of competition just by carrying the rich man's bag. Sometimes caddie-golfer relationships blossomed. Byron Nelson, for example, the best and most popular looper, was befriended by a railroad man who later got him a job in his office. Another member, Judge J. B. Wade, carried Byron's bag in the 1927 Glen Garden caddie tournament.

Bennie also achieved something like a mentor connection with an older man—Marvin Leonard. Leonard, then thirty-two, was one of the department store Leonard brothers. He took up the game in the summer of '27 for stress reduction and began playing nine holes a day at Glen Garden. A disarmingly friendly man—"he had the damnedest grin," says Fred Hodge, an old golf and business associate—the budding millionaire became intrigued by the intense fifteen-year-old. They felt a father-and-son tug, especially early on. There was no older man in Bennie's life, and all four of Leonard's children—Mary, Miranda, Martha (Marty), and Madelon—were girls. Most of all, they were friends. Hogan had few friends during his life, assuming the word is defined as someone with whom you willingly spend leisure time. Marvin Leonard would become his best friend.

They were two poles of a magnet. As one acquaintance understated, "Bennie was not too affable," while Leonard was open to everyone and to anything. Why not pass the time with a busboy, or a caddie, or a waiter? Why not eat breakfast in the company cafeteria with the guys from shipping and receiving? Why not have car tires, barbed wire, feed, seed, groceries, a tub of watermelons in ice water, and the world's largest brassieres under one store's roof? "Why not" made Leonard very rich and very popular in Fort Worth.

Golf immediately gave Bennie at least one other pleasant relationship with a member of the club. One summer day the caddiemaster yelled "Hogan!" and handed him Dan

Greenwood's bag. Bennie accepted reluctantly, because no caddie wants to carry the bag of another kid. There is something undignified about it, and kids never tip. But Greenwood, a smiling, skinny boy about Bennie's size and age, was already a master at putting people at ease. He soon became acquainted with all the Hogans.

"Yes, I knew 'em all," Greenwood recalls, still smiling and still a live wire seventy years later. "Clara was a talkin' dude. Ben didn't take after her at all, she was so gabby. Princess married Doctor Ditto in Arlington [a city between Fort Worth and Dallas], Chester Ditto. Royal was a good golfer, too, a total competitor and a much better putter than Ben. He'd cut your foot off to win a bet. He turned down millions of dollars a few years ago from someone who wanted to buy his office supply business. He still works there every day. And what is he, eighty-six?

"But they won't talk to a writer. Those Hogans are funnier than hell. Real private."

Greenwood's father, a real estate developer, belonged to Glen Garden. Every day during the summer, he dropped his son off at the course at 10:00 A.M. and picked him up late in the afternoon. Bennie caddied for him about once a week. On the third hole, the member's mischievous son would often hand the caddie a club and a ball, and he would play, too, on the three or four holes which were out of sight of the clubhouse. It was exhilarating, dangerous fun for both, because they knew there would be hell to pay if "Captain" Kidd ever found out. Club manager James C. Kidd had a good view of the course from his third-floor apartment in the clubhouse,

HE COULD DRIVE HALF THE PAR-FOURS. BUT BECAUSE HE WAS SO GRIM ABOUT IT, HE WAS NEVER MUCH FUN TO PLAY GOLF WITH. HIS CONCENTRATION SEEMED TO MAKE OTHER PEOPLE DISAPPEAR.

and he never hesitated to suspend a caddie or a member's son for breaching any one of his many rules.

The very first time they pulled this scam—both would have been thirteen or fourteen—Greenwood was impressed both with Bennie's power and with how seriously he took what was for him a lark. Bennie hit a low, hard hook, which ran as though weightless on the sunbaked Glen Garden fairways. He could drive half the par-fours. But because he was so grim about it, he was never much fun to play golf with. His concentration seemed to make other people disappear. In the years to come, Greenwood was struck by one more thing: He had never known anyone so thoroughly broke. He and his mother once took Bennie to a golf tournament at Brookhollow Country Club in Dallas. "Do you have any money for lunch?" she asked him. "No," he said. So she gave him some change and he bought a candy bar.

Social mobility is an underrated benefit of golf. Certainly, Bennie had ample reason to feel socially inferior, but his reserved friendships with Leonard and Greenwood, and his growing skill at the rich man's game, allowed him to hope and to dream.

Glen Garden was an unremarkable nine-hole, sand-green course for the faintly affluent. But in one respect it was extraordinary. Two twelve-year-old country boys who barely knew what golf was began to caddie there at about the same time. Neither came from any money. Both were smitten with the golf bug, practically simultaneously. Both took their first swings with hickory-shafted five-irons. Each held himself apart from the other caddies, although in decidedly different ways. They would become two of the century's greatest sportsmen. But Bennie Hogan and Byron Nelson couldn't have been more different.

No one tried to stuff Byron in a barrel, not because he was too tough, but because he was too nice. Members offered him jobs and rooted for him in caddie tournaments. Bennie was short and deeply suspicious of others; Byron was tall and affable. Unlike Bennie, Byron had both parents. Unlike every other caddie in the yard, Byron didn't swear, fight, gamble, or smoke. The Bible and the Church of Christ were his guiding lights. The pro at Glen Garden, Ted Longworth, hired the only virtuous caddie to work full-time in the golf shop in the spring of 1927, a wonderful promotion from the yard. Bennie sometimes helped in the shop, too, polishing clubs until the wee hours on weekends. But when the PGA Championship was contested in Dallas that year, at Cedar Crest, Longworth took Byron, not Bennie, to watch it. For all their differences, however, Bennie and Byron were united in a fascination with golf and with the discipline and determination to master it. And both possessed talent in abundance, although Byron had a little more.

"The first time I was really aware of Ben was [at] Christmas [1926], when the members put on a little boxing match for entertainment," Nelson wrote in his autobiography, *How I Played the Game*. "Ben liked to box, and so did another caddie we called Joe Boy. They boxed for fifteen minutes, I guess. . . . I was just watching, because I never did like to box or fight."

Bennie and Byron became better acquainted a year later when they tied for first in Glen Garden's annual Christmas caddie tournament. Both fifteen-year-olds shot 39 or (as Nelson remembers it) 40. Byron, the favorite, had to sink a thirty-foot putt on the ninth green to tie.

"Let's play sudden death," said someone, probably one of the members who was watching. Bennie won the first hole with a par.

"Nah, let's play all nine holes," said someone else, probably another member.

Bennie believed he was being jobbed, but he went along. Byron made another substantial putt on the final green to win by a shot with a four-over-par 41. The combatants were given golf clubs, which they swapped, because Byron already had a five-iron and Bennie already had a two. Afterward, all the caddies went to a Christmas party—all except Bennie. Something in him would not permit the familiarity of raising a glass of cider with the other kids. "I felt I already had my party when I tied Nelson," he said years later. But if that was true, it was the only time in his life he was happy with second place.

The caddie tournament was the start of a trend. Byron would best Bennie, personally and professionally, for most of the next twenty years.

Byron over Bennie continued the following spring, when Glen Garden members asked Captain Kidd to nominate a caddie for an almost unprecedented honor, a junior membership in the club. It sounded like a setup. Who else could it be but Byron?

"Byron Nelson is the only caddie who doesn't drink, smoke, or curse," the conservative Scot said. "I think he should have it." And he got it. At about this time, Bennie asked Kidd if he could continue to practice in the Glen Garden caddie yard, even though at sixteen he was now too old by the club's rules to caddie. Kidd said no.

Byron won several big country club members-only tournaments that year, events in which Bennie could not play. He seethed; Bennie lacked the psychic elasticity to slough off rejection, not exactly an unusual trait in a teenager. It's possible the insults and outrages committed against him piled up to form a wall that no one could get through and from which he could not escape.

Thus began his brief career as an amateur golfer. Bennie, at sixteen, had attained his adult height of five-foot-eight, and his weight would stay in the 130s for years. His hands and arms looked too big for his body, as if they had been transplanted from a much larger man. He had a wide, somewhat bony face, with large, perfect teeth, and an I-can-kick-your-ass disposition. He now had a matched set of wood-shafted irons, which had replaced the mix-and-match set he had scavenged or bought one at a time at a discount store. The new sticks cost his mother forty dollars, a purchase that could be construed as an endorsement of this game she hadn't approved of before. His base of operations shifted from Glen Garden to three scrubby daily-fee courses: Katy Lake, which was built on land owned by Dan Greenwood's father; Worth Hills, which Dan Jenkins immortalized in one of his stories, "The Glory Game at Goat Hills"; and Z-Boaz (pronounced "ZEE-boze").

He walked everywhere. Central High was an unexciting two-and-a-quarter-mile stroll through plain vanilla middle- and lower-class neighborhoods: west on Allen, and over to College or Hemphill, past scores of claustrophobic houses just like his. Outside the red brick Gothic fortress of Central High, he might see his classmates Opal Chambliss, Atys Gardner, Effie Moss, and Furlow Owsley. Imogene Tidwell, Lula Lane, Essie Jones, Elberta Peach, and Ida Fae Woody were the best-looking girls. Ellen Zent and Wendell Smitherman were studious; Dan Greenwood was popular; Lloyd Clark had a mustache; and Jack Cabaniss was a jock. The girls bobbed their hair, and the boys applied brilliantine to theirs for their pictures in the Panther yearbook. Bennie never showed up for the photographer. He never joined a club or a team. He would be the guy the class reunion committee couldn't find ten years later.

Bennie took algebra, plane geometry, English, history, chemistry, and shop—no foreign languages, no music, no art. During the second ninety-day semester of his senior year, he was absent sixty-five days. He received no credits and was in no danger of graduating. He dropped out.

"I think about then Ben got the idea he was gonna be a pro," says Matty Reed, a particularly good local golfer five years older than Bennie. "He started practicing constantly. Sometimes he wouldn't even go out with us to play."

As Reed remembers it, Hogan carried his practice balls in his golf bag. He would dump them on the ground, then hit them to a kid he had hired to stand out in a field to act as a target and to shag balls. His fantasy companion, Hennie Bogan, would watch. Hennie was an insatiable practicer and a greater golfer even than the great Bobby Jones. Hennie told Bennie to hit more balls.

Bennie, Greenwood, Reed, Royal (who had taken up the game at age seventeen), and several other young golf nuts would gather at one of the three courses and tee off in a "gangsome." Nelson played occasionally but would not participate in the betting, which mystified the others. It wasn't like he couldn't play.

"We played cats ["skins" is the more common designation; the low scorer on a hole wins the money] for dimes or quarters," Reed recalls. "Or dimes-and-double or two-bits-and-double [an individual bet; win a hole with a birdie and get a double payoff from your opponent]. A big game had five or ten dollars in it."

That summer Reed took Hogan to his first real golf tournament, the state public links championship in Waco. The two-and-a-half-hour drive in Reed's canvas-topped 1926 Ford touring car was mostly silent. "Even before Ben got famous, he didn't talk to you," Reed says. He didn't pay for gas, either. As usual, he was broke. Remarkably, Hogan finished second in his first tournament.

"We played thirty-six holes, two days in a row," Reed says. "Jack Dold of Houston won. They gave you a ball for every birdie you made. Ben made thirteen birdies for thirteen balls, and I won six in a pitch-and-putt contest. So we had nineteen balls. After the awards dinner we gave two caddies a ride and dropped them off somewhere in town. 'The balls still there, Ben?' I asked. He looked in the back seat. 'Damn!' he says. So we drove around the block and found the two boys. Ben didn't say a word, just looked at 'em. They handed the balls back to him."

Bennie finished second in another major amateur event the following summer of 1929, revealing both his promise and his basic problem with golf.

"Skill from tee to green triumphed over the slugging type of golfer here today as Gus Moreland, nineteen years old of Dallas, defeated Ben Hogan, seventeen years old of Fort Worth, four up and three holes to play in the finals of the Southwestern Amateur played over the Shreveport [Louisiana] Country Club," the local paper reported. "Hogan, a very long driver, was in trouble many times off the tee . . . while Moreland, a much shorter driver, was consistently down the fairway."

Long driving had been a macho thing in the Glen Garden caddie yard. Whatever caddies were still around at the end of the day would hit one ball each from the first tee: the shortest hitter had to run out onto the deserted course and pick up the balls, then they would do it again. As Longworth recalled it for a story in the PGA Championship program for 1946, a few members always emerged from the nineteenth hole to watch. "Yah, Bennie, get ready to chase 'em again," the other boys would say, according to Longworth. Nelson never lost; Hogan never won. Bennie tried hitting it cross-handed.

"Bennie, if you don't change that hog-killer's grip, you may as well take up cattle rustling," Longworth told Hogan. The tall, stoop-shouldered pro bent down and untangled the boy's hands. Since distance was the name of this game, he gave Bennie a distance grip, turning his left hand to the right and his right hand underneath the club, thus helping him close the clubface during the swing and producing a left-curving shot, a hook. Hooks roll.

Longworth's story suggests that all the improvements in Bennie's nascent golf game were made in one or two lessons and were a gift from Longworth. They weren't. Bennie Hogan would be the champion of figuring things out for himself. On his own, he lengthened his stroke so far that his hands were up by his left ear at the top of his backswing. And, on his own, he increased his strength by doing the perfect golf exercise, hitting lots of golf balls. He stopped losing the long-driving contests, but the caddie grip and the circle-and-a-half swing would haunt him when he became a tournament player. His shots were too low, too long, and too far left.

His compensating strengths were considerable, however, and none of them had to do with the way he hit a golf ball. Practice was his greatest insight and his biggest advantage. Whether it was due to his world weariness, his dislike of company, or a Calvinist belief in redemption through work, Bennie Hogan could stay on the practice tee like nobody else. His diligence was amazing because he had no model for it and because he got almost no immediate rewards from it.

No one ever saw him throw a club in anger. Testosterone and temper ruined thousands of young golfers—and ruins them still—but not Bennie. Just as he had done since he was nine, he internalized the anger. He took it in and showed nothing. He was far from being unemotional, but the only clue that he was miffed was when he burned an inch of his cigarette in one vacuum-cleaner-like inhalation. He was now what he would always be, a man with a plan. Revealing anger or elation was not part of the program.

Another strength—or perhaps it was the same strangely complete emotional control—was his ability to shoot low scores. Lots of would-be champion golfers become conscience-stricken when they get a few under par: "Pars in will give me 68," they tell themselves, consciously or unconsciously. "That's low enough. Better protect, better play defense." With Bennie, however, there was no bottom. He did not aim for *target* scores; he shot for the *lowest* scores. In a recurring dream later in life, he made seventeen consecutive holes-in-one. When his tee shot on the eighteenth lipped out, he would awake, "mad as hell." Even as a teenager, Bennie could put up the numbers.

"One time in '29 or '30, Smiley Rowland and I played Hogan and Jack Grout [the new assistant pro at Glen Garden] at Z-Boaz," Reed says. "You talk about birdies flying. Smiley and I shot 62, and they shot 61. But I still never dreamed Ben would get that good. He had such a lousy hook."

Bennie's big hook kept him just out of the top level of local golf. He could usually hold his own with the Mangrum brothers, Ray and Lloyd, cool, narrow-faced young men who ran the golf operation at Cliff-Dale Country Club in Dallas, but Nelson and Reed of Fort Worth usually beat him. The best of the amazing Dallas/Fort Worth bunch were two caddies from Dallas, Gus Moreland and Ralph Guldahl. Moreland, a tall, intense young man with a penetrating voice, liked to hit a putt and immediately stroll behind the ball while commenting on its progress. "That one's got a chance; go left; come on, baby!" he would say. "Gus the Walker" they called him, or "Victrola." Guldahl was a gentle man whose parents had both been born in Norway. His swing was an ugly fire-and-fall-back contraption, and his posture was bad, but his composure was a gift from God.

The funny thing about these guys was how good they were, how thoroughly they outgrew Fort Worth and Dallas. Except for Reed, who went to work for the railroad, all became national and international figures in golf. In fact, a case could be made that Moreland inherited Bobby Jones's mantle as the best amateur golfer on the planet. Later, in the thirties, Guldahl was arguably the very best in golf, and Nelson succeeded Guldahl. At the close of the decade Byron and Sam Snead were undoubtedly golf's superior players.

Meanwhile, Bennie Hogan was nobody from nowhere. He hadn't won a tournament—not even the Fort

Worth City Championship—and he didn't have a job or a high school diploma. Then things got worse, dramatically worse, for him and for everybody else. On Black Tuesday, October 29, 1929, the stock market imploded like an old building being demolished. More national lottery than solid institution, the stock market allowed you to buy a dollar of stock for just a dime and put the rest on your tab. "Speculation with other people's money," Franklin Roosevelt called it at his inauguration in 1933. Nearly everybody played this big casino game, including legions of small-timers. The economic disaster affected everyone. Truckers didn't ship, farmers didn't harvest, factories and their workers were idle, and no one had any money.

Economies don't turn off or on like refrigerator lights, however. The Great Depression did not create an immediate national blackout, and its effects were blunted for families such as the Hogans who were already struggling to make it. But in time, as families farmed out kids to relatives who could afford to feed an extra mouth, as large numbers of out-of-work men took walks after dinner and never came back, there came to be a sort of national what-the-hell attitude. Since nearly everyone was just trying to survive this mess, mothers sent their beloved sons to stay with Uncle Walter, and legions of men rode the rails from town to town doing nothing more than breathing in and out and searching for a meal. What the hell.

In February 1930 Bennie Hogan sat down in the back seat of Ted Longworth's Ford in Fort Worth and got out in San Antonio to play in the Texas Open. In another example of the what-the-hell spirit, he registered as a professional. He was seventeen.

## CHAPTER 2

# DUES

THERE ON A LONG BENCH BETWEEN THE TWO ROWS OF LOCKERS WAS A LARGE TRAY. SITTING ON THE TRAY WAS A BIG BOWL OF ICE, FOUR GLASSES, AND A "SCOTCHMAN" WEARING THE LABEL OF HAIG AND HAIG. SINCE I'M A HOLLAND DUTCHMAN AND THE CHIEF HAS INDIAN BLOOD, WE WEREN'T BASHFUL ABOUT TAPPING THAT SCOTCHMAN. . . . THE LOCKER ROOM NOW SOUNDED LIKE BEES SWARMING—SOME GOLFERS WERE CELEBRATING AND SOME WERE CUSSING THEIR LUCK. CLAYTON WON THIS TOURNAMENT, AND STOPPED BY FOR ONE QUICKIE BEFORE HEADING TO THE PRESS ROOM. OLD PORKY CAME IN AND STATED THAT HIS THREE PUTTS ON THE EIGHTEENTH COST HIM FOURTH-PLACE MONEY ALL TO HIM-SELF. . . . HE PROMPTLY ORDERED A DOZEN BEERS.

AFTER A COUPLE OF HOURS OF THIS PARTYING, THE SCOTCH-MAN WAS DEAD, THE LOCKER ROOM WAS QUIET, [AND] PORKY WAS HEADING FOR THE BAR. MY MIND WAS FOGGY AND I FOUND THAT MY LEGS FAILED TO RESPOND TO THE DEMANDS THAT IT WAS TIME TO WALK. I BUMPED INTO THE LOCKERS, FIRST ON ONE SIDE, THEN THE OTHER. UP THE AISLE I WENT, TAKING A FEW STEPS FORWARD, THEN A COUPLE BACKWARD, DOING A SORT OF HEEL-AND-TOE DANCE AS I FOUND MY EQUILIBRIUM ENOUGH TO WABBLE AND STAGGER OUT THE DOOR. . . . I FINALLY GOT TO THE ROOM, FELL STRAIGHT ACROSS THE BED, AND PASSED OUT. AWAKENING NINE HOURS LATER, I NOTED THAT I STILL HAD ON MY CAP, MY SHOES, AND MY CLOTHES. BESIDES ALL THAT, ALL I KNEW WAS THAT I FELT

31

TERRIBLE. SO I GRABBED THE PHONE AND TOLD THE BELLBOY TO
RUSH ME TWO BEERS BEFORE I DIED.

—FROM THE DIARY OF WILBURN
ARTIST "LEFTY" STACKHOUSE, A
TOURING GOLF PRO

The pro golf tour of the thirties was as divorced from reality as a double scotch. It resembled the escapist musicals Hollywood was putting out. It was *Footlight Parade* or *The Gold Diggers of 1933*, with choreography by Busby Berkeley, dancing by Ruby Keeler, synchronized swimming by Esther Williams, and rags-to-riches story lines from a million poor people's dreams.

The strangest period in American history was also the most confusing era in American golf. Steel shafts replaced hickory. A handsome Atlanta aristocrat named Bobby Jones did the heretofore impossible, winning the two major amateur and open golf tournaments in the same year, 1930. His Grand Slam drew new players to the game in droves, but Jones abdicated the throne immediately after ascending it. The stress of top-level golf had upset his stomach for the last time. "Golf without Jones," lamented historian Herbert Warren Wind, "would be like France without Paris."

Just when the game lost its brightest star, the depression hit. Courses closed their doors, and golfers new and old discovered they could no longer afford to play. Many decided they could no longer afford even to watch. Resort hotels and chambers of commerce, the main sponsors of pro tournaments, were forced either to cancel or cut back. The purse in the Los Angeles Open, for example, fell in three years from ten thousand dollars to seventy-five hundred dollars to five thousand dollars in 1932. After it lost its sponsor, the Oakland Open survived by dunning 250 civic-minded East Bay residents one hundred dollars each.

Yet, in a strange way, golf actually expanded during the depression. People couldn't afford the real game, so millions of new enthusiasts took up miniature golf. And a lot of depression-era golfers made golf their life's work simply because there was nothing else to do. Byron Nelson, for example, would have remained a railroad company clerk for a long time if he hadn't been laid off. Partly because there were plenty of unemployed pros around and partly because tournaments were seen as cost-effective commercials for this city or that resort, the golf tour began to include some summer events—more tournaments for less prize money. Still, it was a net gain.

Even before the economic tailspin of the depression, the tour had never provided a way to get rich. "You wonder why I quit playing tournaments? You couldn't make any money in it," said Wild Bill Melhorn, one of the top players of the twenties. Melhorn quit the tour after 1930, the same year Bennie Hogan attempted to join it. "What are you going to do?" he added. "You're there almost a week, and if you win, you only win five hundred dollars."

Melhorn actually won five thousand dollars at the LaGorce tournament in Florida in 1930, which up to then had been the biggest prize ever. Earlier he had earned fifteen hundred dollars for winning the Texas Open in '28 and the same amount for winning again in '29. But that doesn't change his point. As it had been since golf took hold in the United States in 1888, a professional had to have a job at a club to make any financial headway. The lone exception to the rule was the charismatic Walter Hagen, the first full-time, unattached touring professional. After winning the 1919 U.S. Open, he resigned his post at Oakland Hills Country Club for a life of tournaments, exhibitions, and drinking champagne from women's spike-heeled shoes. But just as the Jones/Hagen golf boom made more people interested in golf, the depression market for golf instructors and pro-shop operators dried up. But you didn't need to have a job to play in a pro tournament. All you needed were a bag of clubs and the entry fee.

Most of the tournaments were held in the South in the winter, when the snow-coated courses in the North were closed. As the excerpt from the diary of the wondrous Lefty Stackhouse reveals, the atmosphere of desperate fun resembled college boys on spring break more than the activities of serious athletes. Not that many of them had ever been to college. Hagen, the brightest light on the tour, was typical, having retired from formal education at age twelve. Due in part to the lack of schooling of its members, the tour had more characters than the Sunday funny pages.

Stackhouse, for instance, felt forced to fortify himself against a volcanic temper. He kept a bottle in his golf bag. Once, while at the top of his backswing in a bunker, he fell face first into the sand, exhausted from the sun and fun. On another day when he didn't get his medication quite right, he shocked his playing partner, Hogan, by raking his right hand back and forth in a rose bush as punishment for its contribution to a badly hooked tee shot. "And don't think you're gonna get away with it, either," he snarled at his left hand, and whipped it into the thorny bush until it too was torn and bleeding. A product of a broken home and the Texas oil fields, Lefty had a childhood almost as rough as Hogan's—but obviously he handled adversity much differently.

"The Chief" in Lefty's reminiscence was Ky Laffoon, the pride of Zinc, Arkansas, and a frighteningly strong man. He would offer his hand as if to make peace with his antagonist in a bar fight, then squeeze the other guy's palm so hard he would collapse in pain. In a locker room Johnny Bulla once slapped Laffoon playfully, but the Chief—who may or may not have had any Native American blood in him—was in no mood for it. He picked up Bulla, threw him on top of some lockers, and would not permit him to come down.

34

"Porky" was short, stout, curly haired Ed Oliver. "Porky would bet anything, blow it, and laugh it off," says Herman Keiser, another old pro. "He had a new Packard. . . . After he won his first tournament [in 1940] he got in this dice game, and well . . . the next morning he comes to me and says, 'Herman, have you got room for me in your car?' Lost his car and the money!"

Clayton Heafner was Lefty's rival for worst temper on the tour. He withdrew from one tournament after hitting only one shot and from another before even striking the first ball, because the first-tee announcer had pronounced his name "Heefner." "Screw this, I'm outta here," quoth Clayton.

Drinking on the tour was widespread but it wasn't all Stackhouse style. "Twenty years ago, they could have blindfolded me, placed me at one end of the bar, read the drink orders, and I could have told you who was in the room," says Hogan disciple Tommy Bolt. "Not all of the players drank, but most of them did. . . . They really put on the dog at the clubs we visited." Bolt turned pro in 1946, but he could just as well have been describing 1936 or 1956.

Yet in the thirties, even among the ex-caddies who were its professionals, golf was in many ways quite civil and gentlemanly. A pro dressed for the game in a tie, long-sleeved shirt, and pleated slacks or plus fours (or plus twos, or sixes, the number referring to how many inches below the knee the britches terminated). Fedoras or flat tweed caps finished the look. Golf shoes were custom made from dress shoes. The modern golf shirt—the "polo shirt" invented by French tennis star Rene "Le Crocodile" LaCoste in 1927—did not appear on American backs until after World War II.

Travel on the loosely organized tour was as quaint and uncomfortable as a pair of tweed knickers on a hot day. Little convoys of cars gathered after a tournament in Miami to proceed to North Carolina, or after the Phoenix Open to drive to the Texas Open, with two or three passengers per vehicle.

Golf pros, America's first automobile nomads, helped each other with directions and with flats. Ten or fifteen thousand miles was all you could expect out of a set of tires. They deflated the tires before long drives across the desert Southwest to help them run cooler and thus prevent blowouts. To prolong battery life, drivers sometimes switched off their headlights on night trips and drove by the light of the moon. To ward off the chill of winter travel, Louise Nelson, Byron's wife, heated bricks in an oven, wrapped them in paper, and put them on the floor of their '32 royal blue/cream top Ford roadster. There was nothing that could be done about spark plugs, however. When they gave out after about eight thousand miles, a backfiring Model T would start to sound like firecrackers exploding in a garbage can. There were no car radios, so the riders talked to each other, loudly, because the roads were rough, the drivers were fast, and the high-pressure cotton or rayon cord tires were noisy.

Another boon to conversation was the lack of air conditioning or television in hotel rooms. Lobby sitting, the alternative to doing laundry in the bathtub back in a stuffy room, was enlivened by lobby betting. Every lobby was a little Las Vegas. Bookies followed the tour in informal shifts: "Eddie" from Dallas did the Texas tournaments and New Orleans; a guy from New York handled the Florida and Carolinas swing; and another bookmaker followed the tour in Arizona and on the West Coast. Players wagered on themselves, on each other, and on complicated team bets and parlays the bookies devised. Keiser made thousands of dollars betting on Bobby Locke of South Africa when he came to the United States after the war. Locke heard about it and approached Keiser. "I say, Herman," Locke said, "I'd like to wager a few bob, too." Thereafter, Locke bet at least four hundred dollars per tournament—on himself.

Drinking, gambling, long car trips, hanging out in various hotel vestibules, and a daily round or two of golf—

those were the main activities of the touring professional's life. No one practiced very much. The way to improve, it was thought, was to play a lot, buy a better player a beer, and get him to talk about his game and yours. The strong link between the modern lesson and high-volume practice had not been established. A student might hit as few as a dozen balls in a session with the pro.

DRINKING, GAMBLING, LONG CAR TRIPS, HANGING OUT IN VARIOUS HOTEL VESTIBULES, AND A DAILY ROUND OR TWO OF GOLF. THOSE WERE THE MAIN ACTIVITIES OF THE TOURING PROFESSIONAL' LIFE.

"There was a lot more demonstration in a lesson back then," second-generation golf pro "Lighthorse" Harry Cooper says. "My father concentrated on getting people into the right frame of mind for golf."

The newest player on the tour turned every theory of golf improvement on its ear. Although virtually all his peers were instructors, he didn't believe in lessons. He didn't drink with them and ask how they beat him. Instead, Hogan hit practice balls, hundreds of them, for hours at a time.

"So It's an Old Man's Game, Eh?" asked the headline atop the *San Antonio Light* sports page on January 31, 1930. A boxed caption below read: "These young men, both famous in state amateur golf, played for the first time as professionals here Thursday. Ben Hogan, Fort Worth, and Ralph Guldahl, Dallas, both turned pro for the Texas Open. Hogan ranks as Fort Worth's best; while Guldahl is the champion of the city of Dallas." Both teenagers were pictured in full follow-through, wearing plus fours, sweaters,

Still a teenager, Hogan prepares for his first professional outing, the 1930 Texas Open. (Courtesy of Texas Golf Hall of Fame, from the *San Antonio Light* collection, the Institute of Texan Cultures, San Antonio, Texas)

and grim expressions. Hogan and Guldahl had ridden down with Ted Longworth, the former Glen Garden pro who by now was working at Texarkana Country Club.

Hogan's first round as a professional began at 12:30 P.M. at Brackenridge Park in south-central San Antonio. His playing partners were W. F. Olathe of Dallas and "the Human Two-Iron," Ray Mangrum, late of Dallas but now living in Los Angeles. Ropes defined the borders between rough and fairway. Without the ropes, it was hard to tell where one stopped and the other started, since the entire course—including the greens—was the shredded-wheat color of dormant bermuda grass. Soldiers from nearby Fort Sam Houston—in their wide-brimmed brown hats, puttees, and jodhpurs—acted as gallery police. They looked like forest rangers. The air was cool, about fifty degrees at midday, the ground was wet, and the skies were overcast. Hundreds of men in overcoats and gray and brown fedoras milled around the first tee, situated fifty yards from the front door of the big stone clubhouse.

Hogan's first swing as a professional was with a driver on Brackenridge Park's first hole, a straightaway par-four. He shot 38 in his first nine holes as a pro, then 40, for 78. Ray Mangrum shot 71, Guldahl a 74, and Densmore Shute, who would win the tournament, shot 68. Both of Bennie's acquaintances from Dallas also did well in the succeeding three rounds. Guldahl and Mangrum finished eleventh and twelfth, respectively, and won seventy-five dollars each. Ten bucks for the hotel room, ten bucks for the caddie, maybe another ten or fifteen for everything else. It was a good payday for Ralph and Ray. But Bennie won nothing. He shot 75 in the second round and withdrew. "I found out the first day I shouldn't even be there," he said years later.

Strange, but true: Ben Hogan quit in the middle of his first professional tournament. It was an immature decision and a breach of etiquette. You don't spit into the wind or ask a woman her age or her weight, and you don't drop out of a golf tournament without a doctor's excuse.

In Houston the following week, Bennie and his best-ball partner, G. W. Beardsley, shot a lousy 78 in the pro-am preliminary, thirteen strokes higher than the winning teams captained by Wiffy Cox and Craig Wood. In the main event, Bennie scored 77-76 and again quit before the finish. Two tournaments, two withdrawals: there was petulance in that, an attitude of I-won't-play-if-I-can't-win. At least he had had the chance to stress-test his golf game. When he saw that it was not ready for professional competition, he went back to Worth Hills, Katy Lake, and Z-Boaz, back to beating balls for six-hour stretches. And that was about all he did, for a solid year.

> Question from a 1991 ESPN interview: "The
> Ben Hogan work ethic . . . who instilled that
> in you?"
> Hogan: "Hennie Bogan."

It must have been lonely, even for a loner. Cars had been affordable for the middle class since the twenties, but the Hogans didn't have one, so Bennie couldn't cruise. High school fraternities were a big deal at Central High. They threw enormous parties, especially during the Christmas holidays. But Bennie had never been part of the social whirl and now, as a dropout, he had lost almost all connection with his peers. In the spring and summer, the other kids his age would drive northwest out of town on Jacksboro Highway, leaving the heat of the city behind. They would go to the Casino on Lake Worth, a glittering palace on the water, to dance in the giant ballroom or to rent a rowboat. Or they would drive to the Showboat or to the Ringside Club. Afterward, it was Ball's Hamburgers or the Ballenger Street drugstore, but Bennie didn't date. He had no car or money, he was too shy, and he was too focused on golf for frivolity. Hennie Bogan did allow Bennie to attend Sunday school, however..

Hogan lived at home. He practiced, while Hennie Bogan perched on his shoulder and whispered, "Can't you hit it any better than that?" Bennie practiced more. He played death matches for a dollar or two at the public courses and took mostly menial odd jobs—in the oil fields, in a bank, as a busboy. He hauled suitcases in a hotel and slapped wrenches as a mechanic. Royal gave his little brother money to play in a few golf tournaments.

Longworth helped him, too. In 1931 he drove Guldahl and Bennie, who had just turned nineteen, for their first real try at the tour.

"Who are these guys?" a sportswriter asked at a small warm-up tournament in St. Louis.

"They're a couple of real good kids—Bennie Hogan and Ralph Guldahl," Longworth answered.

"Never heard of them," the reporter said.

Guldahl finished in the money in St. Louis, but Bennie didn't. In December, the three pros headed west. In Phoenix, Bennie won fifty dollars, his first check as a pro. But he arrived at the Los Angeles Open with just fifteen cents in his pocket and had to wire back to Fort Worth, presumably to Royal, to get enough money to return home. Oranges swiped from the trees bordering the Southern California golf courses had been the staple of his diet for weeks.

I went to the West Coast on the tour in 1932. I went broke. I left here with seventy-five dollars in my pocket to go to the West Coast. Would you try that today?

I went with Ralph Hutchison and Jack Grout. The first tournament was Pasadena. I didn't get any money there. Next one was . . .

41

I can't think of the name of it. The next was
the Los Angeles Open, then Agua Caliente. I
would win twenty-five or fifty dollars. I was
always last if I got in the money at all. As I said,
I was a terrible player.

Anyway, we played Agua Caliente,
Phoenix, the Texas Open, and New Orleans.
After New Orleans, I wasn't in the money and
I was broke and I had to come home.

So. I spent five years compiling this time
fourteen hundred dollars. And in the mean-
time I'd gotten married, Valerie and me, and
I told her I'd like to go back on the tour.
She said, "I knew you had this in mind all
the time."

—Hogan, from the 1983 interview with
CBS

Hogan's Hemingwayesque sentences revealed his unusually organized mind, but this account simplified things
quite a bit. Most importantly, he omitted entirely two other
failed attempts at the tour, in '31 and '34. The thoroughness
of and number of these early failures is the key to an appreci-
ation of his later success. What persuaded him to keep at it?

Before he hit the road, Bennie borrowed $50 from
Marvin Leonard to supplement the $75. Still, $125 was a pa-
thetically small bankroll, even for 1932. Bennie scrimped and
skipped meals, but he couldn't make the money last because
there was almost no income to offset the outgo. Leonard
helped, sending him another $100 in November '31, then
$75 two months later. Hogan's 1932 Texas Open scores typ-
ified his performance: 75-80, WD.

When he returned to Fort Worth a couple months
after he had left, Bennie took the only golf job he could
find—as the pro at Nolan River Country Club. Nolan River

was in Cleburne, Texas, in the cotton country an hour's drive south of Fort Worth, or about a half-hour northeast of Dublin. In 1932, the worst year of the depression, he was lucky to get anything. One out of every three bread-winners was unemployed, a total of thirteen million people. Dance marathons were a melancholic symbol of America's desperation.

Hogan's new position at Nolan River consumed lots of hours in return for little pay, a time-honored tradition in the golf business. He got the bags out in the morning and put them away at night; kept the golf shop clean; sold golf balls for thirty cents each and thick wooden tees shaped like carrots for a dime a pack; and gave a few lessons, although he was never any great shakes as a teacher. He cleaned the dirt off the members' clubs and scrubbed off the rust with a buffing wheel for those who still had iron heads made out of iron (rustless stainless steel irons had been available since 1925).

Many budget- or tradition-conscious Cleburne Country Club members still had wood-shafted clubs. Wood shafts broke a lot, so Bennie was continually doing club repair. It was an intricate process. He would select a raw hickory shaft, file it at the bottom, drive it into a clubhead, and fasten it with a nail, not glue. Next he would shape the shaft by whittling it with a piece of glass and rubbing it with sandpaper, wet it with a rag to raise the grain of the wood, then rub it with linseed oil and pitch to help repel water. The final step was to wrap on a strip of cowhide for a grip, fasten the grip at the top and bottom with tacks, and wrap whipping—string—over the tacks. Done. Bennie deeply enjoyed building clubs and was far better at it than he was at asking Mrs. Jones how she enjoyed her round today. Small talk stuck in Hogan's mouth. He was as stingy with words as with dimes or friendships.

Yet he was quite capable of sociability. He began to date Valerie Fox. He had been friendly with the brown-eyed, fawnlike Valerie since they had first met in Sunday school back

43

in Fort Worth when both were twelve or thirteen. She and her family subsequently moved to Cleburne, where her father, a man as extroverted as she was shy, was the projectionist at the local movie theater. History does not record the details of Ben and Valerie's first date in Cleburne, but given the suitor's budget, it would be no surprise if they had gone to the movies on a pass from Mr. Fox. The least expensive and therefore the most popular depression-era date was to simply sit in the parlor and listen to the radio.

In November '32 Bennie accepted an invitation from Longworth to come up to his club in Texarkana for a little five-hundred-dollar tournament. Byron was invited, too. On the long bus ride to northeast Texas, Byron decided to turn pro, even though he knew his parents might object because of all the drinking the golf pros did. Longworth won, Ky "the Chief" Laffoon took second, and Bennie finished out of the money. But Byron finished third, won seventy-five dollars, and felt encouraged to try the tour. Almost immediately, a five-hundred-dollar advance—not a loan—materialized from some friends in Fort Worth. The contrast with Bennie's borrowed seventy-five dollars was stark.

Things looked up for Byron even more that spring. Longworth, the new professional at the Waverley Country Club in Portland, Oregon, wrote Byron suggesting that he apply for the professional's job in Texarkana. Longworth didn't contact Bennie about the opportunity, which paid only sixty dollars a month. So Bennie rented the golf shop at Oakhurst Country Club, a nine-hole course in Fort Worth, and hung out his shingle.

"No friend *ever* showed up," Hogan told golf writer Herbert Warren Wind twenty-three years later. Said Wind, "I've never heard a man so bitter."

Oakhurst was almost deserted in the morning, so Hogan typically practiced for four hours. First an hour of chipping, then irons, woods, and the putter. Around noon the men who owned or operated Fort Worth's card and dice games arrived, many of them from the Green Oaks Inn in west Fort Worth, their unofficial headquarters. Like gamblers everywhere, they loved golf. They loved to win money, too, so their backing Bennie against anyone who wanted a match was a clear signal his game was improving. Bennie played one pigeon while standing on one leg. In another game of chance, a caddie would sidle up to whoever might be watching Hogan rocketing out drives on the practice range. "Bet I can catch them balls in the air, barehanded," the caddie would say to a potential bettor. A few minutes later he would split the winnings with Bennie. They had practiced this beforehand, of course.

It's tempting to picture the custodians of the local gaming industry as cowboy-hatted or golf-shoed yahoos, but they were as unpleasant as the criminals in Cleveland, New York, or Pittsburgh. Lester "Benny" Binion ran most of the gambling in Dallas and west to Fort Worth. From time to time, as author Carlton Stowers pointed out in *Men in Blue,* Binion found it necessary to kill people. Two homicides he did himself were the shootings of a liquor runner in 1931 and of a competitor to his numbers business in broad daylight on Allen Street in Dallas in 1936. Benny's big rival was Herbert Noble, nicknamed "the Cat" for his marvelous ability to survive the many assassination attempts apparently ordered by Binion (a mailbox filled with dynamite finally got Noble in 1951). The Cat was strongest in Fort Worth and Binion had Dallas, but neither respected the other's trading zones. As a result, low-level guys on both sides would shoot each other—"misdemeanor murders" some called them. Marty "the Ox" Ochs, Paul "Needle Nose" Labriola, and others from Chicago tried to muscle in and take over the local vice from these goons, but to no avail.

One of the dangerous men in the local gambling business supposedly lent Bennie the money to try the tour again,

THE THUMP, THUMP, THUMP OF HIS PUTTS INTO A WALL OR OF HIS CHIPS INTO A CHAIR CAUSED THE OCCUPANTS OF ADJOINING ROOMS TO COMPLAIN TO THE MANAGER.

although this often-repeated story is impossible to corroborate. But eyewitnesses say that between stints on the tour Hogan took a low-level job in the gambling industry dealing cards and handling dice.

Hogan didn't win a dime in his third try as a tour player in 1934. The other pros were beginning to regard him as something of a crank. Who the hell was this silent kid who practiced all the time, yet still hit enough low, hard hooks to keep from winning any money? He seldom drank with the boys and he never asked for help, even though virtually all his fellow competitors were also instructors.

"No, he never came to me for help," said Sam Snead, who joined the tour in '37. "I don't think he messed with any of the pros. Hogan's gotta do it the hard way."

Demaret turned pro in '34 and was amazed when he saw that Bennie and Byron "would put in hour after hour on the practice tee, something unheard of. The old-timers in golf rarely practiced. They'd take a few swings and then go out and play in a tournament. Hogan and Nelson began almost a new concept."

Demaret erred in putting Byron in Bennie's league as a ball beater. Nelson never practiced nearly as much as Hogan. After 1936 Byron gave up serious practice altogether. But Bennie never let up, even when there was strong evidence that he was wasting his time. He took his putter, a wedge, and some balls back to his hotel room at night. The thump, thump, thump of his putts into a wall or of his chips into a chair caused the occupants of adjoining rooms to complain to the manager.

It was a unique way to assuage the boredom, loneliness, and creeping feeling of failure. Hundreds of golf professionals before Hogan and thousands of pros after him would feel those same three emotions and try to relieve them in a bar. Even with the comforts a beer and a friend can provide, playing badly far from home creates a sense of despair, a spiritual illness akin to the flu. You feel sorry for yourself, and you start to give up, a little at a time. The other pros would party harder and gradually fade from the game, but Bennie Hogan quite literally did not know how to have a good time. His answer to poor play was hard work, a homely virtue he took to the extreme. For him, golf combined the refuges of religion and war. Golf was a holy war.

Despite the obsessive drilling, Bennie found himself bounced from the tour for the third time, jobless and alone. It was a desperate time. His usual anxiety about getting back on the road was exacerbated by his strong desire to marry Valerie, and he had no money to do either. So when one of the guys from Oakhurst offered him a job in Fort Worth's most prosperous industry, he took it. For the next year or so he dealt cards in various back rooms and hotels around town and worked as a croupier—a "stick man"—at a regular dice game at a place between Dallas and Fort Worth.

Gambling wasn't completely wide open in Fort Worth, but anyone could tell you where a game was. The bellman at a hotel would say, "Go to room so-and-so." Matty Reed played in a blackjack game at the Blackstone Hotel where Bennie dealt. Dan Greenwood played in a craps game in a basement on Ninth Street where his former caddie presided. Hogan supposedly was embarrassed by his brief stint in the gambling business and would not discuss it ever after. Occasionally, however, he couldn't hide his skill with a deck.

"I tell you, when Hogan dealt the cards he did it so fast they just spilled out of his hands," says Paul Runyan, the PGA champion in '34 and '38. "It didn't look like *he* was doing what *we* were doing. He not only had fast hands, he had fast eyes. When anybody else was dealing, he would say, 'Deal your cards lower. I know what you've all got.' "

Bennie and Valerie took the big gamble on matrimony on April 14, 1935. The *Cleburne Times-Review* announced the union on an inside page: "With only a few relatives and friends in attendance, the marriage of Miss Valeria [*sic*] Fox and Mr. Ben Hogan was solemnized Sunday at 12:30 at the home of the bride's parents, Mr. and Mrs. C. M. Fox of 808 Prairie Avenue. Dr. Albert Venting, pastor of the First Baptist Church, officiated. The bride wore an attractive white tailored crepe frock with white accessories. Her flowers, pink rose-buds, were arranged in a corsage. After the ceremony, the couple left for Fort Worth, where they will reside. The bride-groom is a well-known golf professional in Fort Worth." Mr. and Mrs. Royal Hogan attended; Mrs. Clara Hogan, the groom's mother, did not. She and Valerie did not get along, and never would.

For two years, the newlyweds lived cheaply. Green-wood was awed by his friend's ability to stretch a buck: Hogan didn't drink, gamble, or even eat very much.

On January 29, 1936, Marvin Leonard opened his new golf course in Fort Worth, Colonial Country Club, and installed slot machines in the basement to help with the over-head. Grandpa Hogan, the old Civil War veteran of the First Mississippi Cavalry Reserves, died in Dublin in March 1936, at age eighty-nine. Clara attended the funeral but none of her children did. In June 1936 Bennie participated in his first U.S. Open in two years (he had shot 79-79 at Merion in '34) at Baltusrol in New Jersey. He played ingloriously, however, and shot 75-79 and missed the thirty-six-hole cut. Byron shot 79-74 and missed, too. The Hogans somehow found the money to buy a used Buick for $550. It was maroon, a rich man's car with a long wheelbase and suitable for cross-coun-try travel. In May '37 the couple packed their home on wheels with their clothes, Bennie's clubs, and their life savings, and drove fifteen hundred miles to Niagara Falls, Ontario, for the General Brock Open.

The Buick was a dignified-looking machine, with its eyeball headlights, running boards, and spoke wheels, and it rode like a dream on smooth roads. But it bucked like a mule over the far more common surface of coarse gravel, potholes, and bumps. Progress was slow and exhausting. With no heater, air conditioning, defroster, radio, or tape deck to fiddle with, both passengers had plenty of quiet time to decide if this trip was high adventure or one last, desperate try.

Seven months later, there was no question. By the time the tour had traversed the country to California in January 1938 the Hogans were subsisting on hamburgers and Bennie's West Coast staple—stolen oranges.

Anyway, I played the summer tour and then we started for the winter tour. And we played again the Pasadena Open, the Los Angeles Open, and I missed the money in the Los Angeles Open. And we were driving to Oakland, California, and Valerie said, "You know how much money we have?" and I said, "Yes, I know." We had $86 left out of the $1,400. So she said, "Well, what are we gonna do?" And I said, "Valerie, we made a deal to spend $1,400. We have $86 left. And we're going to Oakland."

So, we shopped all around for a hotel room, the least expensive we could find, and we weren't eating very well and buying no clothes at all. . . . In the first round of the tournament, I had a fairly early starting time and left the hotel after breakfast and went across the street, and my car was jacked up.

And my two rear wheels were sitting on rocks. And they'd even taken the jack. So I came back to the hotel and I bummed a ride with somebody, I can't remember who, now. Anyway. I got to the course and I was late. . . . So, I played. I won $385. It's the biggest check I'd ever seen in my life.

And I'm quite sure it's the biggest check I'll, I'll ever see.

   —Hogan, from the 1983 interview with
    CBS

Hogan's voice cracked at the end of the story and his eyes misted over.

It didn't happen exactly as he told it, however. Capitulation, not determination, was his first reaction to losing his wheels. More than anything else at that moment, he wanted to get back to Fort Worth and find a steady job. He actually won $285, not $385, on the strength of a final-round 67 at Sequoyah Country Club. It was Nelson who took him to the golf course after the tirejacking. His car rested on cinder blocks, not rocks. The car was insured.

No matter. Bennie Hogan, dangling at the end of a very long rope, played the round of his life.

While Oakland represented a genuine turning point, Hogan's future as a golfer remained very much in doubt. He was remarkably self-contained and inward-looking, but he was also a merciless competitor, and competitors know when they're getting beat and by whom. The same guys who had always defeated him, the other caddie/golfers from Dallas and Fort Worth, still beat him, and that irritated him like poison ivy in his shorts. Gus Moreland, for instance, had won a flock of amateur events, played in the first Masters in 1934, and was an undefeated member of two Walker Cup teams—the all-star competition between the United States and England. This was big, because amateur golf held a good deal more prestige than the professional variety, thanks in part to the lingering influence of Bobby Jones. Guldahl had also been spectacular despite his funny swing and pace of play that made spectators check their watches. Not only did he win fourteen tournaments during the thirties, but Big Ralph won the biggest tournaments. The Western Open was only slightly behind the U.S. Open in prestige when Guldahl won it three times in succession. He also took the U.S. Open in '37 and '38 and the Masters in '39. Even Ray Mangrum had won a tour event, the Portland Open in '36, and he wasn't even as good as his younger brother, Lloyd.

Then there was Nelson. The recurring pattern of Byron beating Bennie carried over from the '27 Glen Garden caddie championship to the pro golf tour. Byron won tournaments in '35, '36, then twice in '37 and '38, and four times in '39. He made the Ryder Cup team. Just how far Bennie was beneath Byron's level was illustrated each April during Masters week. Byron was invited to participate in Bobby Jones's tournament in east Georgia—it was called the Augusta National Invitation then—starting in '35, the tournament's second year. He won it in '37 by two shots over Guldahl. The clubby atmosphere at Augusta National intoxicated the players lucky enough (or good enough) to be part of it. Members sponsored dinner parties for the participants—"country ham and all the trimmings," Nelson recalled, and "a Black quartet that went wherever the party was. They were mighty good." The papers made a big deal about the Masters, too, marveling over the beauty of the course, the quality of the field, and Jones's ability to create a new "major" tournament. Newspapers were the only contact Bennie had with the event. He was not invited until 1938.

If Bennie Hogan was a mile behind Nelson as a player, he was light years in arrears in a more important aspect of the pro's life—his club job. Given their personalities, it was no surprise. Byron met people easily and put them at ease, whereas Bennie's politeness with new people could seem like stiffness. Byron had left Texarkana in '35 for a better job as the assistant to PGA president George Jacobus at Ridgewood Country Club in New Jersey, which was hosting the Ryder Cup matches. In '37 likable Byron became the head professional at Reading Country Club in Reading, Pennsylvania. There, he was given an annual guarantee of $3,750 plus the profits from the pro shop, revenue from lessons, and plenty of time off to play golf tournaments. Added to the $6,959.50 he won on the tour, Byron was doing well enough to afford a new car, a four-door Ford touring car with side curtains. Meanwhile Bennie had no club affiliation of any kind.

Fortunately, the Century Country Club in White Plains, New York, was looking for an assistant pro. The CCC search committee had just two requirements: The new man would have to be an excellent player, and he would have to accept a salary of five hundred dollars a year. At about the time thieves in Oakland were lifting his tires, Ben Hogan's name came up at a meeting three thousand miles away. It seemed a little expensive to the New Yorkers to bring him in for an interview, so a West Coast friend of a friend was asked to go to the tournament and check him out. "Saw Ben Hogan. He makes a nice appearance," the secret agent reported by telegram. The job was offered and accepted, and he was to report to work in the northern suburb of New York City in May. But that was months away, and the Hogans nearly went broke again. In this crucial moment, a near-stranger bailed them out, someone who believed in Bennie. That someone was Henry G. Picard.

Picard (pronounced "pick-CARD") was a pro from Plymouth, Massachusetts, midway between Boston and

Cape Cod, and he had the "chow-dah" and "lob-stah" in his voice to prove it. He was also one of the best players on the tour. He had won a dozen tournaments between '35 and '37, and he would win the Masters in '38 and the PGA Championship in '39. Since his home base was the Hershey Country Club, the newspapers called him "the Chocolate Soldier." A sharp-dressing Bobby Jones devotee and a man of very few words, Picard was the second prescient pro, after Ted Longworth, to see something in Bennie besides a big hook and a bad grip. In the next three years, Picard's four favors saved Hogan's career as a tournament golfer. Since Picard's help involved an expenditure of no more than fifteen minutes, he never thought of himself as Hogan's savior—or as his great friend.

"My finances were low and I was a long way from home," Hogan recalled later. "Henry must have sensed my predicament because he came to me before a tournament and said, 'Look, Ben, I don't know what your financial situation is and it's none of my business, but I want you to know that if you ever need any help to stay on the tour you can always come to me.'"

According to Picard, however, his promise to back the unsuccessful young pro resulted from a flukish meeting in the lobby of the Blackstone Hotel in Fort Worth, where only a little more than a year before Bennie had dealt cards in a smoke-filled back room.

"I was going across country with Jack Grout," Picard said. "Why we stopped in a hotel in Fort Worth I don't know, because I went across the country many times and never stopped in hotels during the day to eat or anything else."

Picard recognized Hogan in a corner of the lobby, "talking rather loudly" with Valerie. He approached and asked what the trouble was.

"I've got to quit," Hogan told him. "If I go back on the tour, we don't have the money for her to go with me."

The two spouses eyed each other silently.

"I'm not the richest man in the world," Picard said, "but go ahead and play. If you run out of money, I'll take care of it."

Bennie accepted.

He never had to call Picard for backup, "but knowing that help was there if I needed it helped me forget about my troubles," Hogan wrote ten years later in *Power Golf.* His game picked up. He won a little money with a third-place finish at Sacramento. He played in his first Masters, although an incident before the tournament illustrated the experts' indifference to Hogan's game. As the defending champion, Nelson was invited to the Calcutta party at the Bon-Air Hotel. Calcuttas were effectively horse races: the best "horses" sold for thousands of dollars. If the horse/golfer you bought finished in the top eight, you would get your money back, and usually a lot more.

"Hey-what-am-I-bid-for-Ben-Hogan-a-fine-young-player-from-Fort-Worth-Texas-in-his-first-Masters-can-I-get-two-hundred-dollars," the auctioneer began, but except for the clinking of glasses the room was silent. "Can-I-get-a-bid . . . "

"One hundred dollars," someone finally called out. It was Nelson. It was as much a gesture of friendship and support as an investment. Bennie asked Byron the next day if he could purchase a half-interest, which he did, but he shot 75-76-78-72 and each man was out fifty dollars.

In July Picard invited Bennie to Pennsylvania to play in the Hershey Four-Ball Invitation golf tournament, a prestigious two-man team event scheduled for later that summer at Picard's home course. He needed someone to partner with Tommy Armour. Only sixteen of the tour's best players were asked to participate—tournament winners from '38 such as Sam Snead, Dick Metz, and Ky Laffoon; the nearly invincible team of Picard and Johnny Revolta; Paul Runyan, the new PGA champ; Guldahl, twice in a row the U.S. Open champion; and Nelson, who had won the '37 Masters. Bennie clearly didn't belong, and Picard caught some flak for asking him.

"Who the hell is this Hogan?" several important members wanted to know. Fair question. In one of its preview stories about the big event, the *Hotel Hershey High-Lights* published a list of the participants opposite their prize money for the year. Snead led with $7,112, "Lighthorse" Harry Cooper was second with $5,861, and the list went on down to Ed Dudley, the Augusta National pro who didn't play the tour much, who had amassed $1,312. The paper chose not to embarrass the tournament or "Ben Hogan, a rising star of golf" by printing his winnings or his tournament record. Hogan's lone tour highlight was a second-place finish in the Miami International Four-Ball with his teammate, the even more anonymous Willie Goggin. Not that the rising young star of golf had played so terribly. He had finished twenty-fifth at the Augusta Open, seventh in the Metropolitan Open, twentieth at Cleveland, and seventeenth at Glen Falls in his four most recent tournaments. Trouble was, on the depression-era tour, purses were small and only the top fifteen finishers got a check.

Mr. Hershey himself questioned Picard about his friend Hogan. Hershey was the president of both the club and the Hershey Chocolate Corporation that was the heart of local industry. "I think Hogan will be a great player," Picard told his boss, although he had never actually seen him play. He had, however, seen him practice. Everybody on the tour had seen Bennie Hogan practice.

When Hogan arrived in Hershey and Picard took him out to show him the golf course, he was sure he had been right all along about this kid. The third hole at Hershey's West Course was a shortish par-four through a chute of trees. Bennie stood up to his ball, a coiled, erect little man in the late August sunshine. Then he slashed. Although he had the biggest swing imaginable, with a full wrist break that pointed the clubhead straight to the ground at the top of his backswing, it was also the fastest swing around, about a full second faster than Snead's languid stroke. He seemed to be swinging a willow branch or a bull whip. The club swung with the whippy hiss of a willow branch. The trees amplified the concussion of wood on ball . . . *shhhwhack*! "With your swing, you can beat the world," Picard said.

Bennie caught a break when Armour dropped out a week before the event because of a broken bone in his hand. At age forty-three, the silver-haired former U.S. Open, British Open, and PGA champion was now primarily an instructor who drank a breakfast of scotch and Bromo-Seltzer—in separate glasses. The tournament's seven rounds in four days would surely have tested Armour's endurance. Victor Ghezzi, a beak-nosed, lantern-jawed, wavy-haired young man from Rumson, New Jersey, replaced Armour. Ghezzi (pronounced "GEZZ-zee") was good. He had won twice on the tour in '38, including another best-ball tournament while partnered with Snead. Vic was twenty-five, while Bennie had just turned twenty-six. They were the youngest of the eight teams and judged most likely to finish eighth.

Ghezzi-Hogan shocked the field with a twelve-under-par 61 in the first round, leading Nelson-Dudley by three. The Calcutta bettors who had invested so much in Nelson, Snead, Cooper, Picard et al, were astonished and dismayed when Ghezzi and Hogan carried their lead into the final round. Four thousand people clustered around the four foursomes on the final day, September 4, 1938. Byron-Eddie shot 69, but Vic-Bennie shot 64 to win by eight. Bennie had made thirty-one birdies, more than anyone else. A check for eleven hundred dollars awaited.

Euphoria gripped Ghezzi as he walked the last nine holes. But he noticed his partner was unable to lighten up, despite their huge lead. "If we had lost," said Ghezzi, "I am quite certain that he would have jumped out of a window."

After at least a decade of unremitting effort, the Hershey Four-Ball was Ben Hogan's first win in anything. His will and perseverance had overcome a bad grip, faulty technique, poverty, and tragedy. No one had ever paid more dues. Now he was ready to collect.

# CHAPTER 3

# BYRON

OVER THE MOUNTAINS, MOUNTAINS.
—KOREAN PROVERB

Ben Hogan and Byron Nelson knew they had hit the big time when they got out of the car and looked up at the 425-foot radio tower, glowing red and white in the cool, blue February sky. They hadn't even had time to change clothes. A tournament official had hustled them into his Packard for the seventeen-mile drive to the station as soon as Byron, the last to finish, had signed his scorecard. The building by the tower was nothing special—it looked like a little church—but WOAI was one of a handful of the most powerful radio stations in the nation. It transmitted soap operas, news, and sports at fifty thousand watts, the most massive mass media in the days before television. You could hear San Antonio's WOAI in a dozen states and half of Mexico, and in a minute Ben and Byron would be going on live.

Henry Guerra, a dark-haired young man, introduced himself and shook the two golfers' hands. On a table in the tiny newsroom sat a bulky, oblong microphone. The announcer and the golfers huddled around it as if it could keep them warm. On the air Guerra inclined his head slightly to ask U.S. Open champion Byron Nelson about his great 67 in the

BEN HOGAN'S FRIENDSHIPS
WERE RARE, CAREFUL, AND
OFTEN SHORT-LIVED, AND
SO IT TRANSPIRED WITH
NELSON.

just-completed final round of the 1940 Texas Open at Brackenridge Park in San Antonio.

"And what about tomorrow's playoff with Ben Hogan here, who shot 66 in both the final two rounds?" Guerra asked.

"Just happy to be here," began Byron, a born diplomat. "Anytime you can tie Ben, it's a feather in your cap, because he's such a fine player." No bulletin board material there.

It was Ben's turn. While Byron's face was all soft curves, geometric shapes stood out in Ben's eyebrows, jaw line, cheekbones, and the part in his hair. There was a soothing bit of country in Byron's voice and diction, but Ben didn't drawl and his sentences stopped and started as crisply as hand claps. The microphone resembled a very large electric razor, black on the bottom, perforated and shiny on top. Ben leaned into it and spoke.

"Byron's got a good game," he said, "but it'd be a lot better if he'd practice. Byron's too lazy to practice."

By nature and by religion a forgiving and understanding man, Byron recognized Ben's unthinking honesty as the source of this tactless comment. Still, it hurt. He decided to "show him I still practiced a little bit" in the playoff the next day. But one thing confused him about Ben's criticism: How could a friend say such a thing in public?

Ben Hogan's friendships were rare, careful, and often short-lived, and so it transpired with Nelson. After Ben made the tour for good and people stopped calling him Bennie, the Hogans and the Nelsons formed a pleasant, informal alliance. It began as a brotherhood of the road, a two-car caravan of Byron's new gray blue, eight-cylinder '39 Studebaker President and Ben's maturing brownish red Buick. Between tour

stops, they combed the country for filling stations selling gas
for twelve cents a gallon instead of fifteen; for hotels costing
four dollars a night instead of six; and for not-too-greasy
spoons where you could get the breakfast special and a morning paper for a quarter, tip included. Byron wrote down all
the financial data, one incredibly large hand wrapped around
a pencil and the other steadying his little black book. In one
of his regular reviews of their finances, Byron calculated that
he and Louise had set their record for frugality during their
one-month stay in Los Angeles in '37: $9.27 a day, $12.50
per day with lodging included. Usually, pros spent at least
twice that.

The thrifty travelers liked to stop at a little Tex-Mex
joint in Las Cruces, New Mexico, midway between Fort
Worth and L.A., because of its great homemade tamales at a
sensible price. When Ben asked for some to go one day, however, the waitress revealed that not only were the "homemade" tamales canned, they were canned by the Armour
Meat Company in Fort Worth. All four traded blank looks,
then laughs.

The wives got along, providing the main bond among
the four. Perky, self-assured Louise Nelson and the soft-
spoken Valerie Hogan spent a lot of time in each other's company during a typical tournament. Like most of the pros'
wives, they did not go out on the golf course to watch their
husbands play. Instead, they wore dresses and sat in the clubhouse, playing bridge, crocheting, and watching the scoreboard. None of the four drank much—the Nelsons not at
all—and both marriages were exceptionally close, to the point
that Ben and Valerie and Byron and Louise were considered
quite odd by the other golf professionals.

For several years they did the things that friends do.
The Hogans visited the Nelsons for a week in '39 in their
home in nearby Reading, right after Byron had won the U.S.
Open at the Philadelphia Country Club's Spring Mill course.

That week Byron gave Ben a black MacGregor driver he thought would help straighten out his hook. The club became Ben's favorite and he used it until it fell apart. Ben, Byron, and Jimmy Demaret hunted deer together in South Texas in November 1940. And they played practice rounds together on occasion, most memorably in '39 before the Texas Open, when Nelson and Jug McSpaden shot an amazing best ball of sixteen-under-par 55 to win a few bucks from Hogan and Paul Runyan.

None of it was enough to sustain the relationship, however. Ben didn't *need* a buddy. He had Valerie and his practice balls. Byron had long encouraged Ben, especially during the years his friend tried and failed to stay on the tour. He would watch him hit balls and say, "That's it, you've got it now." So when Ben's game improved, an important basis for the relationship was gone. "Have no friends not equal to yourself," Confucius said twenty-five hundred years ago, but it was their growing equality that drove Ben and Byron apart.

PLAYOFF DATA
*San Antonio Light*

Who: Ben Hogan and Byron Nelson. Winner gets $1,500, loser $750

What: Eighteen-hole playoff for 1940 Texas Open title

Where: Brackenridge Park

When: 1:00 P.M. today, Monday, Feb. 12

Price: One dollar and ten cents. Season tickets are *not* good for the playoff.

Gate Receipts: Fifty percent of the net to the players, who will divide their shares equally, and 50 percent to the Texas Open Fund.

About two thousand people watched Nelson strike the first shot 280 yards down the center of Brackenridge Park's first fairway. In their overcoats, ties, and fedoras, the spectators looked like they had just come from church. Most of them were for Byron. As a local reporter wrote in a Texas Open preview, "Nelson plays golf as though he enjoys it, not as though he were fighting a personal battle with the ball."

Ben hit a few seconds later, launching his first playoff drive from the exact spot where ten years before he had hit his first shot as a pro. Brackenridge's tees were unique in bigtime golf: rubber mats with little rubber tubes for tees, just like at the driving range. Shots hit from the tubes sounded like rifle shots. About the only change in the course since Hogan's pro debut there in 1930 was the patch of green at the end of each coffee-with-cream-colored fairway. What the city of San Antonio had saved on tee maintenance it had put into winter grass for the greens.

Ben and Byron had birdied every fourth or fifth hole during the tournament's regulation seventy-two holes, but they filled the playoff with pars. Nervousness, conservatism, or an excess of desire to beat the other guy conspired to keep putts from dropping. Easy wedge shots finished disappointingly far from the hole. Ben nearly drove the par-four fourteenth green but hit his second shot well past the hole and made par. On fifteen he left his wedge second shot far short of the green, into a branch of the San Antonio River for a penalty stroke, and he made bogey. Byron birdied the sixteenth to go one up. Both finished with pars, so Nelson won with a one-under 70 to Hogan's even-par 71.

Their polite war had started.

Like a terrier with a mouthful of pant leg, Ben Hogan would not let go of golf. He had survived ten years of rolling poverty before arriving at the brink of victory in a professional golf tournament.

After the win with Ghezzi in Hershey late in the summer of '38, Ben had made decent money in each of that season's remaining tournaments—a fifth at Westchester; a seventh in Columbia, South Carolina; a ninth in the Augusta Open; a fourth at Miami; and a third in Houston. He won $4,150 for the year. You could live on $150 a week if your car didn't break down and you really liked cheese sandwiches. Ben and Valerie were on the road at least half the year chasing the $4,150, so on average they lost a little bit each week. Still, it was a big improvement over the complete washouts in '30, '32, '34, and '37.

Hogan eked out a living in '39. He was runner-up to Byron at the Phoenix Open—by twelve shots—and made the thirty-six-hole cut for the first time in a U.S. Open before finishing tied for sixty-second, twenty-four shots behind Byron. The summer was spent on the lesson tee at Century Country Club, raking in that five hundred dollars.

"He was a bit shy at first," a member later recalled. "When he wasn't giving lessons, he would practice, practice, practice."

Hogan was back on the tour after Labor Day. Due mostly to an unsatisfying yet fairly profitable ability to finish second, he won fifty-six hundred dollars, seventh on the money list. Again, Ben and Valerie had traveled more than half the year. Maybe they netted a few bucks at the end, maybe they didn't.

Two incidents in '39 addressed old wounds. Around Christmas the members at Glen Garden back in Fort Worth threw a big party for their two former caddies and gave both Byron and Ben honorary life memberships. Earlier in the year, however, Ben had passed up the chance for another symbolic reconciliation. He had played in a little tournament in DeLeon, Texas, just a few miles from Dublin, but he avoided his old hometown and everybody in it. His parents had been arguing about living there just moments before his father's suicide. Dublin still meant death to Ben Hogan.

The year 1940 held the promise of greater accomplishment and further psychic distance from the pain of his youth. The timing was right: Between the end of the depression and the start of World War II, professional golf enjoyed an uneasy but prosperous lull. For touring players, the promotional genius of Fred Corcoran was partly responsible. The tour's charming new tournament director could sell his golfers to sportswriters and sponsors who didn't know Guldahl from Ghezzi. Corcoran's efforts were helped considerably by the emergence of the first marketable star since Walter Hagen, a long-armed athlete from Virginia named Samuel Snead. A pro now could play in a decent-sized tournament almost every week and turn a small profit if he played very, very well. But even for the handful of players who finished in the black, the necessity of a club job for a golf pro remained immutable.

Fortunately, the improved economy resulted in some movement in the market. A representative of Canterbury Country Club in Cleveland whispered a number in Henry Picard's ear, a figure higher than the five thousand dollars he was making at Hershey.

"Done," Picard said.

"Who shall we get to replace you, Henry?" club officials asked. "How about Snead?"

"No, Hogan," the Chocolate Soldier said.

And so it came to pass.

The job required no time in the pro shop, no cleaning clubs, no club repair, and no forced smiles. It was a "playing out of" job, a beautiful setup for someone such as Ben, who had no great aptitude or enthusiasm for the chitchat and teaching of a "real" golf pro job. This had become clear since his boss at Century Country Club had retired in 1940, and

Ben had taken over as the head professional. All he had to do at Hershey was to be around the club often enough during the golf season for the members to see how an expert golfer hit it. There was no television to substitute for a live performance, of course, and there were not enough tournaments around eastern Pennsylvania to satisfy the demand for vicarious perfection. Most of all, Ben was required to do what he had been doing anyway—play in golf tournaments. The club hoped that his finishes would make the members proud to open the sports page and read their club's name next to "their" pro's name when he won a golf tournament. Except for the money, the first yearly contract between Hershey and Hogan was the same as the last one, signed ten years later:

> The Company shall have the right to use the name or picture of *Ben Hogan* in the publicity or advertising in all of the Hershey Companies interest.

> The Professional shall attend and play in such golf tournaments as are mutually agreed upon.

> The Company agrees to pay the Professional a salary of $10,000 for the year during the period of this agreement, in equal semi-monthly installments of $416.66.

> The Company may terminate this agreement at any time for intoxication or unjustifiable misconduct of the Professional.

No records exist showing his original contract amount. Probably, it was three to four thousand dollars.

Ben and Valerie moved to Hershey in the spring of '41 and rented a two-room apartment at the Cocoa Inn, three-quarters of a mile from the club. The story Hershey members always tell about the Hogan years is set, predictably, on the practice tee:

"Gee, Ben, you sure can hit a golf ball," a member says admiringly. "How much would you charge me for a lesson?"

Hogan lights a cigarette, exhales, stares at the man through the blue smoke. "Five hundred dollars," he says.

"Wow," the member says. "Why so much?"

Hogan continues to stare, inhales, lets it out. "Because that's what it'll cost me in the next tournament if I take the time to help you."

He played the course six holes at a time, usually by himself, sometimes in the company of one of the club's better players, such as Hal Brewer, who managed the Hershey cocoa bean extract plant.

"I had a good time watching him," Brewer says. "He had a funny personality to me. Not very jovial. We never had what you would call a relaxing round. He wouldn't say two words."

On one of the few occasions Ben had something to say to Brewer, it was to tell him to get rid of those damn Spalding clubs and get some MacGregors, the brand he played. Brewer complied.

Did he have a sense of humor? "Yes," Brewer says, "Hogan was capable of enjoying a good joke as long as it didn't pertain to golf."

Hogan's standard drill consisted of hitting 150 balls—taking a half-minute for each shot—then playing the six holes, then another couple of hours in a remote corner of the triangle-shaped practice range.

"He never let you around when he was working on a new shot," Brewer said.

The members at the club couldn't believe how much this man practiced. The physical challenge of hitting full shots for even forty-five minutes is substantial for most golfers, but a greater challenge by far is caring as much about the first ball as the last. Your mind wanders; you start to screw around. Is it possible to hit a ball that hooks, then slices? But Ben never gave in to whimsy: he lined up each shot as if he needed it to win the U.S. Open. And he could pretend, thoroughly lost in his game of make-believe, for most of an entire day.

"You could tell this man had a plan," recalls golf pro Jackson Bradley, who first played the tour in the early forties. "Every shot he hit was planned. Every shot was thought out. He exuded energy."

Despite his enormous imagination and concentration, he had not cured his number-one bugaboo—the unexpected, uninvited hook. The hooks haunted him a few weeks after his playoff with Nelson when he and partner Lawson Little lost in the first round of the Miami-Biltmore Four-Ball. On the practice tee after the defeat, Ben broke the habit of a lifetime and asked for help. He approached—who else?—Henry Picard.

"You told me I was going to be a great player," Ben said. "But I hook too much."

He hadn't quite said, "Help me," but Picard understood. "I can change that in five minutes," he said. "Go get your five-iron."

If you don't count Ted Longworth's telling little Bennie the caddie not to grip it cross-handed, and a few brief looks by Jack Burke Sr. in Houston, this might have been the first formal lesson he ever took. And the last.

Years later Hogan seemed not to remember this final favor from Picard, as if he was embarrassed about the time he could not work out a golf problem on his own. And Picard would not reveal any specifics regarding what changes he suggested. But golf is not rocket science, regardless of what

Hogan and generations of golf instructors have tried to make us think. Picard's advice—slice. Move that left hand around to the left. Shove your hands forward. Now hit it.

Learning to curve the ball left-to-right might seem a painfully obvious cure for someone with an excess of right-to-left. But with all the practice Hogan had done, his habits were deeply ingrained. The cure worked immediately. Picard had never seen golf balls hit so straight, so squarely, and with so much force. "You don't need me anymore," he said. Ben thanked him and left South Florida for Pinehurst Country Club in central North Carolina, where he would practice his new grip and setup for two weeks.

Too much has been made about the changes Hogan made in his technique. His mental and attitudinal adjustments were much more vital. He didn't win in the thirties, he said later, because "I hadn't learned to concentrate, to ignore the gallery and the other golfers, and to shut my mind against everything but my own game."

Harry Cooper deserves mention for an earlier anti-hook lesson. "I saw Hogan at the New Orleans Open in 1937 and he was having a hell of a time fighting that duck hook. He asked me for help. On the range I noticed that Ben was letting go of the club with his left hand at the top of his back-swing and then regripping it stronger than he had at address. Ben never made mention of that tip in public, but I think he was grateful. Every time I see him, he comes over and gives me a big hug."

Even golfers read the front page first in 1940. Germany invaded Holland, Belgium, Luxembourg, and France, and attacked London by air. FDR was elected for a third term and everyone wanted to know if he would involve the United States in the European war.

Like many people, an eighteen-year-old boy from Bettendorf, Iowa, studied the sports page with a greater-than-usual sense of relief and escape. Jack Fleck was a golf pro—a touring pro someday, he hoped—so he followed the tournament scores closely. He had seen Hogan's name in the top ten of more and more tournaments in the last year or so, but he was shocked at what he read in March and April. The newspapers kept revealing the same unlikely headline: "Hogan Wins."

> March 22, Associated Press: Ben Hogan, the lad who'd been second in almost everything but never had been first, proved he had the quality that makes champions Thursday when he won the thirty-eighth annual North and South Golf Championship with a record seventy-two-hole score of 277.
>
> Eleven shots under par for the famous Pinehurst No. 2 course, the Fort Worth professional took down first money in beating Sam Snead by three strokes. . . . Byron Nelson was third with 286, nine shots back.

> March 29, AP: Ben Hogan, the little man with a big golf game, cut loose with a seven-under-par finish in the $5,000 Greensboro Open golf tournament today to win first prize of $1,200 with a tournament record score of 270.
>
> The hard-hitting Texas welterweight, breaking 70 on each of his four rounds, won by nine . . . sticking to his fire-for-the-pins tactics right to the final hole . . . so consistently brilliant that it is hard to describe . . .

Hogan's drives, which whistled as they went by. . . . Byron Nelson finished tied for third with 280, ten shots back.

March 31, AP: Ben Hogan, who can make a golf course sit up and say uncle, completed the most sensational streak in the annals of the Professional Golfers Association Sunday when he won the $1,200 first prize in the Asheville, North Carolina, Land of the Sky Open tournament with a seventy-two-hole score of 273.

His scores in his three wins in the last two weeks: 66-67-74-70-69-68-66-67-67-68-69-69. . . . Ben has moved into first place on the money list with $6,438 to Jimmy Demaret's $6,152.

Byron Nelson tied for seventh with 284, eleven shots back.

The irony of Ben's first win and first winning streak was that he did it with brilliant putting. The lesson from Picard and the days of practicing full shots undoubtedly helped, but the least physically demanding part of the game was the least responsive to the all-day drill that was Ben's specialty. Despite heavy rain at Pinehurst, three days of snow at Greensboro, and the resultant disorienting delays, Ben holed lots of birdie putts and three-putted only twice in the twelve rounds spread over the three tournaments.

Putting was in a way the toughest part of the game for him. He found it hard to accept that random and undetectable variations in hardness, contour, grass, and humidity might cause one perfect putt to go in and another to stay out. Putting simply didn't play to his strong suits. Strength was unimportant on the greens and Ben was very strong. Putting technique seemed optional, but the discovery of correct technique in the full swing was his obsession. Despite his ambivalence about the short stick, Ben Hogan could really putt—and now he could beat Nelson.

Sportswriters and sports readers found it impossible not to consider the newcomer in tandem with the king. Editors assigned compare-and-contrast stories to writers who found that Hogan didn't volunteer much and was complex in his motivations and in the way he swung a club. Nelson, however, was accommodating and his golf swing was as simple as a metronome's. Byron apologized for his friend's reticence: "He's just shy. Strange people bother Ben. Well, strangers have never bothered me."

A rivalry was assumed. But it was a one-sided rivalry, if such a thing can exist. Byron did not believe that Ben was an obstacle to a goal, but he could feel exactly that sentiment flowing from Ben to him.

Nelson regained the upper hand in the spring. In an era when touring pros valued their club affiliations like today's pros value their courtesy cars, a great job opened up at Inverness in Toledo, Ohio. This was not a playing-out-of position, but a club professional job with the usual responsibilities of lessons, retail sales, and public relations. Inverness had prestige, a U.S. Open-quality golf course, and a wealthy membership willing to offer its golf professional an attractive financial package. The finalists for the position were Hogan, who was then still making a modest wage at Century Country Club, and Nelson. Predictably, the Inverness representative who interviewed both chose Byron. "I guess he liked the way I combed my hair better or something," Nelson said. Beaten again by Byron, Ben was miffed.

That summer Hershey hosted the PGA Championship, the only match-play major. It would be an opportunity for Ben to get over any disappointment he might have felt about the Inverness job since he had played well there in the past. He beat Frank Champ in the first eighteen-hole round and Harry Nettlebladt after lunch. Al Brosch was no problem in round three. But in the thirty-six-hole quarters on August 29, Ben came up against a recognizable name and an old adversary— Guldahl. Big Ralph, taking as long as five minutes to hit important shots, beat Ben 3 and 2, even though Ben played the thirty-four holes in five under par. Nelson beat Guldahl the next day and Snead the day after to win the tournament.

A year later at Cherry Hills in Denver, the match-play PGA again did what it was supposed to do—settle the score between the game's best players. Hogan played Horton Smith and won. Nelson played Guldahl and won. Snead played Lloyd "Sneaky" Mangrum and lost. Hogan would play Nelson in the thirty-six-hole quarterfinals on a sunny, dry July day in the mountains and this time, dammit, he would win.

Every hole is a little tournament in match play, because you can beat your opponent by two or by ten on any individual hole and all you've won is one hole. This electrifying format exited professional golf's stage as television entered the fifties, because matches might end before they reached the bulky, immobile cameras parked on the last few holes. Besides, advertisers were afraid that unknowns such as Harry Nettlebladt and Al Brosch would somehow make it to the finals. At any rate, players often play a more attacking style in match play, since one bad hole is not nearly as harmful as when you have to count every stroke.

Hogan charged to a 66 in the morning round. Yet he was only one-up at the lunch break. Byron attacked back in the afternoon and evened the match on the eighth hole. Ben birdied the eleventh to go one-up, but Nelson again squared things with a birdie three on the par-four sixteenth.

The thirty-fifth hole would be crucial. The green on the otherwise unprepossessing par-five seventeenth at Cherry Hills held a number of interesting problems for a golfer trying to keep his hands from shaking. The surface was small, hard, backless, and surrounded by water like a moat around a castle. Rarely could you go for this green with your second shot, and hitting it in the right place even in the regulation three strokes was not easy. Both players laid up short of the water in two.

Ben smoked on his cigarette while he weighed the variables of wind, lie, distance, and adrenaline. He was on cruise control now. Because he practiced shots rather than just swings, he had developed an unvarying routine before actually striking the ball: Remove the club from the bag decisively; take one last hit from the cigarette and throw it to the ground; eye the target from the side with a little half-swing; stand with the club behind the ball and the feet together; put the left foot forward then the right foot back; look a final time at the target; look back at the ball; waggle once; pause; hit. But this time something went wrong. Hogan hit it in the water. Byron made par and was one-up with one to play.

Byron hit first on eighteen with his round brown driver, giving the water hazard to the left of the fairway a wide berth, perhaps being "a little too cautious," he said. Then Ben teed his ball and began his precise preshot ritual. One thought always intruded before he hit this particular club, the black driver Byron had given him two years before. It had a noticeable left bias. The first time he had hefted it on the tenth tee at Hershey, he had said, "Byron, I'm gonna hook this thing around my neck." But instead, the club's closed face had shouted a constant reminder— *don't hook.*

He didn't. He played a risky direct shot over the edge of the lake into the left side of the fairway. Both had two-hundred-and-something up-hill, upwind yards to the hole. Ben hit first, a flat-planed slash with a two-iron, a marvelous pressure shot to just twelve feet from the hole. Applause and yells from the spectators. Byron, too, took a two-iron, his absurdly large hands making the club look like a tooth-pick. He swung his upright, up-and-down swing in the silence.

THE FACT THAT HE PRACTICED HIS VICTORY SMILE IN THE MIRROR MIGHT HAVE MADE IT LESS THAN COMPLETELY SINCERE.

Four seconds later, the gallery shouted again, and more loudly. He had hit it inside of Ben's ball. Ben barely missed his putt, but Byron's found the cup. Once again, Ben lost.

Like stooges, musketeers, and french hens, great golfers periodically bunch in threes at the top of the game. The first such triumvirate—John Henry Taylor, a Scot, and Englishmen James Braid and Harry Vardon—dominated golf for the twenty years prior to World War I. Their successors were Americans—Hagen, Sarazen, and Jones. Perhaps because golf's opinion leaders had gotten used to this arrangement, they began to talk in the forties about Hogan, Nelson, and Snead as the latest trinity. The idea caught on, because there was something for everyone in Ben, Byron, and Sam. Their appeal showed clearly in the newsreels, the series of thirty-second snippets of film shown in movie theaters before the feature. "Nelson Takes Los Angeles Tourney!" the first frames would say, and there would be Byron, looking modest and benign, and turning his head chastely when a starlet attempted to kiss him on the lips during the trophy presentation. Snead was a mugger: when he won, he would roll his eyes and do something funny as they handed him the check.

Hogan was quite obviously the least relaxed of the three on the golf course but the most relaxed afterward, with his photogenic piano-key grin and the tilt of his head. The fact that he practiced his victory smile in the mirror might have made it less than completely sincere.

Snead was, for most people, the most fun to watch. Spectators in his gallery would swing their umbrellas, trying to imitate his balletic grace. He would hit a wild shot from time to time, which made him seem like one of them. If he was happy after his round, he would lay out his cornpone country charm like a banquet. Byron the Good was also Byron the Bland. His golf game was built on mistake avoidance, his dipping-at-impact swing was marvelously rhythmic but no aesthetic treat, and his postgame comments had all the fire and spice of rice pudding. Hogan was completely different from these two or anybody else. He was no less graceful than Snead, but his rip at a golf ball reminded an observer less of a ballet dancer than of the violent elegance of a perfect tackle by a football defensive back. And it was so quick a stroke you couldn't really see it. Instead of swinging imaginary clubs, those who watched Ben asked each other, "How does he do it?" With his smoke, his silence, and his detachment, Hogan's style resembled a Catholic mass on Easter Sunday, but without the altar bells. He had some ineffable quality the others lacked, a mystique.

Clothing was part of his quasi-mystical air. Snead and Nelson might use some color, or a pattern; Hogan, never. Gray, white, and black were the only colors in his rainbow. He spit-shined his golf shoes (custom made in London) to a military gloss, wore the best Pima cotton shirts—he had them dry-cleaned, not washed—and bought his white caps from Cavanaugh, an expensive hatter on Park Avenue in New York City. He got his hair cut every week.

Ben, Byron, and Sam were cordial associates, not friends. Even if they had met under noncompetitive circumstances, say, at the opera, they probably would never have sought each other out. Snead thought Hogan was weird and that Nelson was prissy. Hogan kept his distance from Sam and Byron: he had few friends on the golf course and no time for friends off it. Nelson loved thine enemies as thyself, so he never expressed the vague antagonism the other two felt toward him from time to time. Still, Nelson thought Snead was crude. "We were all like priests compared to Snead," says 1957 Masters champion Doug Ford. "And if we were priests, Hogan and Nelson were Jesus." But Hogan, Nelson, and Snead didn't have to be alike or like each other—that was part of the fun. Their differences divided golf fans into three distinct camps.

"The one thing that Hogan and Snead and I had in common was that we wanted to beat somebody," Nelson says.

The only problem with golf's third triumvirate was that Hogan didn't deserve to be in it. Although he had won tournaments—four in '40, five in '41—none of them were majors, the most accepted tests of greatness in golf. By that standard, Snead shouldn't have been included either. He had won twenty-six official PGA events through '41, but no Masters, no Opens, and no PGAs. So who else had a chance to stand with Nelson, winner of three majors, at the top?

The best candidate after Hogan and Snead was the eternally underrated James Newton Demaret. In 1940 he won six of the nine tournaments he played, including the Masters. He didn't take himself or his game very seriously, however, so almost no one else did either.

"You going home, Jim?" someone once asked him as he left the locker room after a tournament in Houston.

"Nah," said Sunny Jim. "I haven't gone straight home in thirty years. Why should I start now?"

He loved to sing, he loved to party, and he dressed like a clown. He spun his club around after every shot in a hot-dog flourish. Demaret was the last guy you would think of as Ben Hogan's partner. But Ben had his reasons for joining Jimmy.

Team events were a big deal on the tour in those days, but so were friendships. In almost every instance, friends chose friends as their partners. Nelson and Jug McSpaden, for example, were as tightly linked as Abbott and Costello. But to Ben, golf had almost nothing to do with camaraderie. He paired up with the best available player and focused on winning. He had won Hershey with Ghezzi, and Miami with Sarazen early in '41. After that, Demaret was his man. They had known each other from golf tournaments in Texas when both were teenagers. "When he played with me, there was no fooling around," Hogan said. "He had tremendous talent as a shotmaker." The strengths of Demaret's game were accuracy off the tee—he had been taught to play a fade by the purest hitter of the old pros, "Wild" Bill Melhorn—and his ability as a wind player. The anchor formed by his short legs and his considerable hindquarters balanced him in a breeze.

"Jimmy was commode-huggin' drunk at 3:30 in the morning the day he's got Snead in the finals of the World Match Play Championship," recalls Demaret's friend Bones Maloney. Mere hours later, his shoes untied, his eyeballs swimming in ketchup, Jimmy swung at his first tee shot and almost whiffed. But then he hit a brassie three feet from the stick and won the hole and then the match. The Demaret legend contains many variations on this theme. Jimmy was a great player, but he just didn't seem like Hogan's type.

The Odd Couple first teamed in the '41 Inverness tournament at Byron's course. As the host professional, Nelson was obligated to take as his partner boozy old Walter Hagen, who played only to hype the gate. Nelson-Hagen finished last, a fact which didn't amuse the competitive Nelson. Hogan-Demaret won.

Hogan and Sunny Jim remained teammates from that point on. And they became friends in the same limited way Hogan later became friends with pro golfers Ken Venturi, Jack Burke Jr., Tommy Bolt, and Gardner Dickinson. Demaret et al were expressive, even emotional men. In 1994 Venturi kissed Ben on the cheek and said tearfully, "I love you, Ben." Said Hogan, "You're not so bad yourself." The vanguard of Hogan men were fonder of him than he was of them, and they knew it. But they were quick to pick up the cudgel if anyone criticized their eccentric friend. They were never fawning, however. Most people walked on eggshells around Hogan, and he hated it.

"I'd just go up and say, 'Hogan, you no-good sumbitch, I'm gonna kick your fuckin' ass today,' " Bolt says. "He loved it. He'd stand there and show those teeth."

Hogan would have a drink with Kenny or Jack or Tommy or Gardner after a round but rarely dinner. Demaret had the *cojones* to kid his partner a little more than the others, but after a beer they went their separate ways—Jimmy to a bar or a party, Ben to the practice tee or to Valerie.

"The strangest thing in the world is that Ben and I have never been close," Demaret said in 1969. "I don't know Ben. We played together in competition, but, actually, on the tour Ben and I never ran together. . . . Nobody gets close to Ben Hogan."

When Demaret wrote in 1954, "Chester Hogan introduced his son Ben to golf," he revealed both how far he was from Hogan's confidence and what a carefree biographer he was. Yet, like many popular people, Demaret was something of a student of human behavior. He noticed during their infrequent meals together that Ben kept his head down and ate without a word. He frequently sent his eggs back at breakfast and his steak back at dinner and sometimes went into the kitchen to instruct the staff on the difference between medium and medium rare. When they were bunkmates at singer/golfer Bing Crosby's ranch in Tuscarora, Nevada, Demaret discovered that Hogan ground his teeth at night. During the day, the tension within revealed itself when someone pointed a candid camera at him. After Ben gave a shutterbug in the gallery at the '41 Colonial a stare that probably exposed his film, Demaret asked him about it. "Jimmy, those movie cameras always sound like rattlesnakes to me," Hogan said. "When I was a kid, rattlesnakes used to scare me to death. When I hear that buzzing sound, I want to jump into the nearest tree." But he also despised still photographers with equal passion—unless, of course, it was after a tournament and he had won. Hogan loved ceremonies.

If Hogan and Demaret hadn't won most of the time, his partnership with this nearly humorless man might have been a trial for the breezy Demaret. Writer Dan Jenkins, Venturi, and other intimates say Hogan could be funny in a heavy, ironic way, but Demaret never saw it. "When he is talking about anything except an out-and-out joke, he remains absolutely deadpanned," Demaret wrote in 1954. "His opinions, when he delivers them, don't have even the hint of a light touch in them." And on the golf course, Ben talked about as much as he did at dinner. Most golf teammates are quite chatty, partly from a desire to help each other and partly out of relief at having the responsibility for a score being shared. Not Hogan. During their rounds together as World Cup partners in 1956, Snead remembers talking with Hogan only once. "That damn [Roberto] De Vicenzo keeps making birdies," Ben had whispered to Sam. "What are we gonna do?" As for Demaret, despite his lime green slacks and lemon yellow shoes, Sunny Jim felt invisible to his partner.

The only part of golf's entourage that Ben consistently noticed was the writers. To Sunny Jim's amazement and veiled disapproval, their relationship was often adversarial. Part of the problem came from the loose way the papers used a player's name with a "Golf Tip of the Day" on the sports page. A reporter would ghostwrite some innocuous bit of golf wisdom— "Don't make up your mind what club you're going to play before you're even up to your ball. Size it up carefully. Select your club with thought"—and put Joe Pro's picture and signature over it, usually with the pro's permission, sometimes without. Everyone else on the tour appreciated the goodwill and publicity such things might bring. Ben did not. He raised hell and threatened lawsuits.

His pique at the unauthorized use of his byline was a symptom of his basic problem with the press. He believed they controlled him in an important way. But just the opposite was true, particularly in those see-no-evil days before Jim Bouton broke the gentleman's agreement with his tell-all baseball book *Ball Four*. A sports star, not some newspaper drone from Dubuque, was in charge of his own image. Ben couldn't, or wouldn't, grasp that a sportswriter on deadline was often quite willing to be manipulated, but if you didn't put the words in his pen, he might put them in your mouth. Every writer misquoted him, he said, except Goldy Goldman of the *Houston Post* and *Chronicle* and Jim Trinkle of the *Fort Worth Star-Telegram*. He reviewed everything that was written about him by guys to whom he barely talked. His conclusion was that writers were nosy, parasitic, inaccurate, and worthy of disdain, since they obviously did not try as hard in their profession as he did in his.

Bob Brumby, a New York columnist, met Ben for the first time at Winged Foot Golf Club in New York in 1942 soon after writing, "Baseball has a press fighter in Ted Williams and now golf, of all sports, has an uncooperative star in Ben Hogan." Ben stared murderously at the writer with his startling blue gray eyes, and the temperature at Winged Foot suddenly dropped twenty degrees. Brumby later joked to Demaret that he was glad Hogan wasn't armed.

HIS CONCLUSION WAS THAT WRITERS WERE NOSY, PARASITIC, INACCURATE, AND WORTHY OF DISDAIN, SINCE THEY OBVIOUSLY DID NOT TRY AS HARD IN THEIR PROFESSION AS HE DID IN HIS.

Yet Brumby had been right: Ben Hogan was an uncooperative star, especially when compared to a charmer such as Demaret. He ignored his partner and fans, would not usually mingle with his peers, and did not much care for Snead, Nelson, writers, photographers, or incorrectly cooked steaks. On the other hand, golf was a business for Ben, and he was the sole stockholder.

"Listen," says a long-time Hogan acquaintance from Fort Worth, "Mr. Hogan wanted to be the best golfer in the world, and he knew it would take every bit of his attention and energy to do it. Some golf champions could smile and sign every autograph. Ben couldn't. Nothing wrong with that."

But something seemed to be wrong, something possibly more substantial and more internal than the burdens of celebrity. Hogan had told no one of the psychological wound he likely was protecting, least of all his so-called "biographer" Demaret, who did not seem to wonder about his partner's motivations anyway. Depression might have been a logical consequence of his father's suicide. Could that have been his problem?

"No, I don't think he was depressed," Dan Greenwood says. "He was pretty dead serious ever since he was a kid, but I always thought he was just like a racehorse with the bit in his mouth. He had his eye on that finish line."

Greenwood believes Ben just overlearned the poker face he had developed from his earlier association with gamblers. Depressed or not, Hogan appeared friendless to Greenwood and others. He rarely laughed and was not noticeably happier after achieving his presumed goal, winning golf tournaments. Although he had had the good sense and luck to channel his rituals into a game that encouraged repetition in a thousand details, he remained anxious. The little ceremonies in golf, although he repeated them endlessly, were still not enough.

Demaret flipped his car lights on and started to leave the Oak Hill Golf Club in Rochester, New York. But he noticed a silhouette of a golfer on the practice tee and stopped the car to investigate.

"Ben, you been out here practicing since you came in?" Demaret asked. Most of the rest of the pros had been drinking and playing gin since finishing their rounds several hours before.

"Yeah."

"Well, Ben, you had ten birdies today and shot 64. What the hell are you trying to prove?"

"Jimmy, there's no reason in the world why a man can't birdie every hole."

Perfectionism works best when it focuses on attainable things, such as keeping one's desktop clear. Perfection in golf is easy to define but impossible to achieve. For Hogan to reach his goal of birdies on every hole, he would have to stay up late, because days were too short to practice adequately. His pursuit didn't leave him much time for himself or for his friends. Minor details and minor problems became major if they interfered with the rituals. And despite all he had achieved, he didn't seem to enjoy life. Hogan's behavior was as classic for obsessive compulsive disorder as red spots are for measles. His obsession helped make him a genius, but it didn't make him happy.

Professional sports and real life once existed without touching each other. The mock importance of the outcomes of games endured no matter what happened outside the stadium walls. The game players we admired were remote and godlike, more connected to golf or football and to previous generations of athletes than to us. A lot of the fantasy has been lost in the modern age, when money and media exposure have created jaded fans and made our heroes mere jock businessmen.

But in the forties, it took a war to remind us on which side of the ropes the term "life or death" really applied. And even after the Pacific fleet was pulverized at Pearl Harbor by some remote Asiatic nuisance, for a few months Americans hung onto their obsessions about who was better. Joe DiMaggio of the New York Yankees or Ted Williams of the Boston Red Sox? Hogan, Snead, or Nelson? It was better than wondering when or if you would be drafted, if you would pass the physical, if you would have to fight, or if you would die. The bittersweet days during the war were filled with portent and finality when you might be doing certain things or seeing certain people for the last time.

For the people of the United States, the war started badly and got worse. Following the Pearl Harbor debacle in December 1941, the Philippines was overrun, Singapore fell, rationing began, and pleasure driving ended. Religious books filled the bestseller lists. Even though professional sports were officially deemed a worthwhile diversion for the increasingly tense citizenship, it was soon obvious that the 1942 professional golf season would be severely diminished. The British Open would not be held, of course, due to the war in Europe; in fact, it had not been held since 1939. The PGA announced that its championship would be reduced from sixty-four players to thirty-two and would be held much earlier than usual, in May, instead of the customary late-summer/early-fall date. The USGA also proclaimed a change. It would not hold its Open in 1942, but would instead cosponsor a tournament with the Chicago District Golf Association and call it the Hale America Open. It would have most of the accoutrements of a U.S. Open, such as qualifying rounds, a good field, and USGA medals for the winner, runner-up, and low amateur. But it would not be called the "U.S. Open" and it would not be contested on a championship course. Hogan would win it, on the strength of an eye-popping, second-round 62. Later, Ben and his supporters—especially Dan Jenkins—would try to keep alive the fiction that this really had been a U.S. Open. It was not. There would be only one real major in 1942—the Masters.

Even without the dramatic context of war, the Masters was the most theatrical of golf tournaments. Augusta National Golf Club in April was an orgy of chlorophyll, flowering trees, budding azaleas, and overheated prose from baseball writers returning north from spring training who stopped in Augusta to attempt to describe it all. Familiarity added to the drama. The Masters was the only major golf championship contested at the same site each year and at the same time. But it wasn't just the voluptuous Augusta National earth and Georgia dogwoods that made the Masters a rite of spring. It was also the guiding hand and presence of Bobby Jones. This was the only time all year the modest yet charismatic retired champion competed, and that was an event in itself. The reverence writers felt for Jones spilled over onto their coverage of his little invitational tournament.

Byron, Ben, and Sam were the betting favorites, in that order, and all three were playing great golf. The tour had begun, as usual, on the West Coast. Byron won at Oakland. Ben won at Los Angeles and San Francisco. As the caravan motored east, gas and golf balls were suddenly harder to come by. Snead won at Saint Petersburg. Ben won twice—the North and South at Pinehurst and again at Asheville. Bit by bit, Picard's antihook lesson had worn off, and Hogan was playing a right-to-left curve ball with every club, even the short irons. On the eighteenth at San Francisco, a dogleg right, Ben had had to aim a four-wood at the trees and spin it left, back into the fairway. His lack of a dependable slice or fade made him feel one-dimensional, like a baseball player who can't hit to the opposite field. Yet the predictability of his shots and the cool, detached way he made each shot set up the next—he called this "management"—enabled him to play any golf course well. And with the extreme length of its holes and its half-a-football-field-wide fairways, a big, running hook was no liability at Augusta National.

Byron got a sweetheart deal by being paired in the first round with his best friend Jug McSpaden and shot 68. Ben teed off twenty-five minutes later, at 1:45, and had to endure more of a late-afternoon thunderstorm than did Nelson. Ben was paired with Lloyd Mangrum, not that it mattered much. Betty Grable could have been his playing partner and he wouldn't have noticed her any more than he did Sneaky Lloyd. He shot 73, well back of the 67s shot by Horton Smith and Paul Runyan. Snead was out of it quickly. He shot 78 and complained of a "bad back."

Nelson took control of the tournament with a second-round 67. Afterward Byron intimated to reporters that he had discovered the secret to playing Augusta National. He promised to reveal it if he won on Sunday.

The wind kicked up during the third round, creating the most difficult combination of conditions in golf—fast greens and fresh breezes. Only three players bettered Byron's even-par 72. Bobby Cruickshank of Scotland and Ernie Joe "Dutch" Harrison of Conway, Arkansas, both shot 71. Ben shot 67, a sensational score.

"Best managing I ever did," he coolly told the press. "I mean manipulating the ball, allowing for wind and roll. You had to do it in that wind."

He had putted only twenty-eight times, a fact he didn't mention. He had the brilliant striker's lack of pride in his little pecks on the putting green. He had picked up five shots on Byron to move into second place, just three shots behind his erstwhile buddy with one round to play. This was getting good.

It came down to the last hole in the final round. Ben hit his second shot to the eighteenth green at about the same moment Byron hit his second to seventeen. Ben nearly holed his; Byron's ball buried in a bunker. The subsequent birdie-bogey tied the score, so Byron would need a three on the difficult par-four eighteenth to win, or a four to tie. It appeared he would get neither when his right foot slipped on his tee shot and his ball flew in a hacker's arc deep into the tall pines on the right. But fortune smiled on Nelson, as it always seemed to. His ball sat nicely on a burnt orange bed of pine needles, no trees impeded his swing, and a twenty-foot-wide gap in the conifers allowed a direct shot to the green. Byron hooked a five-iron through the opening, onto the green, and almost made the fifteen-foot putt to win. Playoff.

At least twenty-five of the pros who had played in the tournament remained for the eighteen-hole showdown at 2:30 P.M. (Eastern War Time) the next afternoon. Nelson faced the day in a weakened state. He had vomited through the night and into the morning. Ben knocked on his door at the Bon-Air Hotel. "I heard you were sick last night," he said. "Would you like to postpone?" Byron declined. Like the tournament host, Jones, Byron usually played very well despite a nervous stomach. Unlike "the Great Bobby," however, he did not cure the problem with a hot bath and a tumbler of corn liquor. Byron went with half a plain chicken sandwich and a cup of tea.

Ben had just as much cause for anxiety, of course. He had built toward this climax for twelve mostly unsuccessful years as a golf professional. He had hit hundreds of thousands of practice balls, exponentially more than anyone else. But he had never won a major. And he had never beaten Nelson head-to-head.

Despite the high stakes, Ben was steady in the playoff, while Byron played like a man who had thrown up all night. Ben parred the first hole routinely. Meanwhile, Byron hit another big slice into the trees, found his ball resting against a pine cone, whacked it left-handed with his putter back toward the fairway, and made a double-bogey six. Three holes later Ben had stretched his lead to three shots.

There was some debate later about the turning point. Was it the three-wood to six feet on number eight or the tee shot to six inches on number twelve? Or was it the entire stretch of holes from six to thirteen which the winner played in six under?

The wives remained in the clubhouse until the playoff reached the final hole. Valerie and Louise walked to the eighteenth green. They hugged when the last putt was holed and applauded with the other fifteen hundred spectators as the victor and the gracious loser shook hands.

The winner revealed his secret about Augusta to the press. "You've got to play your iron shots to the green," he said. "You can't just aim for the flagstick."

Nelson 69, Hogan 70. Ben wondered if he would ever beat him.

# CHAPTER 4

# HOGAN

THE SCHEME THAT SMOLDERED THROUGH WINTER LONG
NOW BURSTS INTO ACT—INTO WAR—
THE RESOLUTE SCHEME OF A HEART AS CALM
AS THE CYCLONE'S CORE.

—HERMAN MELVILLE

THEY USED TO LAUGH AT ME FOR PRACTICING.

—BEN HOGAN

Ben Hogan paced on the people-ringed plateau like an actor on an outdoor stage. Beneath the bill of his deflated white cap, smoke and shadow hid the upper half of his face. His broad boxer's nose jutted above a pair of lips that resembled flat stones clasping a burning cigarette. The lines running from the sides of his mouth to the sides of his nose—the nasolabial folds—were deeply etched. Like Gary Cooper's staring down the bad guys in *High Noon*, Hogan beamed his hidden eyes at eighteen feet of shiny green, the space between his ball and the hole.

Golf tournaments are inherently melodramatic, and the final hole of a major championship can be excruciatingly so. But the wasp-waisted man in the pleated gray pants regarded his putt to win the 1946 U.S. Open at Canterbury

Country Club in Cleveland and betrayed nothing to the three thousand people watching him. He really wasn't much of an actor. He had become Hogan. "Ben" was too familiar for anyone who had felt the arctic cold front of his personality, and the diminutive "Bennie" was a preposterous tag for a man as hard as Hogan. Addicted to alliteration, the newspaper boys referred to him as "Bantam Ben"—or "Little Ice Water"—but no one ever said, "Hey Bantam, what about a beer after the round?" The other pros called him "the Little Man," although they didn't use this Napoleonic reference to his face. "The Hawk" captured him pretty well for the imperious way he held his head with those eyes almost hard to look at. But usually it was just "Hogan." Hogan meant silence and concentration.

Byron Nelson's doctor told him Ben's ability to shut out the world was self-hypnosis, and Byron believed it. Hogan meant a flat, white cap—regular hats got out of shape and white went with everything—and impeccable, almost formal, golf clothing. Most of all, the name came to mean cold excellence. He walked down fairways with his arms extended, holding a club as if it were a picket sign. He was studying his grip, practicing even while he played. The snickering by the other pros about his inability to do anything but practice had been replaced by respect. Hogan was the golfer for the new American technocracy, the most superior athlete of the most superior nation.

He threw his cigarette down.

According to a number of writers, Hogan had "burned" for this moment throughout his years in the service during World War II. They were wrong. Hogan's fierce desire to win did not vary by time or by circumstance. Aside from being incorrect, those writers did a disservice to the thousands who spent the war in mortal danger, burning with the more profound desire to accomplish their missions and to return home.

The tour had stopped in 1943. Hogan got his draft notice on March 1 and was inducted into the U.S. Army Air Corps on March 25. Lloyd Mangrum was wounded at the Battle of the Bulge and Jay Hebert was shot in the leg during the landing at Iwo Jima, but like most professional athletes, Hogan did not see combat. It was a shame, in a way. Many of his contemporaries described the intense Little Man as "someone you'd love to go to war with." But as golf commentator Dave Marr jokes, "Ben fought the battle of Fort Worth, Jimmy fought the battle of Corpus Christi, and Sam fought the battle of Los Angeles." Tommy Bolt was the pro at a golf course in Rome after it was liberated, and Nelson (with a mild case of hemophilia) and Jug McSpaden (with severe sinus allergies) were 4-F. ("Hell, yes, there was resentment" of the nonfighting, high-profile sportsmen, a B-17 bomber navigator recalls.) Not all of the bad feeling was fair, however. Only about a third of the armed forces were directly involved in combat, for one thing. For another, what and where you were assigned were usually a matter of luck.

Private Hogan's war began when he reported to the Fort Worth Army Air Field in the spring of 1943. He led a physical training class for a while. In the summer he rode a C-47 transport plane to Officers Candidate School in Miami. He passed and was promoted to second lieutenant in the fall. Back in Fort Worth, he joined the newly formed Civilian Pilot Training (CPT) program, which allowed him to wear civilian clothes, live at home, and earn $225 a month. During six months of training to become flight instructors, Hogan's CPT unit spent a month in Kilgore, Texas, studying the basics of takeoff, landing, and navigation. That was followed by another month in Shreveport, Louisiana, where they slept in a junior college dormitory and practiced aerobatics in single-

Army Air Corps Lt. Ben Hogan reports to the Miami Four-Ball on March 6, 1945, five months before his discharge. (AP/Wide World)

engine Piper Cubs. A third and final month was spent in Texarkana, their base for cross-country flights. Fliers returning from overseas duty came back to Fort Worth at the same time Hogan did, and they were better qualified to teach than were CPT aviators. So Ben and most of his unit were given a leave of absence.

Jimmy Gauntt, a golf pro from Oklahoma, was among those furloughed. Marvin Leonard gave Gauntt a room-and-board job at the club he had founded, Colonial Country Club in Fort Worth. Private Gauntt gave lessons all morning and played golf with Lieutenant Hogan every afternoon. Like everything with Ben, each day during this four-month period in late '44 and early '45 had the comforting, repetitive feel of ritual. The flyboy pros would have lunch, during which "Hogan wouldn't say four words," Gauntt says. "He never did have much time for conversation." On the first tee, more silence. "He'd never ask you to bet him, so we'd just have a very small bet. He was very impressive, swung fast, and hit the ball real hard. Real long backswing." After the round, Gauntt would pay up and retire. Hogan would remain to hit practice balls until it was too dark to see.

One evening near dusk, Gauntt went out to watch Hogan at work in his personal practice area—the rough to the right of the first hole, hitting toward the second and third fairways. Royal Hogan was there, too, standing behind his little brother as he drilled shots into the dying winter light.

"He doing anything wrong?" Royal asked the teaching pro. Gauntt watched a few shots and considered. "I think he's swinging the club back too far outside," he said softly.

"That's where I want it to go," Hogan said without looking up.

Hogan had an equally strong control of things at the Fort Worth Army Air Field. "Some general knew him real well," Gauntt remembers. "He was treated like the dignitary he was." In other words, Hogan got the shot at Officers Candidate

School—hardly an automatic thing, since he was a high school dropout. He got promoted again, to captain. And he got to play golf. Almost every week, the base commander's secretary would get in touch to request the honor of Hogan's presence on the first tee at Rivercrest Country Club, also in Fort Worth, at 1300 hours. During one hiatus in San Antonio, where he had gone to have a suspected hernia checked out (he didn't have one), Hogan played golf ten days in a row with Tod Menefee, the pro at San Antonio Country Club. He also played in scattered tour events when professional tournaments resumed in 1944 and teed it up in an exhibition or two with Bob Hope.

"His game was very good indeed," says Tom W. Blake, then the director of technical training at the air field and a regular in the foursome at Rivercrest. But was his game as good as it had been before the war? Although he never expressed it to Gauntt or Blake, Hogan must have wondered if he was up to the standard being defined by Byron Nelson. His old friend won eight times in 1944. In 1945 Nelson won an unheard-of eleven straight tournaments and eighteen tournaments in all. Hogan read the papers: The sportswriters were calling Byron "Mr. Golf."

The prologue for the first postwar Open continued when Mr. Golf and Mr. Hogan began dueling in earnest after Ben's discharge in August 1945. But so much had changed since 1942. Although golf ball production had not yet resumed, Gauntt remembers swapping Demaret a bottle of whiskey for a half-dozen hoarded Titleists. Golf in general and professional golf in particular were on the cusp of a boom, and tournaments soon required gallery ropes. For most of the players, however, their club jobs still came first. Demaret, for example, never left his golf shop at Kiamesha Lake, New York, for more than fourteen tour events in a year. Guldahl, Sarazen, and

Craig Wood were fading stars; Snead, Mangrum, and Demaret took their places at or near the top. Before the war, the average age of U.S. Open contestants had been twenty-eight; after the war, it was thirty-four. The tour now had a new set of personalities to go with the old ones and they interacted in new ways.

The two men at the top had changed, too. Nelson didn't fully realize it yet, but he was beginning to burn out. And Hogan had been nearly forgotten. In the 1945 Portland Open, one of Hogan's first tournaments after his discharge, the caddiemaster told sixteen-year-old Rod Slade he would be caddying for Hogan. The boy thought he meant Eddie Hogan, a local pro. Slade didn't realize who his employer was until he followed him up to the practice green where Nelson said, "Hi, Benjie," and shook the little man's hand.

On the back nine in the third round, Hogan pushed his tee shot behind a towering fir tree, 150 yards from the hole. Slade was dumbfounded when Hogan walked all the way to the green to survey the situation and was concerned that he would be penalized for playing too slowly. After what seemed an interminable delay, Hogan took an eight-iron and slashed it right at the tree. He had found a spot thirty feet up where the limbs were relatively sparse, and he threaded the ball through this tiny opening onto the green, two steps from the flagstick.

"Great shot, Mr. Hogan," the caddie said.

No reply from Mr. Hogan.

He spoke to his six-foot-six caddie twice a day: "Good morning, Sonny," and "Good night, Sonny." Valerie got roughly the same treatment. She came out to watch the final nine holes of the tournament and walked most of it between the towering caddie and her husband.

"Where have you been all day?" Ben asked when it was over.

"Right here," she replied in an I've-heard-this-before tone of mild exasperation.

By then they were celebrating. Hogan had shot an incredible 261 (65-69-63-64), the lowest seventy-two-hole score in tour history, two below Nelson's old record.

Demaret shook his hand. "Congratulations, Ben!" he said. No smile from Hogan. "I guess that takes care of this 'Mr. Golf' business," he replied.

It didn't. Hogan's record lasted just two weeks. Byron took it back when he shot 259 in the Seattle Open. "I really was pleased, especially after the drubbing I'd taken from Ben at Portland," Byron wrote in his autobiography. "I was so embarrassed by having Hogan beat me by fourteen that I might not have played as well at Seattle if I'd only been two or three shots back at Portland."

Par on the Broadmoor Golf Club in Seattle was 70 and at the Portland Golf Club it was 72; thus Hogan's twenty-seven-under-par was superior to Byron's twenty-one-under. Hogan's mark for most under par has been tied once, by Mike Souchak in the 1955 Texas Open at San Antonio's Brackenridge Park, but it has never been broken. Neither Portland Golf Club nor Broadmoor were easy golf courses, incidentally, as Brackenridge Park often was.

For a year the two old rivals went back and forth. Nelson had quit his job with Inverness in the fall of '45 and credited his spectacular play to the decision. And early in '46 he and Louise prepared for another big change, a secret Byron planned to share with the world when he would be asked to say a few words after winning the U.S. Open at Canterbury.

Byron won the first tournament of 1946, the Los Angeles Open at Riviera Country Club, in front of Howard Hughes, Hope, Crosby, and all the rest of golf-obsessed Hollywood. But the movie people were much more interested in Hogan, the grim little bundle of fury who finished second. He was such a *type*. You could meet guys such as Nelson and

Snead at the hardware store on Saturday morning, but Hogan had a unique edge, a dangerousness that seemed to simmer just beneath his dignified surface. Most movie stars would give a nonessential body part for a presence like Hogan's.

WHEN THE MOON WAS RIGHT, HE PUTTED AS WELL AS ALMOST ANYONE ON THE TOUR, ALTHOUGH HIS WRISTY STROKE DIDN'T MATCH THE GRACE OF HIS FULL SWING.

The duel continued. Nelson took his fourth tournament of '46 a month before the Open, at Houston, beating Ben by two (Nelson, Hogan, and Snead finished one-two-three, the only time that happened). But Hogan asserted himself with consecutive wins in the next three events, his fifth, sixth, and seventh victories of the year. Now it was June, and all the intricacies of the twenty-year competition between Ben and Byron had come down to one putt on the eighteenth green at Canterbury. If Hogan could make it, he would not only win the first postwar U.S. Open and beat Nelson by one, he would break their perceived tie at the top of the sport.

As shadows lengthened in the four o'clock sun, a hush fell over the crowd, the expectant quiet before the aerial artist attempts his back handspring. Hogan went for it. When the moon was right, he putted as well as almost anyone on the tour, although his wristy stroke didn't match the grace of his full swing. The click of brass tapping rubber was audible in the silence. Eternities passed as the ball, a MacGregor, rolled down the slope toward the right edge of the cup. The crowd shouted at the instant the ball kissed the lip, and murmured as it kept slowly turning, as if saying a slow-motion good-bye to the hole. The ball stopped four feet away. He would need that one just to tie.

Hogan had been in an eerily similar situation two months before at the Masters. In fact, everything about the first major championship after the war had a through-the-looking-glass quality.

Out of giddiness from winning the war and from a party and reunion too long delayed, betting on the '46 Masters was feverish. Hogan, Nelson, and Snead were the favorites, of course. Two of Augusta National's most prominent members bet fifty thousand dollars each on Hogan at four-to-one odds. But Herman Keiser, a short-hitting pro from Springfield, Missouri, who had been discharged from the navy less than six months before, confounded the experts and the bettors by taking control of the tournament from the start. He had wagered twenty dollars on himself at twenty-to-one.

Keiser soon got the distinct impression that certain powerful people didn't want him to win. Officials refused to replace his tired, limping caddie before the second round. His third-round starting time was changed without notice, and Keiser almost missed it, which would have disqualified him. Sportswriter Grantland Rice, although he had no authority to do so, warned Keiser during the final round that he was about to be penalized for slow play. Keiser responded with some phrases he had learned in the navy. Strangest of all to Keiser, by five shots the tournament leader over Hogan, he was assigned a last-round starting time forty minutes before the final pairing. Golfers leading a tournament usually play together at the end of the field.

But the Masters went its own way, since neither the USGA nor PGA had jurisdiction over it. Keiser had spent a recent afternoon with Hogan, losing a Phoenix Open playoff to him, so he approached Ben to discuss the situation. Hogan was sympathetic, Keiser says, "a real gentleman about it."

All but two shots of Keiser's lead were gone when he reached the final hole. But the lanky, long-faced "Missouri Mortician" was one of the tour's best and biggest gamblers; he could play under pressure. His seven-iron second shot hit the cloth on the flagstick and stopped twenty feet above the hole. "You've got it now, Herman," said Byron Nelson, his playing partner, as they walked up the fairway. "You haven't three-putted all week." Keiser, naturally, three-putted, and Nelson couldn't apologize enough.

The lead was one. Hogan, playing in the day's last group, could win with a birdie. He went for it. His second shot was better than Keiser's, but it, too, was a little long, fifteen terrifying feet above the hole, on the middle tier of the stair-step green. "The greens were so slick, you could almost hear them crackle," Hogan would recall years later. "I just touched the ball lightly, and it started rolling so slowly I could read the name on it. It barely missed the hole and rolled on four feet below it."

Keiser couldn't watch. He remained in the clubhouse and waited for a report. Henry Picard delivered the news a few minutes later. "Congratulations, Herman," Picard said, his hand extended. "The Little Man really took the choke. Those were the three worst putts I've ever seen him hit. His third putt was as long as your second."

Now, two months later at Canterbury, Hogan faced another shortish putt on a fast green for a huge prize. If he made it, he would join Nelson, Lloyd Mangrum, and Vic Ghezzi in a playoff the next day for the U.S. Open title. Miss it, and doubts about his ability to ever win one of the major championships would be entirely justified.

The late-afternoon summer sun broiled as he walked around the ball like a toreador around a bull. He assumed his stance, his head suspended over the ball. He putted—*click*—

with his center-shafted brass blade—and missed, by a quarter of an inch to the right.

Hogan's reaction to bitter defeat was his most admirable quality. Some players who later would miss from short range on the final greens of major championships—Doug Sanders at the 1970 British Open, Ed Sneed in 1979 at Augusta, and Scott Hoch in 1989 at the Masters, for example—were devastated by the experience. Hogan was not, just as he had not been defeated by the staggering loss of his father or his repeated failures as a golf pro. In fact, he would endure three more eleventh-hour disasters in the U.S. Open—although the last one, in 1960, would just about do him in.

His resilience was awe inspiring. Or was it really a *lack* of resilience, a refusal to adapt to defeat? He won three of the next four tournaments after his screwup at Augusta; and the week following that mortifying finish at Canterbury, he and Demaret won the Inverness Four-Ball. For so many years success had eluded him, the way a key or a coin under a couch gets pushed away by a grasping hand. Now winning was part of his ritual and the logical conclusion to all that practice. The down side, of course, was that no one could win all the time. Happy endings on Sundays refused to remain happy; another tournament started on Thursday. But if winning a golf tournament allayed his anxiety for only an hour or a day, surely 1946 was the best of times for Ben Hogan. He entered thirty-two tournaments, won thirteen of them, was second six times, and finished third three times. In five other events, he was seventh or better. In other words, he won or almost won nearly every week. He won the most prize money ($42,556). His 1946 was, arguably, the equal to Nelson's spectacular 1945, simply because the competition was better with the war over.

Nelson would probably have been too exhausted from unbroken years of travel and competition to argue the point. Even in 1943, when tournament golf had been suspended, Nelson had stayed on the road and played 110 war-effort exhibitions. Then there was his chronically sour stomach, a sore back, a big chunk of money in the bank, and the perfectly understandable feeling that he had done everything in golf he had ever wanted. In January 1946 he decided to retire. In February Byron and Louise found the 630-acre ranch northeast of Fort Worth they would retire to; and in May they bought it for fifty-five thousand dollars, cash. Since Lloyd Mangrum had won their U.S. Open playoff, Byron had not yet had the proper forum to reveal his plans. Just before the PGA Championship, Byron, age thirty-four, announced to an incredulous golf world that immediately after this tournament, he would be only a part-time golfer. The Wannamaker Trophy presentation would provide a fitting, formal platform from which to say good-bye.

Hogan, of course, had other ideas. The tournament would be held at the Portland Golf Club, where just a year before he had shot that godlike twenty-seven-under. No other course—except, possibly, Riviera, near Los Angeles—would be as important in Hogan's career. Portland Golf Club had been opened for play in 1914, in the days when country clubs actually were out in the country. Following the tradition of the time, the wood-sided clubhouse had an upstairs dormitory for those who wished to save the time and expense of a trip back to the city on the Oregon Electric Railroad, whose tracks bordered the course. With its rolling terrain, a creek meandering through ten holes, and fir trees that became intimidating giants within a few decades after they had been planted, Portland Golf Club looked like a great place for a picnic.

So why did Hogan eat its lunch? At first blush, a tight, relatively short course with small greens didn't seem to play to his first strength, length. And it was obviously not kind to his most glaring weakness, the surprise hook. But it did respond to the cerebral, chess-player approach that he had been working on since he had turned pro seventeen years before, exactly half his lifetime ago. He had begun to control a golf ball almost as well as he controlled his emotions.

The first postwar PGA was refreshingly full-blooded, not the uneven collection of flat feet and on-leave soldiers of 1944 and 1945. All the best American pros showed up in Portland. Nelson, the defending champion, was seeded first. Hogan was placed in the lower bracket, so a meeting in the finals between the "twin Texas terrors," as the *Oregonian* put it, seemed entirely possible. Hogan did his part, winning his first three matches, but the hoped-for death match and the dramatic backdrop for Byron's retirement farewell were flattened by Edward "Porky" (sometimes "Pork Chops") Oliver Jr. Oliver weighed something between 207 (his own estimate) and 270 (Tommy Bolt's exaggerated guess) and he liked to wear tight-fitting, collarless, horizontally striped golf shirts, which only accentuated his heft. But he was an excellent player, and he defeated Byron on the thirty-sixth hole of their quarterfinal match. The *Oregonian* reported that "the deposed mashie monarch" did not blame physical problems for his surprising defeat. If Hogan were to supplant Nelson, he would have to do it with Byron off the stage.

He did. "Hogan just devoured the field," says Peter Walsh, a Portland Golf Club member and a witness. "People didn't realize what they were seeing."

In the thirty-six-hole semifinal, Hogan shot 33-32-31 against Demaret; the final nine was unnecessary, because Ben was ten up. "When was the turning point, Jimmy?" a reporter asked.

"Ten o'clock this morning, when the match started," he answered.

102

In the final match, the austere Little Man beat Oliver, the flashy fat man, 6 and 4.

The one-year contest with Nelson had ended in stalemate. Hogan won more money; Byron had a lower stroke average. Hogan won more often, ten times to Nelson's six, but Byron played fewer tournaments. With Nelson out and Snead winning only once between December '46 and March '49, the triumvirate idea fell apart completely. Hogan was *the* Man.

Yet Hogan didn't believe his success. He remained emotionally grounded in the early thirties, when, as an itinerant golf professional, life and everything in it had been a competition. He gave no thought to resting on his laurels. Hogan believed he had to improve to survive; therefore, constant practice was a necessity. His 1983 videotaped comments to CBS on the subject to his acolyte, Venturi, were telling:

> Venturi: One thing I carried in my wallet was a statement you said: "There isn't enough daylight in any one day to practice all the shots you need to."
>
> Hogan: That's exactly right. . . . I just loved to practice. It was a great satisfaction to me. Not for winning tournaments or anything.
>
> Venturi: The other statement that I carried: "Every day that I missed practicing takes me one day longer to be good."
>
> Hogan: Very few times in my life I laid off two to three days. It seemed like it took me a month to three months to get back those

three days when I took a rest. It's a tough situation. I had to practice all the time.

But did he? Other champions, such as Jones before him, his contemporaries Nelson and Snead, and his successor, Arnold Palmer, were not slaves to the practice tee. They were "feel players," as everyone was until Hogan invented the mechanistic approach. Hogan practiced out of perfectionism and hunger, and he didn't stop even after winning a major tournament, the presumed object of all that work. So how did he know he "had to practice all the time" if he never really stopped practicing? Obviously, something else was at work here.

Hogan seemed obsessed and withdrawn, and practice, he later suggested, had become a repetitious end in itself. On the other hand, his apparent recognition of his need to be consumed by something and his choice of golf, the most hypnotically varied game, revealed a sharp, intuitive mind. Which is not to say Hogan was like other people. Jack Burke Jr., the 1956 Masters and PGA champ, offers a vivid metaphor: "He got up on the cross every day."

Many Hoganophiles attribute the rigidity of his practice routine to another cause, idealism, as rare in golf as atheism in foxholes. Hogan believed in the existence of a Platonic ideal of golf swings, and he believed he could find it and use it if he looked hard enough. Astoundingly, he did find it. The player who had won nearly everything in 1946 was even better in '47 and '48. "I've found the Secret," he told a writer.

It would have been a preposterous claim by anyone else. The hidden keys to golf are not rare; they are instead too numerous and reveal themselves too frequently, sometimes daily. Then they disappear, like ghosts. But even his fellow pros believed Hogan had uncovered the one true Secret. He had, after all, gone where no man had gone before in terms of practice, concentration, and study. It was entirely in character that after announcing his discovery, Hogan did not tell us what it was, a Wizard of Oz act no one else in the history of sport could get away with. Debate about the Secret has raged ever since. At times the debaters sound like clerics arguing over how many angels can dance on the head of a pin, while Hogan has been as coquettish on the subject as Scarlett O'Hara (Hogan's Secret is discussed in more detail in chapter 7).

Mindful of Nelson's flameout, Hogan reduced his tournament load to twenty-five in '47, seven fewer than the previous year. He won four tournaments early on, had his epiphany, then won three more. But he won no majors. Demaret took the Masters and dressed in canary yellow from head to toe on the last day, a color that complemented the kelly green champion's jacket. Hogan finished fourth, three shots behind Jimmy. He never threatened at the U.S. Open and finished tied for sixth. It looked like Snead's tournament. During the break between the two final rounds, Gauntt asked Hogan about Sam's chances. "If he has to think, he won't win it," he said. Snead did have to think—Lew Worsham's famous bit of gamesmanship on the final hole of their playoff induced him to miss a short putt and lose the tournament. Snead was about to hit a two-and-a-half-foot putt on the final green when Worsham stopped him, and asked for a measurement to confirm that Snead was away. He was. At the PGA Championship, Hogan was knocked out in the first round by Toney Penna. One spectator observed such obvious antagonism between the two wiry little men that he half expected a fight.

Was Hogan disappointed with his failure to win his second major championship? Undoubtedly. Yet, as Dan Greenwood says, "I never heard him say how much he wanted to win this U.S. Open or that PGA. He wanted to win 'em all." Besides, majors were different in the forties. The Western Open, the World Championship, the North and South, and even the Los Angeles Open were majors to American professionals—the British Open wasn't. Hogan had won all four of the former and didn't play in the latter. A points system begun in 1947 for Ryder Cup qualifying summed up the matter precisely: Winners of the U.S. Open and the PGA got one hundred points; the Masters champion, ninety-five; the Western Open champion, eighty; and winners of all other PGA-sanctioned events received seventy points.

The Ryder Cup was another event that eventually flip-flopped in prestige. The U.S.–versus–Great Britain all-star match hadn't been played since 1937 and might have remained a dim historical footnote if Oregon fruit tycoon Bob Hudson had not financed the British team's trip in November 1947 to his home course, the Portland Golf Club. The modern Ryder Cup has achieved a transcendent importance, but the Marshall Plan, the death of Henry Ford, the disappearance of street cars from Manhattan, and the first reports of flying saucers all got a lot more ink in '47.

Hogan, the playing captain, noticed that Keiser looked more morose than usual just before the competition was to get underway.

"Herm, something on your mind?" he asked.

Keiser nodded.

"Sit down and tell me about it."

It seemed some cupcake Keiser had recently "dated" for twenty dollars had found out he was a bigtime golfer and presumably wealthy. Now her fee-after-the-fact would be one thousand dollars. If she didn't get it, her attorney promised, she would sue and declare their night of magic had actually been rape. Hogan took out his wallet and extracted ten one-hundred-dollar bills. "Just pay me when you can, Herm," he said.

The perfect ending to this vignette would have had a relieved Keiser playing spectacularly to lead Team USA to victory. Instead Keiser was the only player to lose a point in the Americans' 11-to-1 win. But the incident was notable for revealing a facet of Hogan's personality that he preferred to keep hidden—his generosity. He never forgot the kindnesses shown to him by Marvin Leonard and Henry Picard during his bad old days, and he would repeatedly return the favor in years to come.

Like the others Hogan would help—Bolt, Gardner Dickinson, Don Cherry, John Schlee, and a dozen others—his gesture made Keiser a friend for life. Keiser had already been favorably disposed to Hogan for the gracious way he had handled his defeat in the '46 Masters. Now, Keiser was telling anyone who would listen that Hogan was "the finest gentleman I ever knew." From time to time he would take a lawn chair to the practice tee just to watch the Hawk practice.

"I'm gonna be here a while, Herman," Hogan would say.

"That's why I brought a chair," Keiser would reply.

Biological clocks tick loudly at the approach of middle age, and Valerie and Ben were in their midthirties in the late forties. So why didn't they have kids? Money was not the problem. After winning forty-two thousand dollars in '46 and twenty-three thousand dollars in '47, and with the added income from playing MacGregor clubs, the salary from Hershey Country Club, and a few bucks from product endorsements and exhibitions (three hundred dollars for weekdays, five hundred dollars for weekends), Ben and Valerie felt sufficiently flush to start looking at houses. Childlessness was then seen as a somewhat peculiar condition for a young, healthy couple. But the postwar baby boom left the gate without the Hogans.

Several explanations present themselves. For a man compelled to obey his time-consuming rituals, the prospect of shattering routine with an infant would not have held much appeal for Hogan. Adults who've survived sad childhoods often choose not to become parents. All the interpretations boil down to this: couldn't or wouldn't. "Ben Hogan lived his life by plan," a friend of the couple says. "And children just weren't in his plan."

Ben's plans, not Valerie's wishes, were the driving forces in their very traditional marriage. No one who knew them doubted who was in charge. "I always had the feeling she was afraid of Ben," another friend says.

The Hogans did, however, act on another aspect of the nesting instinct, and Valerie participated in the decision, at least a little bit. They had been on the road for twelve years. Since 1941 their rooms at the Cocoa Inn in Hershey and an apartment in Fort Worth had been the closest they had come to having a home. Their only question on the subject of houses was not if but where. Valerie wanted to live in Fort Worth, where she could be close to family and friends, and Ben went along. He picked out the house himself. Dan Greenwood, his old friend from Glen Garden, had gone into the real estate business, and drove him around. Hogan saw one he liked—a square brick colonial on Valley Ridge Road in Westover Hills, Fort Worth's best neighborhood—and said, "How much?" Greenwood said he thought they could get the place for twenty-five thousand dollars. "Then do it," Hogan said. The Hogans moved in, in October.

Soon after, Hogan told a *Time* writer he eventually wanted a ranch, again possibly emulating Nelson. Over the years he looked at scores of them—spreads as small as three hundred acres and as large as several thousand acres—in a 150-mile radius around Fort Worth. On one of these real estate shopping trips, Hogan and Greenwood stopped at a little country store for a snack. Ben selected a large jar of green olives, and Greenwood watched in wonder as his friend ate every last one.

If Hogan had not felt required to consult Valerie on the location of the new house, he would have chosen California. "Anybody who doesn't live in California is a victim of circumstances," he told *Time*. The epicenter of Hogan's affection was Riviera Country Club, a heavenly 243 acres of Santa Monica Canyon in Pacific Palisades, a suburb of Los Angeles. Walt Disney and Spencer Tracy played polo there. Greta Garbo had a house from which she could look down on the thirteenth fairway and perhaps see Katharine Hepburn and Clark Gable out playing golf. That Hogan would be enamored of this playground for Hollywood seems incongruous, until it is remembered how often he was drawn to very expressive people, and they to him.

Two such outgoing movie colony friends of Ben were Sidney Lanfield, a director, and Bob William, a publicist for Warner Brothers. "Ben wasn't at all like the way he appeared to the public," says William, who helped keep Bette Davis in the public eye. "He wasn't mean or difficult, just very, very sincere." Lanfield and William admired Hogan so much that since the early forties they had walked every step of every Los Angeles round with him. William and Lanfield also played golf at Riviera.

Riviera fit them. It fit all of Hollywood. Riviera had been a Cecil B. DeMille epic of a golf course from the start. George C. Thomas Jr. got off his 110-foot yacht to design it and accepted no fee for his work. He did, however, spend $250,000 of the members' money—an unofficial world's record—but the results were spectacular. At 7,020 yards, Riviera was unusually long, exceptionally varied, and a subtle fooler of the eye. The course was just two years old when it hosted its first Los Angeles Open in 1929, and the prestige of Riviera and of the venerable tournament enhanced each other. The presence of movie stars—America's royalty—and its being the first event of the calendar year gave the Los Angeles Open a further boost.

The length of the course played into the steel-banded hands of the strongest man in golf, and the optical illusions caused by its hills and Rorschach test bunkers did not fool his eyes. But the obvious reason for the Hogan-Riviera attraction should not be overlooked. When they asked Willie Sutton why he robbed banks, he replied, "Because that's where they keep the money." And Hogan won at Riviera because he was playing great, and that's where they held the tournaments.

Hogan shot a course-record 66 in the second round of the 1947 Los Angeles Open and won. In 1948 he led from start to finish, winning again with a tournament record, nine-under-par 275. Six months later the U.S. Open came to Riviera.

In the interim between the L.A. and U.S. Opens, Hogan finished third four times, second twice, and first once. The win was a big one—the PGA Championship. Much was made of the stamina required by the thirty-six-hole final round in the U.S. Open, but the Open was a walk up three flights of stairs compared to the marathon of the PGA. With thirty-six holes of qualifying and mostly thirty-six-hole matches, Hogan had to play 213 holes for the week—that's almost twelve rounds, or the equivalent of three weeks' competition in one. For a man who played each round as if it were his last shot at the SAT or the bar exam, the mental toll was as severe as the physical. Hogan, exhausted, said he didn't think he would ever again play in the PGA. For the next twelve years, he didn't. But a tenth chance to win the U.S. Open revived him two weeks later.

Big golf tournaments in very tony settings always have an amusing snobs-versus-slobs undertone. The guy from Bakersfield who parked his Plymouth on Riviera's emerald green polo field would have felt it right away. At Riviera in '48, an onlooker could play guess-that-starlet, try to eavesdrop on Gregory Peck's conversation, or stand next to Humphrey Bogart and try to figure out what was in the Thermos he was clutching. A relaxed-looking Byron Nelson also watched while holding a pair of binoculars that really were binoculars.

Snead led after thirty-six holes, with Hogan and Demaret two shots back. Sam started the third round eagle-birdie and it looked like he would finally win the only major that had evaded him—or that he had evaded. But he suddenly became nervous with the putter and faded to a 73-72 finish and fifth place. Demaret, playing in a group an hour ahead of Hogan's, charged to a third-round 68. Hogan charged with him; his 67-72-68 led Sunny Jim by two. Demaret counterattacked. His two-under 69 on Sunday gave him a 278 total for the four rounds, which smashed Ralph Guldahl's eleven-year-old record for the Open by three strokes.

**HOGAN WATCHED THE SCOREBOARD. HE ALSO ATE HERSHEY BARS, DRANK COCA-COLAS, AND LIT THE NEXT CIGARETTE WITH THE SMOLDERING BUTT OF THE LAST ONE.**

Hogan watched the scoreboard. He also ate Hershey bars, drank Coca-Colas, and lit the next cigarette with the smoldering butt of the last one. Hogan marched up the final fairway with a two-shot lead and the applause and cheers of the throng in his ears. A friend of a friend fell in step a few yards from the green.

"Ben, how would you like a nice cold beer?" the grinning man asked.

Hogan gave the man the Look. "I think I'd throw up," he said. The stranger slinked back into the gallery.

Demaret's U.S. Open record had lasted just fifty-six minutes. Hogan matched his friend's final-round 69, and his

276 beat the old standard by five, a huge jump forward. Demaret noted that Ben seemed unbeatable on this course and referred to it as "Hogan's Alley." Riviera had become his course and the U.S. Open his tournament.

After the Open, Hogan kept winning and winning and winning . . . five in a row between June and August. First was the Open, then, two weeks later, the Inverness Four-Ball, with Demaret. No one could beat the man in gray and his partner, whose clothes looked like popsicle flavors. In July he played in three and won three—the Motor City Open, the Reading Open, and the Western Open in another playoff with Porky Oliver. His club manufacturer, MacGregor, matched his prize money for each victory; top money in these tournaments averaged $2,090.

He was getting rich, and he should have been getting happy. But Hogan's try at a sixth consecutive win revealed him as a flawed champion.

A high, hot sun illuminated the final round of the Denver Open on August 22, 1948, eight days after the death of Babe Ruth. Hogan had been in the running all the way. When he birdied the final three holes for a 67 and an eighteen-under-par total, it looked good enough, at worst, for second place. Hogan signed his card, then, inexplicably, left the course. Meanwhile, Fred Haas Jr., the leader, was losing his nerve. On the final two holes he hit a spectator with a tee shot, topped a four-wood, missed a six-foot putt, and, *bad-aboom*, he had lost the tournament.

"And now, I'd like to present our new champion with a check for $2,150," Denver Mayor Quigg Newton said to the three thousand attendees of the awards ceremony. "Ladies and gentlemen, Ben Hogan!" Long pause. "Ben, are you here?" Longer pause. With the winner embarrassingly absent, it was left to Haas to speak and to receive the runner-up's check. The papers ripped Hogan, and he deserved it. "Insufferable," said the *Rocky Mountain News*. The *News*'s account continued:

> Hogan's walkout climaxed a long series of unpleasant incidents in which the Hershey prima donna let one and all know that he is good—and that he knows it. He refused flatly to appear in Wednesday's clinic. Asked by a respectful radio reporter to say a few words to listeners, he refused flatly. With oaths, he refused a most reasonable request of photographers who sought to snap him along with the obliging Haas and cooperative Cary Middlecoff. But it was noted that Hogan—the same Hogan—was running after and pleading with photographers to picture him alongside some noted army brass in the gallery. He refused a seven-year-old an autograph, saying "Go away."

Hogan denied the stuff about the photographers, the radio, and the autograph. He admitted turning down one of several radio interview requests but didn't address his refusal to participate in the pretournament driving range golf clinic. His explanation for not attending the presentation party: "I had to catch a 5:30 train to Salt Lake City [the next tournament was the Utah Open]. When I finished, I didn't think I had a chance to win—but as I entered my hotel my wife said the radio reported I had won. I immediately called the tournament headquarters and asked Mr. Dawson [a tournament official] to accept my apologies. He said he would tell the other officials—but apparently my message went astray."

The incident confirmed what many already knew, that Hogan was extraordinarily driven and had no particular interest in savoring a win in public or in public relations. He was a shy man trying to hide while everyone watched, a sad impossibility.

The Associated Press disseminated a report on the affair to its hundreds of member newspapers, and Hogan's image took an important step backward. But as he lay dying six months later, his popularity skyrocketed past presidents, prime ministers, and kings. He hated it.

Hogan finished ninth the following week at Utah, won at Reno, took a break, and returned to the tour at Portland. In the second round on the fifth hole, Hogan topped a brassie, a shockingly bad shot. Then he birdied the next seven holes in a row. "Oh, good, I won't have to shag," his caddie, Robert Atkinson Jr., remembers saying to himself. Instead, Hogan hit two-woods to the boy for more than two hours. "But I hardly had to move to pick up the balls," Atkinson recalls. "The other caddies who were shagging ran around like they were in a tennis match."

With two holes remaining in the tournament, someone in the gallery told Hogan he needed two birdies to tie for first. He did it. But he lost in the overtime to Fred Haas, 70 to 71.

One more tournament—and one more win—and Hogan's 1948 season was over. He had won ten tournaments and was in the top three in seventeen of the twenty-five events he entered. Perhaps Hogan's '48—and his '46, for that matter—have received short shrift from golf historians because, unlike other famous years, they were not isolated flashes of brilliance. In the three and a half years bracketed by his discharge from the Army Air Corps and his 1949 automobile accident, Hogan won thirty-seven tournaments. No one had ever been better in a similar amount of time. Hogan had his own little era. It took a ten-ton bus to stop him.

Ben Hogan's career stopped dead on Groundhog Day 1949. It was Chester Hogan's birthday. He would have been sixty-four. Had Chester still been around, it's doubtful he could fathom what his son had accomplished. More amazing than his house, his twenty-eight-hundred-dollar car, and the cash in his wallet was his youngest child's fame. That was Bennie's face on the cover of the January 10 issue of *Time* magazine—a somewhat silly portrait, with his chin on a tee and little golf clubs surrounding his head. Below that, a quote: "If you can't outplay them, outwork them." *Time* was no mere sports page or golf magazine; everyone read it. And, my God, didn't Ben look just like his father! Chester had been thirty-seven when he died; his son would be thirty-seven in six months.

"I love the competition," Ben said in the concluding quote in the article. "I hope I'm not at the top of my game; I hope I'm getting better."

If not better, Hogan's game was still surpassingly good. He had played the first four events of the 1949 winter tour and had won two of them—the Bing Crosby Pro-Am and the Long Beach Open in a playoff over Demaret. In the most recent tournament, the Phoenix Open, he had finished second, this time losing another playoff with Demaret. The pros hit the road for Texas after Phoenix, but instead of heading for San Antonio and the Texas Open, the Hogans would veer north to Fort Worth and home. "It's not the golf, it's the traveling" that wearied him, Ben told *Time*. "I want to die an old man, not a young man."

Hogan stopped the car on the evening of February 1 in Van Horn, a small town in middle-of-nowhere West Texas. Perhaps he had passed the hotels in El Paso and continued another eighty miles because Van Horn marked the halfway point between Phoenix and Fort Worth. Six hundred miles down, six hundred more to go; Hogan appreciated symmetry. Maybe he found El Paso hotels too crowded or too expensive (the El Capitan in Van Horn cost the Hogans just $4.50 for the night). Possibly, he had instinctively separated himself from the pack. Whatever it was, the little decisions about where to sleep, when to leave, and how fast to drive locked the Hogans into a collision course with Alvin Logan, the twenty-seven-year-old driver of Greyhound Bus 548.

Bus 548, a General Motors Super Coach, had eight windows, eight rows of seats, a white roof, blue below the windows, and a seven-foot-long brown greyhound logo painted on either side. Company people call their emblem "the running dog." The big dog weighed 19,500 pounds empty. With thirty-four of the bus's thirty-seven seats filled, more than twenty thousand pounds of steel, rubber, luggage, and humanity were coming at the Hogans at about fifty miles per hour. Logan left Pecos, Texas, and headed west for El Paso at 7:00 P.M. Hogan left Van Horn at 8:00. They met at 8:30, on a little bridge in a valley on Highway 80.

Logan was late. Despite the fog that cut visibility to several hundred yards, the bus driver tried to pass a truck at exactly the wrong moment. Hogan, creeping the Caddy cautiously along at twenty to thirty miles an hour, suddenly saw four mist-diffused headlights barreling straight toward him. The concrete bridge abutments left no room to bail out. Valerie, petrified, could not move or make a sound. "It was the end," she recalled a few days later. "We had no chance."

Just before impact, Hogan let go of the steering wheel and dove across his wife's lap. Almost simultaneously, the steering column shot into the car like a two-hundred-pound arrow, fracturing Hogan's left collarbone at the arm's end, and impaling the now empty driver's seat. By trying to save Valerie's life, Hogan had saved his own—but at a cost. When the car's five-hundred-pound engine followed the steering column through the firewall into the car, it snapped Hogan's left ankle and mangled his left leg. It also broke his pelvis—a tough bone to crack—and fractured the seventh rib on the right. His face smashed into the collapsing dashboard and his internal organs sloshed violently, as though they had been thrown against a wall. Fog muffled the shriek of metal on asphalt as the car skidded backward on the road.

A DOZEN TIMES HE WOKE, AND A DOZEN TIMES BREATHTAKING PAIN STABBED AND THROBBED THROUGH HIS BODY.

They couldn't get out. Valerie was trapped by suitcases, the compressed car interior, and her husband who lay face down with his head below her knees. For a few moments, she thought he was dead. She wriggled out of the car, and with the help of a man and a woman who had stopped to investigate, she extricated Hogan's limp body. They laid him out on the back seat—the front of the car resembled a crushed aluminum can—and he regained consciousness. He told Valerie that of all his injuries, his crushed left leg hurt the most. It felt chilled; he asked for her to cover it. Then he passed out again. He was in shock, a serious circulatory disorder characterized by weak and rapid pulse, falling blood pressure, and loss of consciousness. A dozen times he woke, and a dozen times breathtaking pain stabbed and throbbed through his body. Had the jagged edge of his rib punctured his lung, he probably would have died.

Eventually, there were thirty-eight people milling around Ben and Valerie, but none of them took charge. "Ambulance? I thought you called the ambulance." As a result, no medic saw Hogan until ninety minutes after the crash, too late for local anesthetics to do much good; too much blood had pooled around the broken bones for painkillers to work. Hogan's unstable vital signs ruled out general anesthesia. After a brief stop for x rays in Van Horn,

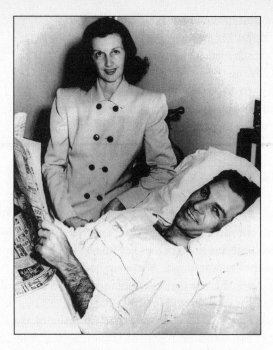

Hogan looked good ten days after the accident. Ten
days later, however, he would become deathly ill.
Valerie, incidentally, lived in the hospital throughout
this period. (AP/Wide World)

the ambulance continued west to a hospital in El Paso. During a lucid moment, Hogan said he wanted to go east to
Pecos, toward home, but the ambulance did not turn
around. And during his periods of delirium, he gripped and
regripped an imaginary club, and waved back an invisible
gallery. "Fore left!" he said.

A number of golf pros on their way to the Texas Open
drove slowly through the confused and eerie aftermath of the
accident. They saw a bus in a ditch, a jackknifed truck, police
cars, fire trucks, bus passengers (none of them were hurt),

118

strobing lights from the emergency vehicles, and fog. The ambulance and a couple of police cars zoomed west past Jack Fleck as he approached the scene of the wreck from the east. Fleck didn't recognize Hogan's flattened Cadillac when he came to it. But when Herman Keiser and Dutch Harrison passed through, Harrison said, "Hey, that's Hogan's car!" Keiser found out where they had taken his friend, turned his vehicle back to the west, and drove the 119 miles to the Hotel Dieu Hospital in El Paso.

"He was all strapped down," Keiser says. "It didn't look like he was going to make it." Hogan gestured for Keiser to come closer. A bandage covered his left eye and the right eye was swollen almost shut. Under the sheets, a cast encased his lower body.

"Herman," he said, "would you check on my clubs?"

Meanwhile Valerie spoke to a reporter: "We crashed head-on. He threw himself in front of me to protect me." And with that, Hogan's popular image underwent a sea change. He had been revealed. He was flesh and blood, not granite. He was vulnerable yet brave and—at least before he was hurt—nearly unbeatable at a popular sport. Somewhere, someone wrote the first get-well-soon letter. Soon three hundred cards a day were arriving.

Royal flew out as soon as he heard the news about his brother. "Ben's not hurt as badly as we thought," he said the next day. "He's going to be all right."

His condition improved from critical to fair to good in the ensuing days, and he moved to a bigger room to accommodate all the cards, flowers, and visitors. Almost everyone in Dublin, Texas, signed a telegram wishing him well, and Hogan sent a written thank-you to each one. A group from Hollywood, in town for the premiere of the movie *El Paso*, came for a visit and a photo op. "Yes," the doctors told the writers who crowded the hospital, "he'll play golf again." But four days after Valentine's Day, the

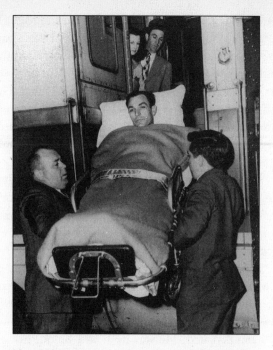

Note Valerie hovering above Hogan as they take the train home to Fort Worth from the hospital in El Paso. Mrs. Hogan never left her husband's side during his long convalescence. Royal Hogan, Ben's older brother, stands next to Valerie. (AP/Wide World)

anniversary of Chester's death, Hogan complained of a sharp pain in his chest.

A blood clot had traveled up from his left leg to his right lung. Pints of blood had congealed where Hogan's insides had been crushed or scraped by broken bone. Clots were breaking loose—particularly in his legs—and they were dangerously large, large enough to block the bigger pipes, the veins to his lungs. The next embolism—clot—could kill him. Nowadays, a patient would be administered anticoagulant or

120

effective blood-thinning drugs for the same thing, or a surgeon might implant a little jagged-toothed screen to trap any embolisms floating upstream. But in February 1949 the drugs they gave Ben Hogan were ineffective, and Greenfield filters had not been invented. His doctors thinned Hogan's blood practically to water, and still the clots came. With their patient losing weight and strength, they decided to operate. Newspapers prepared Hogan's obituary.

Dr. Alton S. Ochsner, deemed the best vascular surgeon in the country, agreed to do the operation. But air connections from New Orleans—where Ochsner was a professor of surgery at Tulane—were very slow because of a rainstorm in South Louisiana. No charters were available, and Ben was sinking fast. Royal convinced the commander at El Paso's air force base to pull some strings for his brother, the former Army Air Corps captain. Brig. Gen. David Hutchison agreed with Royal and immediately sent a B-29 bomber to New Orleans. Eight hours later, Ochsner transfused Hogan with three units of blood. Then he cut.

Ochsner (pronounced "OX-ner") was the Ben Hogan of vascular surgery. He had trained in Europe, as all the best surgeons did early in the century, and he pioneered a number of surgical techniques. He introduced blood transfusions to the United States, and he trained Michael DeBakey, the first man to successfully implant an artificial heart. The Ochsner Clinic in New Orleans would become the Mayo Clinic of the South. When an assassin shot Louisiana governor Huey Pierce Long in 1935, they called Dr. Ochsner, but a traffic jam on the road between New Orleans and Baton Rouge, the state capital, prevented his timely arrival. Long died.

Hogan might also die. No surgery could have been more invasive than what Ochsner planned. He would be going almost all the way through Hogan's body, through the abdomen to get to a blood vessel on the right side of his spine. The cage formed by the spinal bones, vertebrae, and nerves made carving from the back impractical. The goal was to get to the inferior vena cava, the main return line of blood from the lower body ("inferior" refers to the vessel's position in the body, not its size or importance). When he reached it, Ochsner would loop it a few times with surgical thread and ligate—tie off—the soft, pliable vein with a square knot. Any future clots following that route would run into a dead end.

Tying a knot sounds simple enough, but vascular surgery is a good deal trickier than removing an appendix or a gall bladder. Moreover, the patient was weak and the operation would take two hours. If Hogan made it through, more problems awaited. Tying off this large vein was like building a dam. Until Hogan's smaller veins dilated—enlarged—enough to take the increased flow, very low blood pressure was probable. And as those collateral veins got bigger, they, too, might become big enough to carry a deadly clot.

Ochsner sliced an eight-inch horizontal incision in the patient's lower abdomen. An assistant peeled the skin back with retractors and suctioned off the blood. Then Ochsner cut into the abdominal muscle, red with white fibers. A transparent zip-lock bag called the peritoneum lay on the other side; it holds the guts in place. Ochsner cut it. In the center of the trunk, all the visceral organs had to be pushed to one side to reach the far side of the peritoneum. Another cut and there it was, the inferior vena cava. It was impossible to miss—a light blue, shiny, oval tube, about the diameter of a fifty-cent piece. Ochsner tied it off with surgical string, then, exiting, did the entire operation in reverse.

While Ochsner performed his magic with scalpels and retractors, Valerie Hogan knelt in the hospital chapel and prayed. Her prayers to get her husband back were answered. However, Hogan's left shoulder under the broken collarbone would hurt every day for the rest of his life. Same thing with his legs. With smaller, less efficient veins transporting blood back up to his heart, his legs would ache and swell every time he walked. And he would never see very well again.

Pain was in Hogan's future, but was golf? And what would happen to him mentally if he would be denied the game that kept his demons away?

Hogan left the hospital on April 1, almost two months after he entered it. Valerie drove him to the train station. She could have carried him. His weight had fallen to 120 pounds, and he looked like hell.

# CHAPTER 5

# ANGER

HE STAYED RIGHT THERE IN HOLLYWOOD, MOST OF THE TIME ON
THE SET, BOTHERING THE LIFE OUT OF EVERYONE. "THAT DOESN'T
LOOK LIKE ME AT ALL," HE'D SAY. "I'D NEVER DO A THING LIKE
THAT!" . . . HE DROVE EVERYBODY NEARLY MAD.
                                        —JIMMY DEMARET

Sam Engel hung the strap of his new golf bag around
his neck and walked uncertainly out of the Riviera clubhouse.
Engel, the producer of such films as *Sitting Pretty*, *Rawhide*,
and *My Darling Clementine*, had recently committed to producing Hollywood's first golf feature film, a biography of Ben
Hogan. Engel had never hit a ball or set foot on a golf course
before, a problem made abundantly clear by his feedbag approach to carrying a golf bag full of clubs. Worse, he was
about to play his first round of golf with the perfectionistic
subject of the new movie. Engel pushed through the door, his
new MacGregors clattering noisily under his chin. Hogan
looked up from the putting green and collapsed in laughter.
Red-faced, Engel turned around and walked right back into
the clubhouse.

The producer's Jed Clampett act symbolized the
problems Hogan and Hollywood would have with each
other. By agreeing to cooperate—reluctantly—in the production of a movie of his life, Hogan hoped to quench the

almost insatiable demand for the details of his background. *Collier's, Life,* the *Saturday Evening Post, Reader's Digest,* and seemingly every newspaper in the country wanted an hour or two, a couple of photographs, a quote.

"We just couldn't have that. They wanted to know when he blinked," Valerie remembers. "He was a golfer, not the president."

The Hogans objected particularly to a story by Jack Murphy in the June 1949 issue of *Collier's* entitled "Battle of the Crippled Champ." The article wasn't particularly intrusive, and it repeated the usual mistakes Hogan let stand—where he was born, where his father died. Perhaps the frequent references to Hogan as "bite-sized," "pint-sized," and "the tiny terror of the fairways" were galling. He wasn't *that* small. Maybe this passage embarrassed the Hogans: "But in adversity and pain, Ben gained the affection that had eluded him. A trace of moisture still creeps into Valerie's eyes, and Ben's voice grows husky, when they discuss the biggest rooting section that ever shooed Ben home to victory. 'People've been great,' Ben says wonderingly. 'People I didn't know, never even heard of—people from all over the country wrote to us.' "

That people were so interested overwhelmed the Hogans, and they were confused about what to do about it. "Don't waste your time writing about me," Hogan told *Life.* "People are tired of hearing about Ben Hogan. They're interested in the guys who are playing now. It won't be long until they forget about me." Valerie Hogan recalls being afraid "people would start to resent us" from all the publicity.

The Hogans considered the movie, to be titled *Follow the Sun,* as a way to relieve the media pressure. Sidney Lanfield, Hogan's old fan and a friend from a score of Los Angeles Opens, would direct. This alliance would enhance Hogan's control of the finished product. Lanfield, a former vaudevillian, joke writer, and jazz musician, specialized in light comedies such as *My Favorite Blonde*. After *Follow the Sun*, he would direct only one more movie—*Skirts Ahoy!*—before moving on to television. *Follow the Sun* was shot in the winter and spring. Most of the golf course scenes were shot at Riviera, and the "interiors" were filmed on the sound stages and back lots at Twentieth Century-Fox.

Although in its details the film was far from what Hogan had in mind, it provided a fascinating peek at how he saw himself and his peers and how he wished others to see him. Subsequent written biographies had far less of his input. Trying to guess how much was Hogan and how much was Hollywood is the only reason to watch the movie now. Like *The Story of Louis Pasteur* (1936) and *Young Mr. Lincoln* (1939), *Follow the Sun* was the story of an idealist at odds with society. Sort of.

For those with no knowledge of golf or the facts of Hogan's life, the film was like having two desserts, tolerable but way too sweet. For aficionados, however, *Follow the Sun* was laughably bad, from the leading man to the ridiculous things screenwriter Edward Hazlitt Brennan had him say. Glenn Ford, a lowercase Gary Cooper, was horrendously miscast as Hogan. He got roles that idealized common men. Ford's forte was portraying earnestness, hard work, and bashfulness. Hogan was earnest and hardworking, all right, but there was assertion and self-interest in his shyness, and he was tougher than a truck stop steak. Ford's Hogan was an irresolute little flower. A tough guy, such as gangster actor George Raft—who resembled Hogan—would have been a better choice. From a golf standpoint, any actor who knew his nose from a brassie would have been an improvement. Ford, an unathletic man whose hobby was gardening, held the club as if it were a trowel and swung it like a rake. He marked his ball incorrectly and illegally in one scene. He couldn't even carry a golf bag believably.

Hogan and the stars of *Follow the Sun* in March 1951. Anne Baxter played Valerie, and Glenn Ford portrayed Hogan. Ford's clumsy efforts to hit a golf ball frustrated Hogan, who acted as technical adviser for the film. (AP/Wide World)

Hogan, of course, missed none of this. The filming would stop so he could show Ford how to grip a club or how to stand, but the actor still looked like a hacker. Hogan stood in on the long shots of his swing, but Ford had to handle the close-ups.

Hogan's friend Bob William frequently watched the production. "Ben was very annoyed throughout the filming," he says. "He just smirked all the time."

"I was ready to shoot one scene when Ben noticed that the clubs weren't the type used in that particular year,"

128

Lanfield recalled later. "He insisted that we get the exact models of that year. I explained a day's delay in shooting would cost us about one hundred thousand dollars in overhead, that movie audiences wouldn't even notice the error. Hogan said no. I could have killed him in cold blood, but I admired him all the same."

While Hogan chafed under the restrictions of drama, Hollywood, and Glenn Ford's awkwardness, Engel, Lanfield, and Brennan tried to accommodate him as best they could. Hogan refused to sign a contract, a fact he recalled aloud on the frequent occasions when he threatened to wash his hands of the whole mess. Obviously, the people of Twentieth Century-Fox could not afford to have the subject of the film biography disavow it, so they made him "technical advisor" and gave him a little camp chair with his name on the back and script approval. And they held their breath.

The Hogan-approved depictions are remarkable. The press, symbolized by columnist Jay Dexter (actor Larry Keating), drips with vitriol and sarcasm. Dexter purposely misspells Hogan's name, refuses to shake hands when they're introduced, and hates Ben for his quietness and modesty. Dexter plainly wants Hogan to suck up to him, and Hogan, of course, will not.

Hogan's chief friend/antagonist, Chuck Williams (played by Dennis O'Keefe), appears as a backslapper and a sloppy drinker, beloved by fans and the writers. A lampshade-on-the-head kind of guy, he wonders why Ben won't stick around for the party.

"Who was that supposed to be?" someone asked.

"A composite," Hogan answered.

Anne Baxter played Valerie as saintlike but simpering, with, as one reviewer said, "lines that jump from cliché to cliché about a woman's place at a man's side." Ford, a graduate of the Jimmy Stewart stuttering school of acting, played a nonsmoking, diffident, and painfully shy Hogan. And the lines they gave him!

> "It's no good, Val," complains Ford/Hogan early in the movie. "People have got me pegged as a grump and a grouch."

> "Wh-wh-wh-what's that, Val?" he says, when Valerie, who had forbidden him to play golf following the accident, coyly relents. In an earlier scene, Baxter/Valerie announces to a mildly surprised Ben that *she* has purchased their first house.

> "Gee, that was swell of the gang, wasn't it, Val?" Ford/Hogan says after Jimmy Demaret and Cary Middlecoff, playing themselves, come to his hospital bed to ask him to be the 1949 Ryder Cup captain.

> "You know, Val, I shoulda, shoulda taken my eye off the ball once in a while and taken a good look at people," Ford says, in a postaccident reflection on the goodness of mankind. "I've really been a jughead, Val."

Despite these groaners, the movie got it right in some details. His rehab, for instance, really did begin with squeezing rubber balls and doing chin-ups on a bar suspended over his bed. Twelve days after the surgery, he took his first painful, shuffling steps behind a wheeled walker. At home, he soloed by circling his bed, one hand on the bed for support. Next were laps around the bedroom, then the living room. He counted each circuit and increased his regimen every day. His feet and legs throbbed after the exercise, and they ballooned so much that his ankle bones disappeared. Then he would lie down, sweating and weak. In August, Doctor Ochsner discovered another reason Hogan's right leg hurt so much—torn knee cartilage. "We should operate," said the doctor. "No way," the patient replied.

Just as in the movie, when Hogan finally ventured outdoors and went too far, Valerie picked him up in the family car (another black Cadillac; Hogan credited the weight of the Caddy with saving their lives in the accident). In the late fall he occasionally hiked to Colonial Country Club and back, a twelve-mile roundtrip.

HOGAN REQUIRED THE TEAM TO GET UP EARLIER AND PRACTICE MUCH HARDER AND MORE OFTEN THAN THEY WERE USED TO. DEMARET SPOKE UP: "HEY, HAWK! WE TRAINING FOR GOLF OR THE ARMY?"

"It took me eleven months to get where I could play a little bit," he recalled. "Not as good as I could before. I was better in 1948 and 1949 than I ever was."

The part in the movie about the Ryder Cup was true, too, although Hogan had been out of the hospital for months when the captaincy was offered and he accepted. Middlecoff, who helped Demaret offer the job, didn't make the squad. The movie doesn't show it, but Hogan sailed with the team to England in September.

"The road smash in which he had nearly been killed had left its mark, both psychologically and physically," British golf writer Louis T. Stanley recalled after the match. "I drove him from Southampton to London, but every oncoming car so tensed his nerves that we reduced our speed at times to a crawling pace."

Having glimpsed his own mortality and given his diminished capacities, a kinder, gentler Captain Hogan might have been expected. But no. Hogan required the team to get up earlier and practice much harder and more often than they were used to. Demaret spoke up: "Hey, Hawk! We training for golf or the army?" Hogan also had the U.S. team bring its own food—eleven hundred pounds of steaks, ham, and bacon—because he knew of the postwar rationing still in effect in the United Kingdom. That was six hundred steaks, twelve sides of beef, a dozen hams, and twelve boxes of bacon. A bit insulting, the hosts murmured, that a guest brings his own dinner. And although Hogan shared the beef with the carnivores on the British side at a dinner before the match, the press sunk their teeth into the issue. "Meatgate" plagued the captain all week.

"The subject should be dropped," Hogan said. "We came over here to play golf, not talk about meat. If the British public wants it, we'll come over next time with a meat exhibition instead of a golf team." After that, Hogan added some comments which, as an English writer delicately reported, "contained more heat than accuracy."

Nor was that the only controversy. The night before the match, Hogan complained formally about the depth and spacing of the grooves on several of the opponents' irons. He didn't agree to the changes made by Richard Burton, the 1939 British Open champion, until five minutes before the "friendly competition" was to start. Burton, it turned out, had been hollowing out the little holes in his dot-punch wedge with a drill before the competition. The club conflict was no coincidence: Henry Cotton of the British side had lodged an identical complaint against the Americans at the previous Ryder Cup match in Portland, and Hogan did not forget. Hogan's coaching seemed to light the British fire. Only a second-day rally by the Yanks enabled them to retain the Cup. Demaret and Clayton Heafner—Jimmy's partner in Hogan's absence—played particularly well.

A storm hit the North Atlantic on the return crossing, and the *Queen Elizabeth* pitched and rolled through the night.

On his way to the bar at 5:00 A.M., Demaret found Hogan trudging around the deck. While Demaret drank and Hogan watched, they noticed a quiet gathering by the rail, investigated, and found a burial at sea in progress—for a crew member. Hogan grabbed Demaret's arm. "Jimmy, please. You're my friend," he said. "Don't let them do that to me if I die on this thing."

Hogan survived the voyage and soon hit his first full shots in the seven months since the accident. In the movie version, Ford's gardenerlike golf swing came in handy. His stiff-legged karate chops were his most accurate scene in *Follow the Sun*. He falls like a redwood at one point. Just then Anne/Valerie drives the Caddy right onto the practice tee. "I fell," Ford says goofily, while Anne/Val cradles his head tearfully.

For the real-life Ben Hogan, the pain of shifting weight and moving muscles diminished with several thousand repetitions. On December 10, 1949, he played eighteen holes for the first time in almost a year, riding (reluctantly) between shots at Colonial on a motorcycle-like precursor to the golf cart. Two weeks later he checked in as a contestant at the Los Angeles Open at Riviera. For the first time in his life, he would be the sentimental favorite in a golf tournament.

Sportswriters and fans were shocked to see him. Demaret was not. When he went down to the practice tee to check out Hogan, Demaret found him still looking a little skinny, but his golf shots zinged with all the startling force and accuracy they had before the accident.

"You've been practicing a bit," Demaret said.

"No," Hogan answered. "I'm just going to try my luck here."

But Demaret said later that when he shook Hogan's hand, his calluses made it feel like "putting your hand in a meat grinder."

*Follow the Sun* ends with this tournament. It's the Bataan Death March without the fun, a melodramatic

The playoff for the 1950 Los Angeles Open, won by Snead, 72-76. This might have been the only time in his competitive career Hogan sat during a round. (AP/Wide World)

crescendo of string music: Ford overdoes the limp, Ford falls in the rain and mud as he tries to get up a hill, and Anne Baxter/Valerie gazes at her man with a look of syrupy devotion.

Despite the pain and his long layoff, Hogan played a sensational tournament, but Sam Snead tied him for first place with a late run of birdies and then beat him in an eighteen-hole playoff. Yet Hogan "didn't lose," concludes sportswriter Grantland Rice, playing himself in the movie, "his legs simply were not strong enough to carry his heart around." It was corny, but true.

In real life no violins played as Hogan walked slowly to the first tee for his playoff with Snead. His friend Bob

William and *Sports Illustrated* correspondent Jack Tobin strolled along, talking about this and that, with Tobin scribbling in a notebook.

"For crissake, Jack," Hogan suddenly growled. "You don't have to write down every damn word I say." Tobin and William froze, while Hogan limped away.

William asked him about it later. "I had to get mad at something," Hogan said. "I use anger to drive away fear."

The automobile accident had changed everything. Hogan's public image, for an obvious example, spun 180 degrees. He had been the lion among the Christians. Now he was seen as an appealing underdog. During the forty-one-month postwar period in which he had won thirty-seven tournaments, he had more or less handled a great deal of attention. Now he faced the far greater burden of being deified.

Even the other pros assumed a reverential posture. That was something to see, since most of them were up-the-hard-way former caddies like Hogan himself. Ex-marine combat veteran Jay Hebert, for example, spoke to Hogan only when spoken to. "You were always afraid of saying something stupid around him," Hebert says in his Cajun lilt. Often his fellow professionals gave him their ultimate salute: When Hogan hit practice balls, they stopped and watched.

His heightened status fit him like a key in a lock. This was the way for Hogan and his peers to interact—at arm's length, with deep but often one-sided respect, and at Hogan's discretion.

"It's standard procedure now for Ben to sit around after a tournament and chew the fat with the boys," wrote Demaret in 1954. "And he's made a lot of friends doing it, too."

He had more time. He didn't have a train to catch to the next tournament because he wasn't playing in the next tournament. So he took more time. With just a word or two, he became a mentor to a number of awestruck younger or less-accomplished pros.

Relationships deepened with a few of the older guys, too, such as with Claude Harmon, the pro at Winged Foot and the 1948 Masters champion.

"When he was in New York, he'd come to our house for a cookout in the back yard," says Harmon's son Butch, one of three Harmon boys who would become famous teaching pros. "They'd have a few scotches. . . . Hogan relaxed around my dad."

Chew the fat. A few scotches. Whether from pain or sociability, or both, Hogan drank a good deal more after the accident than before it. At Colonial he tipped Beefeater martinis with Marvin Leonard. On the tour he would occasionally join Cary Middlecoff, the former army dentist. The Middlecoff martini consisted of an olive, a mere vapor of vermouth, gin, and vodka. Root canal, anyone?

Don January, a tour rookie in 1956, once tried to keep up with Middlecoff and Hogan. "Man, fasten your seat belt. Martinis, straight-up. I got so loaded I couldn't play the next day," January says. "But they were fine. It's what you get used to, I guess."

Here was something else Hogan did better than the others. He practiced more, won more, and held his booze better.

Those who got closer to Hogan felt the force of his personality, a personality that demanded obedience to his ideas and his style. You could see it for years to come on the heads of Bob Toski, Ken Venturi, Jack Fleck, Gardner Dickinson, Fred Wampler, Tom Weiskopf, Marty Fleckman, and others who continued to wear the "Hogan cap" long after it went out of fashion. Like a good poker player, he never gave away what was in his hand or in his head. Even talkative or emotional guys, such as Dickinson and Billy Casper, imitated his silence and his reveal-nothing body language. The Hogan influence also showed, of course, on the practice tee. Golf pros began to hit more and more practice balls. At age thirty-seven, before he was gray, Hogan was golf's gray eminence.

None of this implied any drop-off in his competitiveness, however. Everybody knew it, or they found out. One of the younger pros ventured a question while the Hawk was hitting balls. Hogan cut him off. "Don't talk when I practice," he said.

"You've got no friends out here," he told Jack Burke Jr., a son of the great teaching pro from Houston. "If you've got a four-foot putt to go home, you don't need to worry about who you'll beat." Not that Burke, another tough customer, needed to be reminded. Hogan advised Dickinson to stay serious on the golf course, saying, "There's nothing funny out there."

What about the world outside the gallery ropes? A few captains of industry were allowed into his circle. These included several of Fort Worth's oil elite, Dallas construction tycoon Pollard Simon, and Phillip Morris Companies chairman Joseph P. Cullman. Retailing magnate Marvin Leonard continued as Hogan's closest friend.

*Follow the Sun* intimated that the outpouring of sympathy following the crash had transformed Hogan's outlook the way the ghosts changed Scrooge in *A Christmas Carol*. Yet he did not suddenly become "Mr. Warmth."

"Hogan didn't like anybody, except maybe his wife," Snead says, overstating a little but not by much, when comparing Hogan to his predecessors, Jones and Nelson, and his successor, Arnold Palmer. Hogan had not lost his disillusionment with people. He was still distrustful of the casual intimacies others found so routine and so easy.

Hogan was a Texan, but he could just as well have been from Japan with his politeness, love of ritual, formality, stoicism, humility, and remarkable discipline. He was acutely aware of status and uncomfortable in circumstances where he didn't know someone's name or job. As with the Japanese, friendships with him were far more likely after proper introductions.

His face spoke clearly of another change since the accident—he had aged. Hogan's granitic face seemed more deeply etched, and with his customary concentration—and anger—now blended with pain, the face looked even more masklike. His hair had grayed slightly at the temples and there was less of it. And his body had thickened through the middle, either from relative inactivity or from the onset of middle age. After several decades at 138 pounds, Hogan's weight reached the 160s a year after the accident. Snead believed Hogan's postaccident workouts had actually made him stronger than before. But whether muscle or flesh, the extra pounds looked good on him.

Other changes were harder to detect, such as Hogan's not being able to see as well. He didn't let anyone know about the near-blindness in his left eye, especially not the press. "It's none of their business," he told Hogan Company president David Hueber many years later. How he had changed his swing to accommodate a body that had endured thirty years of stress in three seconds was also difficult to pinpoint. And except for the subtle clues in his face and his slower walk, you could not discern his pain, which remained like an unwelcome houseguest for the rest of his days. Aspirin and Ben-Gay became as much a part of his day as cigarettes.

Too often his injuries were considered discrete units, but the body is a system. Just as snow in Detroit can screw up a flight out of Des Moines, virtually any part of Hogan could ache whether or not it had had a cast on it. For example, he had broken his collarbone near the acromio-clavicular (AC) joint at the top of the left shoulder. That injury resulted in chronic pain eight inches away, down his back and behind his shoulder blade. Tendons and bursas from his neck to his toes could develop a painful "itis" almost at random.

For Hogan the golfer, the most profound fallout from the accident was his permanent loss of stamina. Five or so tournaments a year would be about all he could stand. He had averaged about thirty a year before the crash. The rarity of his appearances would add to his aura—which he didn't give a damn about—but he most assuredly cared about the disruption of his tournament routine. Two of the four most important events were summarily dismissed: the PGA, which was a week's worth of double rounds; and the British Open, in which he had never played, but which was now too many exhausting miles away to even contemplate. For the rest of Hogan's career, the Masters, the U.S. Open, Fort Worth's Colonial, and the Seminole Amateur-Professional would be the only fixtures on his calendar.

A handful of tournaments a year, Hogan knew, would not be enough to occupy his restless mind and spirit. He would need something else.

For the 1950 U.S. Open at Merion, Hogan added another hour to his three-and-a-half-hour preround ritual. During the first hour out of bed, he soaked in a tub full of hot water and Epsom salts. In the second hour, he swallowed his aspirin, rubbed on his liniment, and wrapped his legs from ankles to crotch in elastic bandages, which were supposed to minimize swelling. He dressed, then had his usual bacon and eggs. Two hours gone. Hogan stayed at the Barclay Hotel in Philadelphia during the Open as a guest of his lawyer, Frank Sullivan. Sullivan lived in a suite at the elegant old hotel.

Hogan's morning ritual allowed a one-hour commute from hotel to golf course. Sullivan drove. As always, Hogan walked into the locker room one hour and twenty minutes before his starting time. For twenty minutes he would change his shoes, comb his hair, maybe drink a glass of ginger ale—

he believed it had diuretic properties that reduced swelling—and put on his cap. As he pushed on Merion's locker room door precisely one hour before show time, he forced his mind into a kind of numbness, a dream state that made him oblivious to the mouth-breathers watching his every move. "My round begins the minute I step out the door," he once confided to Jackson Bradley, a fellow pro.

He hit practice shots for forty minutes—putts, chips, pitches, and full shots, in that order. Then it was back to the locker room, where, if he felt chilled, he would soak his hands in hot water. At ten minutes to launch, Hogan stood on the first tee, doing the things all the competitors did: he shook hands with fellow competitors, exchanged scorecards, announced his golf ball make and number, and carefully read the rule sheet.

The rule sheet held the key to the most amusing subplot at Merion in 1950 or at any U.S. Open. For the pros, the Open was the only tournament they played in run by the United States Golf Association and not the Professional Golfers' Association of America. To put it politely, the PGA and the USGA had different attitudes on a variety of issues, including the rules. More bluntly, the pros regarded the USGA as a bunch of blue-blooded horse's asses who refused to believe it wasn't 1910 anymore. And the amateur volunteers of the USGA considered the pros to be uncouth mercenaries who were pitifully willing to bastardize the game of golf and pee in public. Until 1959 the PGA permitted its players to carry sixteen clubs. The USGA allowed just fourteen. The PGA deemed it okay to mark and clean a ball on a green and to repair impact craters. The USGA said no to cleaning and no to fixing pitch marks and ruled that you can put a dime behind your ball only if it's in someone else's way—and you can't clean it even then. Some sort of trouble always seemed inevitable.

Hogan's own trouble started on Friday, but it had nothing to do with the rules. He had played fairly well up to then, with a two-over-par 72 in Thursday's first round followed by a solid start in round two. But on the eleventh green, where twenty years earlier Bobby Jones had completed his Grand Slam on a conceded ten-inch putt, Hogan's Open almost ended. He holed out, put the putter in his brown leather bag, started the two-hundred-yard walk to the twelfth tee, and stopped dead in his tracks. Cramps shot through his legs like electric shocks. Surprisingly, standing still was harder on his legs than walking. Leaning hard on his caddie, he made it to the next tee and through the round. Given Merion's high rough and marbleized greens, and constant pain that alternately throbbed and stabbed, Hogan's second-round 69 was a minor miracle. He trailed the leader, Dutch Harrison, by just two shots. But for all the obstacles in his path, it might as well have been twenty shots.

Hogan had been brave, but he also had been lucky. What if a spasm shot through his body during a shot, for instance, while he attempted a two-iron to the seventeenth green or drew back his putter on a downhill putt? Merion's greens were so quick that on one green during the first round, as Hogan stood next to his ball, the ball rolled four feet closer to the hole before he hit it (no penalty was assessed—he hadn't grounded his club so, technically, he had not addressed it). And just as he needed continued good fortune if he were to prevail in the next day's two-round, ten-mile march, he would need some bad luck for those in front of him: Harrison, the slick hick from Arkansas; Australian Jim Ferrier, whose omnipresent wife acted as his on-course valet; Julius Boros, a mooselike CPA from Connecticut playing in his first Open; and Johnny Bulla, who played a cheap drugstore ball and flew his own plane between tournaments. Not the least of Hogan's problems was fatigue. His stamina was way down, and he had been getting less sleep than usual. With Saturday's double round and a 9:30 starting time, he would have to get up at 5:30 to bathe his legs, rub them, and wrap them.

"THAT'S IT. I JUST CAN'T MAKE IT," HOGAN SAID THROUGH CLENCHED TEETH TO HIS CADDIE. "NO, MR. HOGAN, YOU CAN'T QUIT," THE BOY SUPPOSEDLY SAID, "BECAUSE I DON'T WORK FOR QUITTERS."

Newspaper editors across the nation recognized the appeal of the limping Little Man's attempted comeback and put the story on the front pages of their Saturday morning editions. Although television had lately enjoyed a growth spurt, thanks to cameras being allowed in the room at the Kefauver Committee's organized-crime hearings, it had yet to make a mark in golf. In fact, no network televised a U.S. Open until 1954. Until television matured, only newspapers, newsreels, and *Life* magazine covered sports. *Life* specialized in a new genre called photojournalism and boasted a huge circulation. The magazine employed the country's premier sports photographer, Hy Peskin, and directed him to patrol Merion and snap the one perfect shot.

That Saturday Peskin had good light in which to shoot, as gauzy sunshine and warm, spring breezes kissed the historic old course. All the contenders played cautiously. Only Boros played himself out of it, with a 77; and only Mangrum shot his way into contention, with a 69. Hogan hung in until cramps hit him hard about noon. After putting out on the thirteenth green, his legs seized up so badly he decided not to continue.

"That's it. I just can't make it," Hogan said through clenched teeth to his caddie.

"No, Mr. Hogan, you can't quit," the boy supposedly said, "because I don't work for quitters."

The caddie's astonishing reply became part of Merion's lore, but it's impossible to verify since no one got the cheeky kid's name and he has never come forward to talk about it. But from *some* source, Hogan found the strength to struggle on. His 72 kept him within two of the lead, now held at one-over-par 211 by Mangrum. Harrison held second place. Johnny Palmer and Cary Middlecoff were tied with Hogan.

No one played well after lunch. Mangrum, Harrison, and Palmer shot 41s on the front nine, and Middlecoff scraped out a 39. While the others collapsed, Hogan's normally ordinary one-over-par 37 seemed superb. It put him in the lead with nine holes remaining. "Neither yet bread to the wise, nor yet riches to men of understanding, nor yet favor to men of skill," the Bible says. "But time and chance happeneth to them all." Life is luck, life is random. Hogan's luck was holding, and there was something almost biblical in his struggle to finish.

The throbbing in his legs grew worse. After holing out on each green, Hogan's caddie retrieved his ball from the cup. Under USGA rules, you couldn't mark your ball on the green unless it interfered with another player's line to the hole. On the few occasions this occurred, Middlecoff marked Hogan's ball for him, a fitting gesture of sportsmanship. Unrestrained by gallery ropes or by any familiarity with the situation, most of the thirteen thousand people on the course scrambled to watch Hogan's struggle. Football fans get to see this sort of irresistible drama once in a while: A running back or a linebacker makes play after heroic play in the Big Game despite being hurt, then slowly limps back to the huddle, to heartfelt cheers. But golf had no precedent. Golf inflicts invisible agonies. Physical pain added to the lip-biting mental stress that seemed beyond endurance.

Hogan made a few pars and his lead grew to three shots. But immediately after driving from the twelfth tee, he staggered as if he had been hit with a knockout punch. "Let me hang on to you," he said to the owner of the shoulder he grabbed onto. "My God, I don't think I can finish." He continued, but not very well. When he reached the final tee, his lead was gone.

Now Hogan faced precisely what he didn't need, a very long par-four. Given the 10-percent inflation in the distance the modern ball goes when hit with the modern club, the 448-yard eighteenth hole at Merion would be today's equivalent of 492 yards from tee to cup. The home hole began with a blind tee shot that had to carry 210 yards of a grassed-over quarry, a shale mining operation abandoned before the course was built in 1912. As always, Hogan took a final pull on his cigarette, tossed it right-handed down to the tightly mowed grass on the tee, swung a little half-swing behind the ball, and assumed his stance in three steps, like at dance school—feet together, left foot forward, right foot back. He aimed at the left side of a tall maple tree on the horizon and fired. The ball hissed, a little white 180-mile-an-hour rocket. Thousands of heads swiveled to watch its flight. Hogan lit another cigarette. The crowd buzzed in the circus-like atmosphere and sprinted ahead of Hogan and Middlecoff into the quarry and up the steep opposite side.

Although his drive had been solidly struck, Hogan had advanced his ball only slightly more than halfway to the hole. He walked slowly to his ball as the murmuring crowd fell silent. He delayed his preshot ritual while he confirmed with PGA tournament director Fred Corcoran that he would need a par to get in a playoff with Mangrum and George Fazio. What should he hit? No wind, flagstick back right behind a bunker, decent lie in the fairway, huge green, dead legs. As Hogan withdrew an iron from the bag—presumably a one-iron—Hy Peskin elbowed his way to a spot directly behind the golfer.

Hogan swung; Peskin snapped. It was the shot of both their lives.

Most of the other photographers disliked Peskin, according to a contemporary, who recalls him as a "typical pushy little New Yorker." But no one denies the greatness of his black-and-white image of Hogan in full follow-through, the ball streaking to Merion's final green in the '50 Open. Powerful context, exquisite framing, and telling details would make this golf's best-known photograph. Details such as the extra spike in Hogan's right shoe under the ball of his foot (he later had a thirteenth spike added to the left shoe, too, for added stability); the number of men in his gallery wearing Hogan caps; and, for the only time in its history, the absence of Merion's distinctive teardrop-shaped baskets on the top of its flagsticks.

The shot was so easy to mishit under the circumstances, but Hogan nailed it. His ball finished forty feet from the hole, exactly where he had aimed. He two-putted, making the four-footer to get into the next day's playoff with seeming haste. When he holed the final putt, he explained later, "I was so discouraged. If you can't hold a three-stroke lead through six holes, you ought to be someplace else."

Given the distance involved, most people assumed Hogan's stroke from the eighteenth fairway had been with his one-iron. It could have been a two-iron, however. Typically, Hogan gave conflicting accounts of what he hit on what was to become golf's most famous shot. He had decreased the loft on his two so that it was a one-and-a-half, enough to carry the 200- to 210-yard shot. Jackson Bradley had missed the cut and watched the shot while standing next to Peskin. Bradley believes Hogan hit the two. A writer asked Hogan what he was doing with a one-iron in the first place. For those pros who reduced their arsenal from the usual sixteen clubs down to the USGA's fourteen-club limit, the usual toss-out was the one-iron and one other. But Hogan kept his knife and pitched his seven-iron. A bizarre choice—the seven has forever been a standard part of the golfer's arsenal. "There are no seven-iron shots at Merion," Hogan said.

Frank Sullivan drove them back to the Barclay Hotel, "since 1929 the pride of Philadelphian society," according to an old advertisement. The Barclay was perfect for Hogan. It was formal and too expensive for the other players. In the next day's playoff, rejuvenated by two baths and a good night's sleep, he played crisply. He fell behind only once, when Mangrum birdied the second hole. The result turned on the fifteenth hole, where Fazio double-bogied to fall too far back, and Mangrum birdied, to close within one of par and Hogan. But on sixteen, Sneaky Lloyd committed one of golf's all-time stupid mistakes, a blunder so huge it made Hogan's eventual victory seem predestined. An insect landed on Mangrum's ball. He marked it with the head of his putter, picked up the ball, held it up to his mustache, blew away the bug, put the ball down, and holed his eighteen-foot putt for a par.

"I'm sorry, Mr. Mangrum, it's not your honor," a rules official told him sadly on the seventeenth tee.

According to the rules, you weren't allowed to clean your ball or mark it, unless it impeded someone else's line. Mangrum had done both. Two-shot penalty. Nothing he had done was out of the ordinary on the tour. It was only illegal in this one tournament.

"What if it had been a snake?" Lloyd lamented.

Now three shots ahead with two to play, Hogan holed from fifty feet on the long par-three seventeenth.

To a lot of people, Hogan's birdie erased the sour taste of Mangrum's breach of an inconsequential rule. But that is balderdash. No stroke in golf is inevitable. They're all at least a little the result of the shot before, or of your opponent's previous shot. Hogan might have three-putted on seventeen if Mangrum had dealt differently with that ladybug, or he might have made a hole-in-one. Who knows? Again, Hogan had been very lucky.

He had also played better than anyone else: Hogan 69, Mangrum 73, Fazio 75. Hogan had won golf's most important tournament just sixteen months after he had nearly been killed. "The most incredible comeback in the history of sports," Dan Jenkins said. "The 1950 Open was my biggest win," Hogan would say later. "It proved I could still play."

Hogan paid his caddie in front of the golf shop immediately after the round. He took his brown street shoes out of the golf bag, put them on, and put his white golf shoes back in the sack. In the next few minutes, someone, somehow, stole Hogan's one-iron—and his shoes.

*Follow the Sun* debuted in Fort Worth in March of the next year, 1951. Its competition did not seem particularly tough. Some of the other movies released at about the same time were *Abbott and Costello Meet the Invisible Man, The Man from Planet X, Cuban Fireball,* and *Insurance Investigator.* The studio pressed its advantage by getting a story—actually a synopsis of the film—in the March issue of *Reader's Digest.* "This article was prepared with the collaboration of Twentieth Century-Fox Film Corporation," the story entitled "He Still Follows the Sun" concluded. "A motion picture based on it will be released throughout the country this month."

Fort Worth did not need to be reminded. The Worth Theatre, which had the honor of hosting the big show, quickly sold out (tickets cost sixty cents each). A day before the March 23 premiere, the distributor arranged for a second Seventh Street theater, the Hollywood, to show the film. The Hollywood sold out. So they added a third theater, the Palace. At least six thousand people attended the biggest movie opening in Fort Worth since the debut of *The Westerner* in Cowtown in 1940.

On World Premiere Day the *Fort Worth Press* ran a quarter-page ad in its movie section showing Ford and Baxter embracing. Under them, a headline covered every promotional base except God and country: "A Woman's Story of a Man's Great Comeback . . . and a Love Big Enough to Make the American Dream Come True." The *Press* editor gave the top of the sports page to golf writer Dan Jenkins. "But the Bantam is still making his comeback," Jenkins wrote. "He is not yet the par-insulting machine which assaulted the U.S. Open record with a screaming 276 at Riviera. That was Hogan at his peak."

The studio sent actors Dennis O'Keefe (by train) and Glenn Ford (by plane) to Fort Worth. Hogan, in a navy blazer, striped tie, and dark gray slacks, met O'Keefe's train in the station where he once sold newspapers. O'Keefe told the press that Hogan had taken five shots off his game during the filming. Ford seemed to be in character when he said, "I feel privileged and proud and humble to play the part of Ben Hogan on the screen." As searchlights combed the sky and the Carswell Air Force Band played, limousines pulled up in front of the theaters. The crowd recognized some of the tuxedoed VIPs as they disembarked: Demaret, Ford, O'Keefe, and another actor, Rory Calhoun, the star of the soon-to-be-released *I'd Climb the Highest Mountain*. Less recognizable were Doctor Ochsner, Brigadier General Hutchinson, and Henry P. Cowen, the president of Mac-Gregor Golf.

A crisis loomed when the Hogans walked to their reserved seats and found them occupied by two poachers, but they scurried off when Hogan suggested they do so. When the lights came back on ninety-three minutes later, five hundred of the moviegoers attended a party hosted by Marvin Leonard at the Fort Worth Club.

It had been a big day for Fort Worth—but did the movie ruin it? For most people, no. Although Sam Snead and

Byron Nelson roll their eyes when asked about *Follow the Sun*, most reviewers were kind.

> BUT WHEN HE SAW FOLLOW THE SUN FOR A SECOND TIME FORTY YEARS LATER, TEARS STREAMED DOWN HIS FACE.

"It is the study of a sensitive right guy whose conscientious craftsmanship was misunderstood," said the *Dallas Morning News*. "Unusually absorbing and occasionally moving."

*Variety* called it "a basic human drama of love and courage with appeal for adult filmgoers. . . . When carefully sold, its box office possibilities are sound."

Not everyone liked the film, of course, far from it. "Unctuously ingratiating," Ronald Bergen commented in his book *Sports in the Movies*. Demaret avoided an outright pan. Hogan, he said, "should have left the job of directing to Hollywood professionals." Clara Hogan objected to Valerie's getting all the credit for his eventual success. The movie made it seem like Ben Hogan didn't have a mother. Hogan himself didn't talk about it, a silence that could be interpreted as disapproval. But when he saw *Follow the Sun* for a second time forty years later, tears streamed down his face.

Two days after the movie premiere, Hogan arrived at Augusta National, ten days early for the Masters. America's best-known members-only playground was a unique combination of haughtiness and hospitality, a place where the president of the United States liked to hang out. Hogan enjoyed the gracious atmosphere, too, but privately he disparaged the golf course. His ability to hit long, straight drives gave him no particular advantage. Long and crooked worked almost as well. Augusta had generously wide fairways, no rough, and its trees were smaller and less numerous than they are today. "You can drive it anywhere," Hogan said. And its greens were so steep and fast he felt forced to play defensively from the fairway, to make uphill putts his target, not the flagsticks. In eight previous tries he had been second a couple times, to Nelson in '42 and to Keiser in '46, but he had never won the Masters.

In the ten days before the tournament, Hogan hit a few thousand practice balls to his caddie, Willie Lee Stokes, and developed an intricate plan to win. He didn't just hit four-iron shots on the practice tee, he hit the punch four-iron he would use on the sixteenth hole. He developed wind and distance guidelines on when to go for the green in two on the thirteenth. He had hit it in the water on that hole twice the previous year. Because the water hazard protecting the eleventh green had been widened on the left, Hogan decided to intentionally miss the green to the right rather than risk a wet ball and a penalty stroke.

The long preparation had two other purposes: It acclimated his legs to Augusta's hills and allowed him to enter the soothing cocoon of routine. Hogan grasped the connection between mood and performance, of the mental and the physical. He understood himself.

"I couldn't be playing better," he said after the second round. Skee Riegel had the lead at 141, Hogan held second with 70–72—142, and Snead was third with one-under-par 143. After three rounds, Riegel and Snead shared the lead at 211, five under par. Hogan remained one shot back after a 70. "Snead is the man to beat," Hogan said. "The leaders usually fade, but I can't depend on that. I've got to let go."

He was wrong about Snead. Sam hit two balls in the water on eleven—where Hogan played so cautiously—and made an eight. But while Snead was shooting 80, Riegel shot 71.

Hogan would need a 70 to tie, a 69 to win. He birdied two of the first three holes and shot the front nine in three-under 33. He hit a brilliant second shot on ten, but just lagged his six-foot putt for birdie to the edge of the cup. Then he played eleven as if he were disarming a bomb—a careful drive, the intentional miss to the right of the green, a six-iron chip, one putt, par. He drove well on thirteen and seemed prepared to go at the green with a four-iron, but he then thought better of it and laid up short with a six. But he hit a wedge to seven feet, made the putt, and now led the tournament by two shots. Hogan followed with more circumspect pars—he played short of the water on the par-five fifteenth—and so still had two shots in hand as he came to the final hole.

About eight thousand people had walked along with him this day, many of them refugees from Snead's gallery. Hogan smoked, walked—Jenkins said he always seemed to be walking uphill—and appeared not to notice anyone. But you didn't need to be a mind reader to guess his thoughts as he stood in the fairway contemplating his second shot. He was thinking about Sunday, April 7, 1946, and about Saturday, April 8, 1950. He had three-putted this green both days, which cost him a chance to win in '46 and a tie for the third-round lead in '50. They had been downhill putts so friction-free it was like trying to stop a bowling ball short of the pins. That was not going to happen again.

Hogan took out a six-iron and hit the ball thirty yards short of the green. Those who didn't understand his chess game thought he had missed the shot or lost his mind. He bumped a wedge shot four feet below the hole and made the putt. Then the familiar cycle of applause, handshakes, photographs, a hug from Valerie, and ceremony. Bobby Jones helped Hogan slip into the kelly green Masters champion's jacket.

"What would you like to win next, Ben?" a reporter asked. "If I never win another one, I'll be satisfied," he replied.

Hogan chips from the edge of one of the hardest-to-hold greens in the world, the seventh at Augusta National. He bogied the hole, but won the tournament—the 1951 Masters. (AP/Wide World)

It was a nice white lie. The instant he removed the green coat with the little gold crest, Hogan began preparing for the U.S. Open.

Charles Lindbergh and Bobby Jones inspired one of James Thurber's funniest short stories. "The Greatest Man in the World" concerned Jack "Pal" Smurch, who had made the first nonstop flight around the world, a heroic feat. But Smurch himself was not heroic. "Slightly built, surly, unprepossessing," his only provisions on his flight had been a gallon of bootleg gin and six pounds of salami. He had done time for knifing the principal at his high school and for bashing a church sextant on the head with a pot of Easter lilies during his theft of an altar cloth. Naturally, the press and public officials conspired to keep the truth about Smurch from an adoring public. During a meeting in a tall building with, among others, the president of the United States, Smurch leeringly rejected all suggestions regarding a hero's conduct. All he wanted to talk about was money and babes. So an assistant to the mayor of New York City "seized the greatest man in the world by his left shoulder and the seat of his pants, and pushed him out the window."

Thurber was saying something about hero worship, hero protection, and how we often confuse aviation and athletic success with character. Hogan, of course, was no Smurch, but was neither nice like Lindy nor charming like Jones. Hogan's star shone with a different light. While he was still an actor—no, the star—on a very public stage, the movie of his life played at the Bijou down the street, and the print media's interest in him continued unabated. Would the unblinking spotlight reveal some previously hidden Smurch or Jones in Hogan?

If Hogan's frigid facade were ever to break, Oakland Hills seemed the place for it to happen. The 1951 U.S. Open course in suburban Detroit had been sketched out in 1917 by Donald Ross, the Henry Ford of golf course architecture. But important members of the club and of the USGA thought it might yield embarrassingly low numbers to Hogan, Snead, and the rest, even possibly—horrors!—a new Open record. So they hired Robert Trent Jones, the Edsel Ford of golf course architecture, to redo it. Ross had been an innovator; Jones was an amplifier. He put tail fins on Oakland Hills. Bigger, longer, tougher, more: the new Oakland Hills fit perfectly with other examples of fifties excess such as poodle skirts, hula hoops, and Elvis.

153

For the first time in U.S. Open history, the architect and the golf course received more attention than the players. The newspaper guys referred to it in print as "the Monster."

"If the winning score is 286 or higher, we will have accomplished our objective," Jones said in his high-pitched voice.

Par was 280 and it was not threatened. In fact, 290, ten over par, was not bothered much. Strangely, the hardest part of the new Oakland Hills involved a change Jones had not intended. It seemed like such a small detail, compared to the diminution of the fairways and the number (sixty-six) and location (in the middle of a number of fairways) of new bunkers. To prevent erosion, the construction crews had sodded and overseeded rye grass around the new sand pits. The rye grew more luxuriantly than the surrounding grass, and it was a bitch to get out of. Thus Jones's tremendous bunkers became an even bigger hazard.

Not everyone thought the architect and the USGA overdid it, however. The old course had been bunkered for hickory shafts, after all. Balls hit by a good player with steel-shafted clubs flew over those hazards with ease. So Jones filled in the holes two hundred yards out and dug new ones 250 yards from the tee. With its high rough; hard, unwatered fairways eighteen yards wide; and sand right where you didn't want it, Oakland Hills favored no one but Hogan. No one else habitually played his tee shots to tiny targets in the fairway, as if each drive were a par-three. Former USGA official Frank Hannigan once observed that every postwar U.S. Open seemed to be set up for Hogan, with an emphasis on straight driving, accurate irons, and high rough that effectively eliminated chipping.

Yet if the fix was in for Hogan, someone forgot to hand him a script. He had earned a reputation as an excellent defensive player because he won on courses which demanded that style. But he much preferred the creativity of attack, and Oakland Hills didn't seem to present that option. "If I had to play [this] golf course every week, I'd get into a new business," he said.

After five days of analysis and drill at Oakland Hills, he played the first nine holes of the tournament like a five-handicapper with a beer: bogey, birdie, bogey, bogey, par, bogey, par, bogey, par. That was 39, four over par. After a double-bogey six on the final hole, Hogan had a disgusting 76. "The most stupid round of golf I ever played," Hogan said. Snead led with a 71. But Sam could be counted on to screw up in the Open, and he did, with a second-round 78 and some bitter words about the bunkers.

Hogan improved with a 73 in the second round for a 149 total. That didn't seem like much, but it kept him within five of the lead. Unfortunately for Hogan, Bobby Locke owned first place halfway home. Locke, from Transvaal, South Africa, and the first foreign player to win consistently on the American tour, wore plus fours, a dress shirt, a tie, and an inscrutable look. The other pros called him "Old Muffin Face," an uncharitable nickname that hinted at their frustration with his eerily consistent roundhouse hook and his godlike putting touch. He also was five years younger than Hogan and relatively fit. "It would take two subpar rounds for me" to catch Locke, Hogan said. "Even that might not be good enough."

In the morning round of the sunny, hot Open Saturday, Hogan shot 71, the second-best score of the tournament. Although he had pulled to within two shots of the lead, he trudged off, someone said, "like a man condemned to die." He had blown it, or believed he had. With five holes remaining, he had been three under par for the day. But he missed a four-foot putt on fourteen. On fifteen he hit it in the woods, then the rough, then the sand, for a dreadful double bogey. And he bogeyed the par-three seventeenth. Demaret had tied Locke for the lead. Paul Runyan and Julius Boros were one stroke back. Hogan, Dave Douglas, and Clayton Heafner trailed by two.

The 1951 U.S. Open champion holds the trophy after
defeating "the Monster." (AP/Wide World)

Golf galleries usually get bigger, noisier, less knowl-
edgeable, and more fun with each round. So it was at the '51
Open. Hogan, the sort-of movie star, was the people's choice.
"The biggest mob in history ever to follow a golfer," according to an Oakland Hills historian, clustered around the first
tee to whoop it up for Ben. Just before he teed off, Hogan did
something out of character. He turned to a blue-blazered
USGA official and said, "I'm going to burn it up this afternoon." No more defense.

Burn was the right verb. Something in the moment—
the buzz from the crowd, his anger at himself or at this Civil

By the early fifties, Hogan had become accustomed to winning handsome checks, like the one being handed him here by Fort Worth's Amon Carter Sr. on the occasion of Hogan winning the 1952 Colonial National Invitation. (Colonial Country Club)

War battlefield of a golf course—allowed Hogan to find the perfect balance between fury and control. During his four-hour burn, he almost holed a full two-iron shot on the tenth hole, a full six-iron on the fifteenth (where he had made a double bogey in the morning), and a full nine-iron on the sixteenth. He closed with a flourish, a birdie from fifteen feet on the final hole for a 67, a masterpiece.

Locke had teed off ninety minutes after Hogan, but he stumbled a bit on his way in with a 73 and finished third.

The best eleventh-hour effort came from Clayton Heafner, the burly North Carolinian whose temper often obscured his talent. Heafner shot 69, a wonderful score when you consider the field averaged more than 77 for the tournament. But Heafner fell just short. He finished second by two shots to Hogan. It was Hogan's third U.S. Open victory in a row: Riviera in '48, the accident in '49, Merion in '50, and now Oakland Hills.

They gave him the silver trophy and the gold medal and he said, "I'm glad I brought this course, this monster, to its knees." It's the only part of any golf victory speech anyone remembers. But Hogan had had a better line before the presentation. Heafner was sitting in the locker room changing his shoes a few minutes after his charge had fallen short.

"Congratulations, Ben," Heafner said, drained from his pursuit. He extended his hand to the new champion.

But Hogan seemed not to realize he had been pursued. "Thanks, Clayton," Hogan said. "How'd you do?"

# CHAPTER 6

# '53

HE COULD GO A WHOLE TOURNAMENT, THAT'S FOUR ROUNDS, WITHOUT MISHITTING ONCE. I'VE SEEN HIM DO IT. HE WAS QUITE A CONTRAST WITH ARNOLD PALMER, WHO COULD HARDLY GO THREE HOLES WITHOUT HITTING ONE SIDEWAYS. . . . THE PRECISION OF HOGAN'S STRIKING WAS INCREDIBLE. I DON'T BELIEVE ANYBODY TODAY HAS APPROACHED THAT, NOT EVEN NICKLAUS.
—PETER THOMSON

Ben Hogan filled his bathtub with water and poured in the Epsom salts. But instead of getting in himself, he dumped in a boxful of new golf balls. He had put a mark on each ball beforehand, a pinprick or a little dot with a pencil. Then, one at a time, he spun the balls, which were buoyant in the $H_2O$ and magnesium sulfate. If one side of a ball consistently finished floating downward, Hogan knew the rubber bands inside had been wound unevenly. Only perfectly round balls made it into his bag.

His golf balls also had to pass a visual inspection. He held a magnifying glass up to each one and turned it over slowly in his hand, searching for excess paint in each of the 280 dimples. No other player knew what Hogan knew about balls or took the trouble to inspect them the way he did. He could press an unmarked golf ball between the tips of his thumb and forefinger and tell its compression, or hardness.

Although Hogan had no great fondness for rolling golf balls in saltwater, he had felt since the war that it was necessary to do his own quality control, beginning when MacGregor started manufacturing its own balls. Until 1946 the MacGregor Tourney ball had been made by—"outsourced" in purchasing agent-speak—the Worthington Golf Ball Company in Elyria, Ohio. But in 1946 MacGregor moved its factory from Dayton to Cincinnati and started to make its own golf balls. Hogan didn't like the new Tourney, and he let the factory know it. Other players in similar situations surreptitiously broke their endorsement deals by switching brands, but Hogan at times openly played Acushnet's Titleist ball or Spalding's Dot. Byron Nelson, on the other hand, continued to use the Tourney without complaint in the few events he played each year.

Hogan had been affiliated with MacGregor since the midthirties, when he and two other up-and-comers named Nelson and Demaret agreed to play the company's balls and clubs. This was called being "on staff." Then, as they do now, manufacturers scrambled for the best staff members because amateurs buy what the best professional players use. The manufacturers got a vital marketing tool from the deal and the pros got free equipment, sometimes a small salary, and bonus money tied to their performance.

Until the disagreement over golf balls, Hogan and MacGregor got along fairly well, primarily because Hogan loved the company's custom-club-making department, which was the best in the industry. Again, his approach contrasted with Nelson's. When Byron came up to Ohio every year or so for new clubs, he would select his entire set and a few backups after an hour in the stock room. But "Hogan would spend three days with our top custom grinder," recalls Bob Rickey, who succeeded his father, Clarence, as MacGregor's liaison to the tour. "He was brutally honest. . . . The guys in the shop loved him as a person but hated to see him come in."

"Too much bounce in this sand wedge," Hogan would say, or "The toe is too round on this one-iron. This four-iron is flat, the six is too upright, this driver's too light, and I don't like this shaft." It was like he was twenty again, standing in the back room at Nolan River Country Club in Cleburne, Texas, sanding wooden shafts or wrapping on leather grips, totally absorbed in the process of making a club as good as it could be. Perhaps the sparks and smells and hammer blows transported him back even further, to his father's blacksmith shop.

Hogan would leave the factory every year with a perfect set of clubs, a still deeper understanding of club design and construction, and two questions: Why couldn't all Mac-Gregor clubs be as good as his set? Why couldn't they all be perfect? "Look, Ben," Rickey would explain, "it's not practical or necessary to custom make every set." But Hogan was not satisfied, and he was reminded he was not satisfied when the MacGregor Ben Hogan Model BAP 2322 irons came out. They were department store clubs. You could buy them at Sears, for crissake! The Tommy Armour Silver Scot remained the company's top club, the one sold in pro shops, and was the model Hogan used.

The Hogan-MacGregor rift grew worse. In June 1953 company president Henry Cowen asked the only staff member openly playing a competitor's ball to come to Cincinnati for a conference. Cowen, naturally, would have liked to have been able to advertise that Hogan won with the fabulous new MacGregor Tourney. "For three days, we showed him every imaginable test we were doing on our ball," Rickey says. "He never says a word. On the third day, I brought him into the president's office to review the tests. 'Well, Ben,' Cowen says, 'I guess you can see we're doing everything possible to ensure the high quality of our ball. Take that driving machine, you can't get more advanced than that.' And Hogan says, 'Then I recommend you enter the fucking driving machine in the U.S. Open.' A week later he won the U.S. Open using a Spalding Dot."

And a month later, in July 1953, Hogan announced his plans to resolve his conflict with MacGregor by manufacturing his own clubs and (eventually) balls at a factory in Fort Worth. Remarkably, at the very time he was organizing the project that would consume the second half of his life, Hogan won golf's biggest tournament. But that was not all he won. In 1953 Hogan had a year as good as Jones's in 1930, or Nelson's in 1945. Maybe better.

Exactly when he had decided to challenge the golf club manufacturing establishment—or at least join it—is a little hard to pin down. But Hogan was a planner. Undoubtedly, he had thought about this for a long time. It's likely his plans solidified during the previous winter, which he had spent in the Southern California desert town of Rancho Mirage. His ten-year relationship with Hershey Country Club had come to a close. "I don't want to be negative, but there wasn't a lot of communication with him in the last few years of the contract," a Hershey official says. So when Tamarisk Country Club founder and president Lou Halper offered Hogan a job at his new club, he took it, but not for the money. The position paid only about what he was making at Hershey—ten thousand dollars. What Hogan wanted was a warm place to hit golf balls.

Tamarisk, the second golf course in the Palm Springs area, had been started by the Jewish golfers not accepted for membership at the first club, Thunderbird. Tamarisk was a flat, green carpet with a lake in the middle, Lake Halper, a very unusual feature in the southern Mojave. The San Jacinto Mountains surrounded the course, and they were beautifully multihued in the rising or setting sun. Soon after it opened in

1951, Tamarisk became a get-away-from-it-all haven for the entertainment elite. Members included Bob Hope, Bing Crosby, Jack Benny, Kirk Douglas, Clark Gable, the Marx brothers, and Frank Sinatra. One of the Mrs. Marxes, Barbara, divorced Zeppo and married Frank.

"Our members were a tough outfit, not easily impressed," says Nick Turzian, who succeeded Hogan as Tamarisk's golf professional. "Whether they were happy with him or not depends on which member you talk to."

Hogan's job at Tamarisk today might be called "director of golf," although his mere presence was his main duty. You could set your watch by his schedule. He walked into the golf shop at exactly 9:30 each morning, and waved hello to employees Scorpy Doyle, Pete Raynard, and Gardner Dickinson. Then he drew the drapes in his office and read his mail, while nursing a cup of coffee and a cigarette. That done, his golf clubs and a bowling bag full of practice balls came out of a closet, and Hogan and his caddie walked past the practice tee to the ninth fairway. As always, he preferred to practice alone. He gave almost no lessons. He had hired Dickinson for that.

After a couple hours of hitting full shots, then putts, he would play. Pollard Simon, the real estate tycoon from Dallas, often joined Hogan's group. Simon and Hogan bought some land together in Palm Springs. As it turned out, he and Marvin Leonard would be the biggest investors in the Ben Hogan Golf Company.

Hogan occasionally invited Dickinson along, too. Dickinson, twenty-six, idolized Hogan. They had met when they were paired together in the spring of 1953 at the Pan American Open in Mexico City. The next week Dickinson traveled to Fort Worth to watch Hogan play in the Colonial National Invitation. Hogan spotted him in his gallery "and handed me a small piece of paper," Dickinson writes in his book *Let 'er Rip!* " 'Gardner, I don't know what your financial situation is, but if you run out of money, don't

WHAT A SPECTACLE IT WAS TO SEE HOGAN HIT EVERY FULL SHOT LIKE A GOD, THEN TO WATCH HIM PUTT IKE AN EXPECTANT FATHER ON HIS THIRD CUP OF COFFEE.

quit. . . . This is my unlisted phone number. You call me, and I'll get you some money.'" Dickinson adopted Hogan's monochromatic wardrobe, smoked like him, looked mean like him on the golf course, and named a son after him. But he was not blind to a major weakness in his hero's golf game. Hogan couldn't putt anymore.

What a spectacle it was to see Hogan hit every full shot like a god, then to watch him putt like an expectant father on his third cup of coffee. He had putted well but not spectacularly during his comeback years of 1950 and 1951. But in the three tournaments he played during his slump year, 1952, his short putting especially started to become a lottery.

He couldn't be helped. Chuck Kocsis, a top amateur golfer from Michigan, recalls walking off the eighteenth green at Augusta National (sometime in the early fifties) after a practice round with Hogan, Claude Harmon, and Gus Moreland. "Hogan hit the ball so good, you couldn't believe it," Kocsis says. "I was never a big fan of his, but he had been the best putter inside of ten feet I ever saw. Now, he was losing it."

Kocsis watched as Harmon touched Hogan on the arm. "Ben, I can help you with your putting if you'll let me." No response.

"Well, what do you say?" Harmon asked again.

"What do *you* say?" Hogan said.

"Come on, let's go to the practice green and I'll show you." Augusta's putting green was only a few steps away.

"No," Hogan said. "Show me right here."

So Harmon had to explain, rather than demonstrate, that Hogan's wrists were breaking down and he was squeezing the grip too tightly. Kocsis believed Hogan did not want to go to the practice green because he did not want to be seen missing any more putts that day. But embarrassment did not put his putting into its downhill slide and his stubbornness did not keep it there. Hogan's overcaffeinated short putting stroke was an inevitable result of the accident. There was nothing he could do about it.

From the time the dashboard of his Cadillac smashed into his face and nearly blinded him in the left eye, Hogan's depth perception had deteriorated. As a result, the subtle breaks in a green became a little harder to read, and distance was more difficult to measure. Eyesight declines in middle age, anyway, and Hogan had turned forty in August 1952—an old forty due to the crash. His declining visual skills did not affect him on full strokes, because a driver or a seven-iron shot had so many more landmarks and boundaries—bunkers, trees, people—than the blank, unbroken green of a four-foot putt. A full golf shot is like a home run in baseball, a no-brainer in a way because it involves all the muscles and a full extension of the arms. But very short shots require just the finest little bursts of electricity from the brain to the arms, hands, and fingers. And, of course, the little tin cup is a much less-forgiving target than a fairway or a green.

Like most good putters, Hogan had always visualized the ball going into the hole before he putted it. Now he was finding that vision and visualization were so tightly linked they might as well be the same thing. He had begun to fidget and hesitate on the greens because he couldn't picture how the putt would go in the hole. He wasn't losing his nerve; he was losing his eyesight.

Hogan compensated with memorization. He had always absorbed details that slipped past others, and his strangely insular concentration allowed him to recall, for example, how a south wind affects the speed of a left-to-right putt on the back right of the second green at Augusta

National. Refreshing and boosting his store of such trivia was why he had begun to show up so early at Augusta and at the U.S. Open.

But how long could his memory make up for his lack of practice? Not that the world's most diligent practicer suddenly stopped drilling—far from it. But *tournament* practice and the blood-congealing feeling of tournament pressure had nearly disappeared from his life. In 1952, for example, he appeared in only three seventy-two-hole events. He won at Colonial but putted his way out of contention at the Masters and in the U.S. Open at Northwood in Dallas. Because of his detached air, no one could see it, but very high stakes keyed up Hogan like anyone else.

"If you got close to Ben, he'd 'er-er-er-er,' " Snead says, referring to Hogan's throat-clearing tic. He might repeat the grunts at two- to five-second intervals for most of an entire round. Hogan knew tournament pressure could not be duplicated in a round at Tamarisk with guys he knew, no matter how big the bet was.

With all that was going on for Ben Hogan in 1953— the deteriorating relationship with MacGregor, the pending birth of his own company, the slow decline in his ability to see and to putt—it was a wonder he could play at all. But he decided to play in five, maybe six tournaments.

## The Masters, April 9–12, Augusta, Georgia

Hogan left the desert in March for his usual working vacation at Seminole in Palm Beach, Florida.

In his exhausting and eerily precise schedule, he hit six hundred balls before lunch, fifty with each of twelve clubs, three balls per minute. After a snack and some rest, he repeated the routine in the afternoon, occasionally mixing in a round with Claude Harmon, the pro.

He arrived in Augusta two weeks early and prepared for the tournament as if he needed the money. In fact, he could use some extra cash for his still-unannounced golf club company, although the Masters first prize of $4,000 would barely make a dent in the funds he needed to start manufacturing golf clubs. His personal finances, however, seemed secure. In a cover story in January 1949, *Time* had estimated Hogan's 1948 income at $100,000. After the crash, the Greyhound Bus Company settled out of court for a considerable sum. Demaret estimated it at "between $125,000 and half a million." Hogan's lawyer told his son-in-law the total was $150,000, then the biggest-ever settlement in the state. "I don't think that's any of your business," Hogan told a writer who asked for the number, although he might have been prevented by terms of the settlement from revealing the amount. Demaret kidded him about calling the dispatcher every morning to see that "his" buses were running on schedule. "Jimmy, don't say a thing like that," Hogan said. "People will think I've got money. They'll hound me!"

Hogan put his bus money into oil and did very well, according to his friend/adviser Gary Laughlin. But the fact that he continued to play exhibitions indicated that he didn't feel wealthy. Few children of the depression ever felt they had enough. For example, he played an exhibition in the summer of '51 in Logansport, Indiana, then took a train to Detroit for the U.S. Open. Again in 1953 Hogan was back in Indiana—his exhibition fee now was fifteen hundred dollars—and it had to be for the money as well as the practice. It wasn't like he needed the applause.

"He was the perfect gentleman, everything by the book," says John "the Bomber" David, a local pro who played in both those exhibitions and created his own legend by beating Hogan both times. At one point David was surprised to see Hogan play his usual fade on a dogleg-left hole.

"Why don't you play a hook here, Mr. Hogan?" he asked.

"Young man," Hogan replied, "I don't care if I ever hit another hook again."

On the Tuesday evening before the Masters started, Hogan attended the second annual champions dinner at Augusta National, a tradition he himself had started the previous year. "I suggested the Masters Club one night in 1952 when we [Hogan and Augusta National majordomos Bobby Jones and Clifford Roberts] were just sitting around shooting the bull," Hogan recalled. "They thought it would be a great idea, especially since I was the defending champion and would pick up the check."

Snead had won in '52, so he bought in '53 and had a captive audience for his jokes. Every former champion—except Keiser and Guldahl—attended and wore his green jacket with the big circular logo on the breast pocket. Strong spirits were served, but Jones and Roberts did not allow the little band of former caddies to dissolve into giddiness. Thus the dinner was never much fun, according to one former champion. "What a wet blanket that Roberts was," he recalls. "I remember he got a deal on some canned peaches, and we had those goddamned peaches for years."

After this champions dinner, Hogan didn't retire to the Bon-Air Hotel, his regular Augusta address. He had requested a room sufficiently high and wide to allow full practice swings, but the Bon-Air didn't have one, so he went elsewhere. And he didn't bother with another practice round the next morning. He had already lapped Augusta National eleven times in the previous twelve days. Besides, he was hitting the ball so well, it surprised even him. Not coincidentally, he seemed to be in a better-than-normal mood. The year before, when Hogan tied Snead for the third-round lead, a writer had asked him what it would take to win. "The low score will win," he said. Then he went out and three-putted five times to shoot 79. But now, on the eve of the '53 tournament, he told a reporter in his tobacco-tinged baritone,

"I'm in grand shape." His confidence came, he said, from his winter workouts: "I practiced every day of the winter. This is no plug for Palm Springs, California, but the turf there is ideal for development of your swing. It's firm, and the sand under-neath gives it a good cushion."

Augusta National's turf, on the other hand, often re-sembled a two-dollar haircut. "You just couldn't spin the ball out of those fairways back then," Fred Hawkins says. "On the seventh, you had to plan to play your third shot from the front bunker or the back bunker, unless you could hit a spot about this big." But the spring weather had been beautiful, and Augusta National was perfect. So perfect that Lloyd Mangrum shot a 63 in practice—so perfect that Dwight Eisenhower had recently shot a "that putt's good, Mr. President"–aided 79. Hogan predicted someone would beat the tournament record of 279.

Who would win and what he would shoot seemed ir-relevant when you got a look at the founder of the tourna-ment—Jones. He had played his last Masters in 1947, when he went the first two rounds with Herman Keiser, the de-fending champion. By then he already had syringomyelia, a degenerative nerve disease. Now Jones could barely walk or stand. But he rode around in a golf cart and presided over the event with dignity and without complaint.

The tournament began. Hogan missed short putts for par on the final two holes and shot 70 in the first round, two behind Chick Harbert, one behind Porky Oliver. Two other Texas boys made bigger splashes than did Hogan, however, and one of them—Byron Nelson—for the wrong reason. Snead holed a sixty-foot putt for a birdie on the eighteenth hole and a 70, but Nelson, playing with Snead and keeping Snead's card, wrote down a four instead of the three that hun-dreds had witnessed. Snead signed the card before catching the error and thus had to keep the four, and a 71. The other Texan being talked about was Don Cherry of Wichita Falls, a good friend of Jimmy Demaret's. Not only was Cherry a professional singer good enough to have a hit, "Band of Gold," he also was a good enough amateur golfer to be playing in the tournament. Cherry entertained nightly at the Club Barcelona in Augusta during Masters week, sharing the bill with the comedy team of Stuart and Barry and dancer Peggy Adams. Hogan did not attend.

A second-round 69 put Hogan in the lead. He missed a morning thunderstorm that inconvenienced others. "The fact is that he did not make one poor shot in the entire round, except for the putts missed," wrote Al Laney of the *New York Herald Tribune*. Hogan missed from less than five feet three times on the back nine, at eleven, fifteen, and sixteen. He looked particularly unsure on the eleventh green, freezing over his second putt like an actor who had forgotten his lines. He waited and waited and the gallery fidgeted. When he finally hit it, his nervous stab jerked the ball off line.

"I just haven't played in enough long tournaments recently [this was his first in ten months], and I'm not putting well enough to win this one," Hogan said. Then he conceded, "I guess I did hit the ball pretty well." He hit seventeen greens in regulation.

The longest putt Hogan made during the first two rounds had been eight feet. But on Saturday, the hole finally got in the way a few times. He drained a just-get-it-close fifty-footer on nine and made a downhill twenty-five-foot putt on ten. His 66 blew the field away, and his 205 broke Byron's fifty-four-hole scoring record at Augusta by two shots. But he had three-putted twice and missed three short birdie putts. He could have shot 61. He had missed only two greens, both by a yard, one because of a bad bounce. Hogan commented to the press how nice the weather had been, then excused himself to have the club's masseur rub down his aching legs. Then he dressed and went back out to practice his putting.

The halfway leader at the '53 Masters shows his thirty-six-hole score, putting him well on his way to a new tournament scoring record. (AP/Wide World)

The key shot of the final round might have been Hogan's four-and-a-half-foot putt for par on the first hole. He lined it up, stood over it, and backed off. Again, he lined it up, stood over it, and backed off. Hogan finally lunged at the ball. It went in. A tradition had evolved that paired the amiable and supportive Byron Nelson with the final-round leader. "Did you see that?" Hogan asked his old adversary on the walk to the second tee. "Now, how can I miss?"

With his next swing, Hogan drove a little too close to the trees on the left of the 555-yard par-five, then hit the shot

"PRACTICE MEANS AS MUCH

AS PLAYING ITSELF. A

TOURNAMENT IS AN

ANTICLIMAX TO

PREPARATION, THE WAY I

SEE IT."

everybody talked about later. He took a four-wood out of his bag, aimed way right, and from a downhill lie hit a big sweeping hook, the ball describing an almost comic right-to-left parabola. The ball landed in front of the green, rolled gently up to and almost into the cup, and twenty feet past it. Twice more during the round he almost holed full shots, a three-iron and a four-iron, on the fourth and thirteenth holes, respectively.

Hogan won by five shots over Porky Oliver, and his fourteen-under-par 274 (70-69-66-69) set a tournament record by five shots.

"The greatest four scoring rounds ever," Gene Sarazen told the press.

"That's as good as I can play," Hogan said. "Practice means as much as playing itself. A tournament is an anticlimax to preparation, the way I see it."

The nation's sportswriters described his win in much more fulsome terms, partly because the performance deserved it and partly because the press tent ran out of beer by midafternoon and started serving scotch.

"When did you start to play conservatively, Ben?" a writer asked in postround interview.

"On the first hole."

"But you went for the green on your second shot on the thirteenth," one of the reporters said. "That doesn't seem conservative."

"Look, I hit my best drive on that hole and the green is big. If I can't hit it with a four-iron, I don't belong in this tournament."

"But you just cleared the ditch."

"Well, the pin was close to the ditch, wasn't it?"

The writers repeatedly asked Hogan if, under any circumstances, he would play in the British Open, say, if he won the U.S. Open. "I have no plans to go to England," he replied each time. But, as Hogan knew, the British Open would be held in Scotland.

President Eisenhower flew into Augusta the day after the tournament, and Hogan stuck around to meet him. They played the course together on Tuesday, two days after the tournament, with Nelson and Clifford Roberts. Ike tweaked Roberts's aristocratic nose over how Hogan had disassembled par during the Masters. "Ben Hogan made fun of your course, didn't he, Cliff?" Eisenhower said.

**Pan American Open, April 30–May 3, Mexico City**
"Flare Up: Hogan Actions Raked over the Coals by Lloyd"
"Official Denies PGA Criticism of Hogan"
"Jimmy Defends Ben"
*"Hogan No Quiso Comentar"*

For three weeks, sports pages all over two countries trumpeted a controversy about the alleged selfishness of golf's greatest player. Feuds between public personalities were revealed, unnamed sources were guessed at, and opportunities to comment were declined. This tempest in golf's teapot had all the classic ingredients.

The brouhaha started when the organizers of the Pan American Open offered an appearance fee—probably five thousand dollars—to get Hogan to their tournament. He accepted. But they extended no cash offer to defending champion Lloyd Mangrum.

"I don't like it, don't think it's right," Mangrum said. "Hogan can get five thousand dollars or fifty thousand dollars. More power to him. But they turn around after I've won the tournament and offer Hogan a guarantee." His dispute, Sneaky Lloyd said, was with the Mexicans, not with Hogan. Nothing "has caused Hogan and I to be any unfriendlier than we ever were. I've always been friendly with Ben until the past two years or so, but we haven't had much to do with each other. But then, Hogan doesn't have much to do with anyone."

Mangrum refused to play, even after el Torneo Panamericano offered him a one-thousand-dollar guarantee. "Ben's never done anything to help his fellow pros," Mangrum said in a parting shot.

At about the same time Hogan accepted the offer in Mexico, he turned down an invitation to play in the Tournament of Champions in Las Vegas. Like all PGA events in the United States, the tournament gave a portion of its proceeds to charity, in this case the Damon Runyon Cancer Fund. "An anonymous PGA official" told a writer that Hogan was not playing in Vegas because the tournament would not provide the five-thousand-dollar appearance fee he requested. Which official? Apparently, either PGA president Horton Smith—Hogan had had words with him at the Masters, something about slow play—or Fred Corcoran, a former PGA tournament chairman, with whom Hogan had never exchanged Christmas cards. Both Smith and Corcoran denied everything.

Columnist Red Smith pointed out that the tournament was not run for charity, "but to advertise the city and its several thriving industries: slot machines, roulette wheels, and craps tables." Hogan wouldn't talk about it; his above-the-fray posture gave the whole thing its momentum. According to the *New York Times*, he told friends, "If they [officials of the Tournament of Champions] had asked me earlier, I'd have been delighted to play there, especially since it was in aid of the Damon Runyon Cancer Fund. Apart from that, I'm a free man living in a free country. I don't like being told where I have to play and where I can't play. If I have to take orders as to where I can or can't play, I suppose I might as well go to Russia."

Hogan was so upset by the imbroglio that he shot 72-72-68-74—286—and won the *torneo* by three strokes. First prize was thirty thousand pesos, about twenty-six hundred dollars.

### The Greenbriar Pro-Am, May 7–10, White Sulphur Springs, West Virginia

Hogan shot 67-68-68-69—272 in this unofficial, carnival-like event, a score that would beat anyone—except Sam Snead on his home course. Snead won with a 268. Hogan finished in third place.

Meanwhile, the public opinion pot continued to boil. Many sportswriters produced columns in support of Hogan. Few, if any, criticized him. Red Smith referred to the "querulous yapping from other pros resentful of their well-earned inferiority to Hogan."

*PGA* magazine came to his defense in its May issue on another irritating controversy: "Ben Hogan has been greatly upset by criticism which has erroneously arisen regarding his fee for playing in last year's National Golf Day. He did receive a fee, fifteen hundred dollars, from *Life* magazine but immediately turned it over to his church, University Christian. According to Hogan, it has never been his policy to reveal his charities."

Another of Hogan's good deeds revealed itself a month later. He had written an encouraging letter to a Louisville, Kentucky, high school golfer named Bobby Nichols, who had been badly injured in a car accident. This was a more substantial gesture than it might appear, because Hogan wrote his own correspondence and sweated over the wording until it was exactly right. The letter came to light when young Bobby won the Kentucky high school tournament and said Hogan's letter had inspired him to play golf again after the accident.

The public relations counteroffensive showed that many members of the press admired him. The need for it demonstrated that many of his peers did not. As the year progressed, Hogan would become even more of a lightning rod for derision, and for glory. None of it changed him. He continued to be self-absorbed and self-righteous in public, and surprisingly kind and sympathetic away from prying eyes.

### The Colonial National Invitation, May 21–24, Fort Worth, Texas

Hogan dominated on his home course just as Snead did on his. In six tournaments at Colonial, he had won three times. Sportswriters were calling the Colonial National Invitation "Hogan's Benefit," or "the Colonial National Second Place Invitation."

He did not treat it as a party. Scores of friends and acquaintances from Fort Worth marched in his gallery, but he never acknowledged them during play and rarely afterward. To him there was nothing funny out there. Even a return to his home course was not a social occasion. "I'm tired of going off last all the time," Hogan complained after the third round. He had missed from thirty inches on the eighteenth green to fall into a tie for the lead with Clayton Heafner and Jerry Barber. "Every time I looked up to line up a putt, all I could see were footprints and cleat marks," Hogan said. "I know it [a special tee time just for him] is good for the gallery and crowd, but I'm in these tournaments for something besides drawing a crowd. I simply want a fair break."

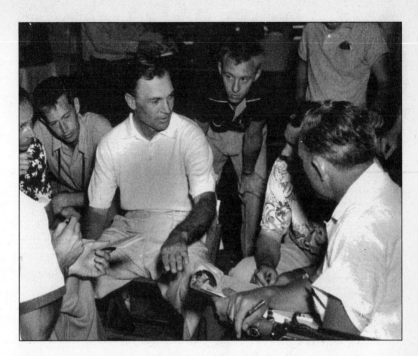

The man of a few words opens up as he meets the press following one of his Colonial rounds. (Colonial Country Club)

Everyone in the field got a tough break the next day, when wind like the high/hot setting on a hair dryer whipped Colonial. All the scores went up—except Hogan's. His final-round 67, the lowest score of the tournament, allowed him to win by five. His scores: 73-71-71-67—282. His money: five thousand dollars. He had now played four tournaments in 1953, and won three.

Hogan's gorgeous teeth caught the popping lights from the photographers' flashbulbs as, for the fourth time, Marvin Leonard presented him with the Leonard Trophy.

It was always a happy occasion for Hogan when he got together with good friend Marvin Leonard, seen here congratulating Hogan for winning another Colonial National Invitation title in Fort Worth. (Colonial Country Club)

"Do I get to keep it this time?" Hogan joked.

"No," Leonard said. But he smiled, too, and his affection for the son he had never had was unmistakable.

The next day, Monday, May 25, Hogan wired in his entry to the British Open.

On Tuesday afternoon, May 26, he left Fort Worth for Cincinnati, where he visited MacGregor's golf equipment factory and made that memorable suggestion to MacGregor's president regarding his ball-hitting robot. He played a few exhibitions on the East Coast, then traveled to Oakmont, for the U.S. Open.

### The United States Open, June 11–13, Oakmont, Pennsylvania

Ben Hogan had won three of the five previous Opens, but the USGA required everybody (except defending champion Julius Boros) to participate in a thirty-six-hole qualifying tournament on the two days before the main event. Making Hogan qualify for the U.S. Open was like running a credit check on John D. Rockefeller, an insult and a waste of time. And although Hogan made the field without much trouble with a 77 at Pittsburgh Field Club and a 73 at Oakmont, the extra rounds cost him some of his limited supply of energy and a pulled muscle in his back.

Monumental and forbidding, Oakmont was the Mount Everest of golf courses. A river ran through it, the Allegheny; as did a turnpike, the Pennsylvania. Some of Oakmont's huge trees met at the top to form canopies, breaking the light into kaleidoscopes of sunshine and shadow. The shifting patterns were pleasant to contemplate even when your ball was hunkered down in the too-tall grass near a too-big tree or buried in a bunker with *furrows* in it for godsakes, like a freshly plowed field. The first, tenth, and twelfth greens

179

tilted *away* from the fairway, a difficulty almost as maddening as the unplayable sand pits. Architect Henry Clay Fownes designed Oakmont in 1903 to be the toughest course in the world and he succeeded. Shots that strayed from the straight and narrow indicated an evil heart, Fownes seemed to say from across the years. Suffering was called for.

Salvation lay not on the greens, which undulated like a belly dancer. Although they were less steep than those at Augusta National, Oakmont's carpets were even quicker. Golf writers searched for similes involving hockey rinks and pond ice. Snead joked that the dime he used to mark his ball slid off one green. Grantland Rice wrote of seeing quite a number of the world's best players take five putts on some greens during the 1935 Open at Oakmont. He even witnessed a *six-putt*—from *ten* feet.

Hogan began memorizing and analyzing the old course nine days before the tournament started. "I have no practice system," he told a *Pittsburgh Press* writer, then described his practice system. "I go over the course a couple of times to decide what type of golf I'll have to play. Then I work on that." For most of three days he practiced high four-woods, for the second shot to the tenth.

Hogan debuted a black cigarette holder in the first round, during which he burned the usual two packs of butts. In warm, sunny weather that had most of the spectators thinking about sunburns and tans, Hogan wore the only sweater on the grounds, a gray cashmere cardigan.

Skip Alexander played in the threesome behind Hogan's. He strode into the locker room after the round and announced, "I know how to shoot 67 on this course.

"Okay, Skip," Fred Hawkins said, "how?"

"You hit every goddamn fairway and every green about ten feet from the hole. Like Hogan did."

Hogan had five birdies—three of them tap-ins—no bogeys, and his chip onto the only green he missed hit the flagstick and stopped two inches from the canister. His 67 led by three over Frank Souchak, a local amateur, and George Fazio, who had been in the U.S. Open playoff with Mangrum and Hogan at Merion.

Hogan said he had no problem with the back after the fourth hole. "I'm filled with ointment and I kept my back warm with this sweater. . . . Don't forget I'm forty years old. I'll have a new ache tomorrow—and I'll still have this one."

Drama returned to the Open the next day. Sam Snead shot 69 to pull into second place, and bitching by the pros reached an unpleasant crescendo. Snead produced the kind of brilliant putting round Hogan never had anymore. He used only eleven putts on the final nine holes and capped it off with a sixty-five-foot, seven-iron chip-in on the last green. Hogan, exhausted from being on the golf course too long, hit uncharacteristically poor iron shots on sixteen and eighteen for two bogeys. His 67-72 and Snead's 72-69 set up a showdown of the two best players in golf for the national championship in Saturday's double round. Just behind them lurked the third-best player, Lloyd Mangrum, and former Oakmont assistant pro Jay Hebert. Who could ask for more?

The USGA could. Actually, it asked for less—less dawdling by the participants, some of whom had spent almost five hours to get around Oakmont in the first round. USGA president Totten Heffelfinger, executive secretary Joe Dey, and others took positions on the course and played traffic cop, and the inevitable PGA-USGA blowup resumed. First it had been those irritating qualifying rounds, then the course itself (Mangrum called the hard, furrowed sand in the bunkers "a disgrace" and the greens "a runaway freight train"), now this.

"We played in three hours and seventeen minutes," said white-haired, red-faced Denny Shute, a normally pacific man who collected stamps. "I want to see them rush Hogan the way they did us."

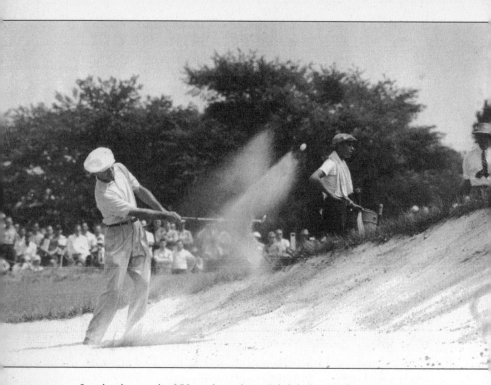

In a bunker on the 253-yard par-three eighth hole at Oakmont, second round, '53 U.S. Open. Hogan bogied the hole, but won the tournament. (AP/Wide World)

Clayton Heafner also claimed selective enforcement. "I want to see what they do with Ben Hogan this afternoon. We played in three and a half hours. . . . It took Hogan four and a half hours yesterday. I told one official I was going out and clock Hogan this afternoon and see how fast he plays."

If Heffelfinger and Dey felt intimidated by Hogan, as Shute and Heafner implied, that would hardly have been un-usual; Hogan scared everybody. Perhaps he should have been asked to get the lead out. He had been playing very carefully,

looking at the clouds, the trees, and the smoke from his cigarette for clues about the wind strength and direction. On the
greens he had slowed down to a crawl. His threesome required four hours and fifty minutes to get around Oakmont
on Friday. But the snail's pace had just as much to do with delays caused by the ten thousand people watching him as with
his own speed, or lack of it. How many had watched Heafner?

The feeling among his peers that the USGA favored
Hogan continued on Saturday. Hogan began play at 9:00;
Mangrum, 9:30; and Snead, 10:00. "It's unfair," said Cary
Middlecoff, "and I don't think it's accidental." The good
dentist quit in a snit halfway through the third round, because, he said, he was mad about starting times. "The late
starters have to play on a course that's chopped to pieces by
ten thousand people," Middlecoff said.

"They shouldn't give the leader the early schedule all
the time," agreed Snead. "They ought to give everybody a fair
chance."

Despite a three-putt from eight feet at the eighth,
Snead took the lead with three front-nine birdies, and thousands of Hogan watchers fell back to watch the new leader.
Snead held the lead until he reached the par-four seventeenth,
an uphill and heavily bunkered hole just 292 yards long. You
could drive it if you could hit and hold a convenience store
roof from three blocks away. Snead could. But he went for his
eagle-two too hard and three-putted. Ben had chipped to a
couple of inches for a three on the same hole an hour before.
Hogan led by a shot with one round left.

He ate a lunch of salad and fruit, a diet that had helped
him lose twenty pounds since February. Between bites, he told
a writer the outcome might hinge on holes fifteen, sixteen, seventeen, and eighteen, "the toughest part of the course."

Hogan still led Snead by one when he reached the
458-yard fifteenth. He drove into one of the cornrow fairway
bunkers and had to wedge out. Then he hit his third with a

two-iron into a bunker by the green. Another wedge, and still he faced a twenty-foot putt for bogey. But he holed the putt. Then he grabbed the Open by the throat, finishing three-three-three—par-birdie-birdie. Just when he might have been expected to lose his edge to fatigue, he hit a cut two-wood into a right-to-left crosswind on the 234-yard sixteenth, drove the green on seventeen—"I never hit a ball harder in my life," he said—and staked a five-iron to two yards on eighteen.

Snead had unraveled by then and would finish second in the U.S. Open for the fourth time. Hogan's final putt would win it by six shots. He stood over it, and again it was like he had seen Medusa. After an eternity, he hit the putt and made it.

Writer Charles Price asked Hogan what took him so long. "I couldn't see it going in," he said.

### The British Open, July 8–10, Carnoustie, Scotland

Thousands of people pressed in around the trim little man on the practice tee at Moon Brook Golf Club in Jamestown, New York. Before an exhibition with Jay Hebert, 1950 U.S. Amateur champion Sam Urzetta, and host professional Toby Lyons, Hogan demonstrated low, long-iron shots, and "emceed himself, and very professionally," Hebert recalls. "Much better than you might think." Hebert got down on his stomach ten yards away and took some photographs with his single-shot Roloflex camera and tried to catch the new Open champion at impact.

After the exhibition—Hebert and Lyons clobbered Hogan and Urzetta—Hogan asked Hebert for a ride to the train station in Erie. He was going to New York, he explained, but didn't want to take a plane because he didn't want to fly on Allegheny Airlines. On the forty-five-minute drive, they talked perhaps five minutes, Hebert says, "and would you

Jay Hebert, professional golfer and amateur photographer, got down on his stomach to shoot these action shots of Hogan demonstrating low iron shots. Hogan's fellow golfers were as intrigued with his swing mechanics as they were mystified by the man. (Courtesy of Jay Hebert)

believe he didn't mention he was on his way to the British Open?" But Hebert later realized that Hogan had been thinking about his first try at golf's oldest major championship. Those head-high one-irons—he was already practicing for Scotland's ocean winds.

When Hogan confirmed the rumors that he was going Over There, it was as if he had announced plans for a polar expedition. Some headlines hint at the breathless interest:

"British May See Hogan"

THE LONG-UNDERWEAR SAGA BEGAN WHEN HOGAN MENTIONED TO A REPORTER THAT HE UNDERSTOOD IT GOT COLD IN SCOTLAND, EVEN IN JULY.

"Hogan Under Unfair Pressure" (from the *Fort Worth Star-Telegram* editorial page)

"Big Ben Ticks off Today Unalarmed by Carnoustie" (he arrived in Scotland on June 23)

"Ben to Get Long Undies"

The long-underwear saga began when Hogan mentioned to a reporter that he understood it got cold in Scotland, even in July, and that it would be nice to have some long handles to ward off the chill. Maybe some in cashmere? Abercrombie and Fitch, a New York retailer of hard-to-get items for the sportsman, cabled Hogan that it had the very item. Hogan ordered two pairs at ninety-five dollars each. A. J. Anderson Company of Fort Worth made a media splash by shipping over a couple of their scarlet cotton-and-wool two-piece long johns. BVD topped that by sending him three pairs. Each shot fired in the underwear war made the first page of most American sports sections. Of course, his golf soon drew the attention:

"Hogan Amazes Scots with 69"

"Irons 'off,' Hogan Shoots 70"

"3,000 Stampede Fairways: Gallery Hinders Ben's Group"

"Hogan Has Greens Trouble, Fires 74 in Practice"

"Hogan Slips Away for Practice Round"

All this, and the tournament hadn't started yet. Why was he there? Why did he enter this cyclone of expectations and publicity? That was the familiar Hogan conundrum, the mystery of a man both drawn to and repelled by the limelight.

"Why are you going to Scotland, Ben?" someone asked during the post-U.S. Open press conference. "Who made up your mind for you?"

Incorrect phrasing.

"I make up my own mind," he answered. "About everything."

Other writers who asked the question more respectfully got the same careful, four-part reply: "Because so many people want me to; it's being held in July, when it might be warm and presents no scheduling conflicts; the Royal and Ancient rules now permit me to use my center-shafted putter, after having banned it for some time; and for the challenge." Of these, the *challenge* was most important. His competitive nature demanded he take this test.

By "people" in part one of his answer, Hogan meant Walter Hagen, Tommy Armour, and Bobby Cruickshank, three of golf's elder statesmen. All three had called him about playing in the Open. Claude Harmon also had urged him to try it "for the good of the game."

Since no rooms with private baths were available at the Bruce Hotel next to the golf course, Ben and Valerie stayed at a private house in Dundee, eleven miles down the coast. They rented a Humber limousine, a big, solid, American-looking car, and hired a driver. National Cash Register Company of Dayton, Ohio, owned the house and lent it to the Hogans— more corporate support for the one-man Olympic golf team. Acushnet donated the British-sized golf balls, in three compressions. The British ball had a 1.62-inch diameter, versus the 1.68-inch American ball. It doesn't sound like much of a difference, but the small ball went much farther, particularly against the wind, and settled more deeply in the grass. After thirty years with one ball, Hogan would be trying a new one in his first attempt at golf's oldest major championship. He had his challenge.

But did he feel the seductive tug of the place? Did he hear the whispers of long-dead ancestors? His British Open experience is usually portrayed as a lovefest between the dour, golf-mad Scots and the dour, golf-mad Hogan, but it wasn't.

Hogan tees off at Carnoustie's first hole during a practice round preceding the '53 British Open, his only appearance in golf's oldest major tournament. (AP/Wide World)

Repeating a familiar pattern, the Scots invested much more emotion in him than he did in them. All of Hogan's mental energy went into winning.

"I went over there, and after I got there and saw the conditions of the golf course and the transition I had to make to play any kind of decent golf, I said to myself, 'I've made a mistake by coming,'" Hogan recalled. He let slip an undiplomatic remark about lending the Carnoustie greenkeeper his lawnmower, but mostly he said all the right things.

"A perfectly mannered American ambassador," commented British golf writer Louis T. Stanley. Meanwhile

Hogan privately deplored the casual, natural maintenance of the course, its burned-out fairways—there had been a drought along Scotland's east coast—and greens that were slower than a Scottish sunset. The adamantine turf jarred the lofts and lies of Hogan's irons out of adjustment; the height of the flagsticks varied mysteriously; and the divot-pocked fairways of heavily played, municipally owned Carnoustie added a variable he particularly disliked. He would never return. "I'm not going back to a place where they never rake the goddamn bunkers," he told a friend later.

"We heard that he was in a bad humor, about the weather, the accommodations, whatever," recalls Peter Thomson, then a twenty-three-year-old Australian professional who would win five subsequent British Opens. "The Scots know golf, and he was the best player, so he had the biggest gallery. But they didn't really want an American to win. I don't think they wanted an Australian to win, either."

As for Hogan's unfamiliarity with Scottish seaside golf, Thomson is dismissive. "A links course is the same as any course. It's all ball striking."

But the Scots really did fall in love with Hogan, and their sense that the romance might be for just these two and a half weeks made it more intense. Seven years earlier Snead had come over for the Open at the Old Course at Saint Andrews, won the tournament, then didn't return to defend. "It's like camping out over there," Snead had said, ungraciously. He also complained about the meager prize money, which had caused him to lose money for the week even though he had won. Snead's negativity further depressed American interest in the Open. That's why the Scots couldn't believe their luck when Hogan bucked the trend and appeared in their tournament. They swirled around him wherever he went, running between his shots, and loving the cool perfection of his golf game. "The Wee Ice Mon," they called him.

Hogan quickly got used to the bewildering series of mounds in Carnoustie's fairways and learned to avoid the fierce tangle of heather, gorse, and broom in its roughs. In fact, he missed the rough altogether, never hitting into it once in the entire tournament. He handled another Carnoustie eccentricity—his caddie—simply enough. Cecil Timms, a tall, handsome man of thirty-four, jabbered excitedly between shots, ate the candy Hogan kept in his golf bag, and actually covered his eyes with his arms when his employer putted.

"Timmy, shut your mouth and stand still," Hogan advised.

"Aye, Mr. Hogan."

But as his caddie's body language suggested, Hogan's putting was a sight. "The least attractive part of his game," said Bernard Darwin, the grandson of the naturalist and Great Britain's foremost golf writer.

As CBS Radio broadcaster John Derr remembers it, he was the only American journalist who accompanied Hogan overseas. Just two other notable American players made the trip, Lloyd Mangrum and amateur Frank Stranahan. "Strannie," the heir to a spark plug fortune, wore tight shirts that showed off his heavily muscled arms and torso, and admired Hogan greatly. "If I could find a perfectly matched set of hickory shafts, I'd go back to playing hickory," Hogan told him one afternoon, perhaps taking advantage of the opportunity to put a strange thought in a gullible opponent's head. He played practice rounds with both the other Americans but didn't hang out with either. The gentlemanly Derr was more his style.

"Ben and I had lunch every day," Derr recalls, "and I walked every hole of his practice, qualifying, and tournament rounds with him, except for the last two holes. We got along like people do when they're countrymen and in someplace foreign."

When they walked together during practice and qualifying rounds, Hogan carried a club in his right hand and kept his left hand on the back of Derr's belt, a ruse of keeping both hands occupied to discourage autograph seekers and handshakers. Legend has it that during one endless Scottish twilight, Hogan walked Carnoustie alone, tracing the holes in reverse. On his greens-to-tees hike, Hogan supposedly was trying to discover any little hill or valley or tilt of ground he had missed. Derr discounts the story. Hogan would have attracted scores of fans in such a circumstance, and he would have had both hands free.

As tournament week began, Royal and Ancient officials protected Hogan from his admirers by employing a half-dozen Scottish policemen to walk in formation around him. There were no gallery ropes. Everybody, even the defending champion, had to qualify for the tournament: It was another policy guaranteed to keep most American professionals from entering. Hogan made it easily, however, with a 70 at Burnside (a course adjacent to Carnoustie) and a 75 at Carnoustie.

He settled on the ninety-compression balls, and used six of them per round: a new ball on the first tee, another on the second tee, and a third on the third. Then the first ball on the fourth, the second on the fifth, and so on. On the back nine, he repeated the procedure with three more balls.

A very strong wind blew in from Carnoustie Bay in the first round of the main event. Hogan shot a bump-and-run 73, a good score for the conditions but three shots behind Stranahan. The greens felt like concrete underfoot but putted like shag carpets. Hogan couldn't get used to them.

When the second round began, the drought ended. Hogan and playing partner Ugo Grappasoni got drenched, then coated with sunshine, then drenched again. His second-round 71 was built on more excellent hitting and more mediocre putting. Dai Rees of Wales and Eric Brown of Scotland shared the lead at 142. Hogan trained by just two.

But he had caught a cold, or the flu, and his temperature hit 103 degrees. Derr found out, but Hogan would not let him go on the air with it.

After a shot of penicillin, Hogan teed off at 10:27 for the first of Friday's concluding double round. The previous day's smorgasbord of rain, sun, wind, and calm resumed, and so did Hogan's uncertain putting. He missed short putts for par on the fourth and fifth, then changed the momentum with a birdie on the long, dangerous sixth. Many of the other competitors played this 565-yard hole on the installment plan. Defending champion Bobby Locke, for example, hit a four-iron off the tee to avoid the two coffinlike bunkers in the middle of the fairway, a three-iron second to avoid the burn (creek) and the out-of-bounds on the left, and a pitch. Most of the fairway was to the right, but Hogan noticed that the hole opened up from the left side. He could hit this green in two if he could thread a driver into a narrow haven of brown grass between the fence bordering the practice ground and a sod-faced bunker deep enough to hide a cow. He went for it, and made it, in all four rounds. His daring drive was "not, if you please, a canny steered shot," wrote S. L. McKinlay of the *Glasgow Herald*, "but a full-blooded bang." From there Hogan fired a wood over the burn and at the green, and chipped and putted for a birdie four.

With a third round of 70, Hogan tied Argentinean Roberto De Vicenzo for the lead. The man from Buenos Aires didn't look like much with his big hands, big feet, and big nose, and a swing as hard and short as an uppercut. Yet Roberto was a superb golfer, possibly the best in the world after Hogan and Snead. He and fellow Argentine Antonio Cerda played a practice round with Hogan. "I hit driver and seven-iron, Hogan hits driver and three," De Vicenzo recalls. "Hogan say, 'Roberto win because he can fly the bunkers.' But I putt so bad."

De Vicenzo started the final eighteen at 1:56, Hogan at 3:27. After Hogan chipped in from forty feet from the edge of a bunker on the fifth hole, a hailstorm hit. Despite this added incentive to play safely, again Hogan blasted a driver along the out-of-bounds line on the sixth. The gallery inhaled . . . then sprinted, relieved, to Hogan's new Alley. From there he striped a wood to the edge of the green and made another birdie.

Did Hogan's gamble give him the lead? No one knew for sure. Carnoustie had no scoreboards. The absence of that basic information caused a great deal of whispering and intrigue, and running back and forth. Like a horse race in the dark, not even the participants knew how they stood.

From time to time Derr used his press badge to get into one of the scorers' tents scattered around the course. They were the only place to get almost up-to-the-minute news on the standings. On the fifteenth tee, Hogan gestured toward him.

"How's Cerda stand?" Hogan asked.

De Vicenzo had finished with a 73. Antonio Cerda was the last remaining challenger.

"He's three under," Derr reported at the green. Hogan led him by two shots.

"What hole's he on?"

"Thirteen."

"Tee or green?"

"He's *through* the thirteenth. He's playing fourteen."

Hogan walked to the sixteenth tee and took a club and a ball from Timms. Then came the usual routine: the cigarette, the stance, and finally the flat, ferocious swing. His ball stopped twelve feet from the hole on the 235-yard par three. Hogan picked up his cigarette, and stood close to Derr. "This tournament's over," he said. "You can go in now and set up for the broadcast."

Later, as his birdie putt from twenty feet fell in the final hole, the Wee Ice Mon acknowledged the deep-chested roar from the largest gallery in Open history. He took off his hat and he smiled. He had shot 68 and would win by four over Rees, Cerda, Thomson, and Stranahan. He signed his card, and walked with Derr to the CBS "studio," the tiny starter's shed by the first tee.

Eight minutes later Derr and Hogan went on the air. Hogan gave listeners a calm synopsis of his round.

"Tell us about the seventh hole, Ben," Derr said, and, having spotted Valerie waiting outside in the drizzle, took off his headset and walked outside to invite her into the cramped hut. She declined—"too shy, I guess," Derr says. Valerie waited outside in the rain with Cecil Timms and the writers, a few of whom were unhappy to have been kept waiting by American radio.

"Ben, the USGA asked me to bring back your golf ball for their museum," Derr said later, sometime after the presentation ceremony.

"Sure," Hogan said, "Timmy's got it." Timms handed Derr the ninety-compression Titleist 2 he had finished with and one more ball. "This is the ball we used to hole that deuce on number thirteen," the caddie said. "Mr. Hogan thought ye might like it for a souvenir."


### Ticker-tape Parade, July 21, New York City

The USS *United States* glided majestically on the morning high tide past the Statue of Liberty. Sirens from police launches filled the air, and fireboats squirted water in glistening arcs. The ship docked at Pier 86 at 8:15 A.M. Down on the dock, reporters, photographers, newsreel cameramen, TV people, and a police detail awaited. Welcome Hogan signs decked the West Forty-Sixth Street pier.

The Hogans disembarked and the police escort whisked them to the Park Lane Hotel at Forty-Eighth and Park. Just before noon Ben and Valerie rode downtown in a

Hogan rides down Broadway in New York City on July 21, 1953, showered by ticker tape, en route to city hall. Gen. Douglas MacArthur had been the most recent recipient of this hero's welcome. (AP/Wide World)

After the ticker-tape parade, Hogan joined writer Grantland Rice and baseball star Stan Musial at a luncheon at Toots Shor's restaurant. (AP/Wide World)

five-car motorcade of new convertibles. The parade formed at Bowling Green near the southern tip of Manhattan and went north ten blocks on Broadway to city hall. An escort of motorcycles led the way, followed by Troops A and B of the Mounted Squad of the New York City Fire Department. A color guard trailed the horses. Behind the flags, sitting on the rear deck of a shiny black Chrysler, was Hogan. He wore a gray suit. He smiled and waved up at the people hanging out from office building windows. They yelled down to him, waved back, and threw ribbons of paper from their telegraph tickers. Lunchtime walkers stopped and cheered. Deputy

Valerie and Ben prepare to board a flight home from
New York to Fort Worth following the Big Apple's
celebration of his 1953 Triple Crown—victories in
the Masters, U.S. Open, and British Open.
(AP/Wide World)

Chief Inspector Patrick Kirley estimated the crowd at
150,000.

"I've got a tough skin, but this kind of brings tears to
my eyes," Hogan said in his brief remarks at city hall. His
voice cracked. "I don't think anything can surpass what's hap-
pening now."

Hogan had accomplished so much in the last four
months. He had played in six tournaments and won five, three
of them majors, a record of undiluted excellence. He had

overcome physical deterioration, the emotional pain of his past, caviling from his peers, and a game that defied mastering. And the ticker tape had officially anointed him as an American hero.

The clock struck one and the fire department band played its final note. Again, sirens wailed as the Hogan party started uptown for a luncheon in his honor at Toots Shor's Restaurant. He would be going on TV the next night, and the USGA was holding a dinner in his honor the night after that.

But in that wonderful glow of achievement and respect, how could Hogan know? How could he know he had won his last major tournament?

# CHAPTER 7

# THE SECRET

YOU KNOW WHY I'M SO GODDAMN GOOD? I NEVER MOVE MY RIGHT
KNEE.

—BEN HOGAN, TO HIS CADDIE

The enduring mystery of Hogan's Secret had no parallel in sports. Other games had fundamentals—only golf had a Secret. Only golf had Hogan.

He claimed to have had a flash of insight into the golf swing while lying in bed one night in the summer of '46. Although Hogan played extremely well for the next several years, Cary Middlecoff remembered a preaccident Hogan who occasionally missed fairways and greens just like everybody else.

"It was in 1950 that he began showing the kind of precision golf that set him apart," Middlecoff wrote in his book *The Golf Swing*. "In 1950 he began to take on the miracleman aura. Small crowds that included a number of his fellow pros would gather around him and try to watch his every move anytime he started hitting practice balls."

"What's your secret?" people wanted to know. Not telling was Hogan's reply, encouraging the question's premise. There was cynicism in this and probably some psych-out value for use against Snead. Yet Hogan knew he did a number of things that made him markedly better than anyone else. One of his advances screamed out at the clusters of practice-tee observers peering at his grip, backswing, and right elbow at impact. *Practice.* He didn't get where he got by watching the next guy. He dug it out of the ground. They were looking for a shortcut from a man who disdained the easy way.

*Golf Digest* came out with the first "Hogan's Secret" cover story in September 1953. The writer was Lawrence Robinson of the *New York World-Telegram and Sun*:

> The secret is out. Ben himself has given it to several friends. It isn't an unusual way of swinging or a matter of grip or stance. It's a twenty-minute-training routine.
>
> When Ben gets up in the morning, he grabs a club, preferably a wood. With his feet close together, the Little Man clamps his arms tight against his stomach [and] starts a short swing of a few inches, arms still close. Then he gradually lengthens the backswing a foot at a time. He does this for twenty minutes each day until he is taking a full swing, all the while from the close-to-the-body position.

The key to the golf swing was a twenty-minute drill he did in his jammies? This bit of classic Hogan misdirection did not gain wide credence. CBS-TV obviously didn't believe it. "They offered him a lot of money to reveal his secret, and they wanted me to do the interview," John Derr recalls. Apprehensive about holding his own with golf's only research scientist, Derr conferred with Claude Harmon about what questions to ask. "Don't worry," Harmon said. "He knows what to say. You just fill in around the edges." But the television deal fell through.

Meanwhile, Hogan disclosed another insight. "You can hit your shots great and still shoot 80 every day because of poor management," he said while nibbling on a lemon rind after winning the Masters in '53. "The shots are 30 percent of the game. Judgment is 70 percent." The profundity of that statement escaped notice. Instead everyone wanted to hear about some mechanical trick that would allow them to play golf like a champion.

In 1954 Hogan accepted *Life* magazine's offer of ten thousand dollars for the Secret. The cover of its April 5 issue trumpeted "Ben Hogan's Secret: A Debate." The seven pros polled for the story came up with seven different answers. They sounded like a freshman philosophy class.

"The left hip leads," Harmon said.

"Level shoulders," George Fazio said.

"He opens the face of the club when he grips it," Mike Turnesa said.

Walter Burkemo: "He drops his hands at the top of the backswing."

Fred Gronauer: "It's his pivot."

Snead was dubious: "Anybody can say he's got a secret if he won't tell what it is."

Gene Sarazen came closest to the mark. "He has it up here," he said, pointing to his head.

Hogan demonstrated how thoroughly he still had it up there the same week the article appeared, when he tied Snead for first in the Masters. Seekers of the secret didn't take to heart the obvious, that he concentrated and controlled himself better than anyone else in golf.

*Life* ran its "Hogan's Secret" story in the August 8, 1955, issue, in which "Ben Hogan Finally Reveals the Mysterious Maneuver That Made Him a Champion." There were actually three mysterious maneuvers, Hogan wrote: He weakened his left-hand grip, that is, moved it to his left; he fanned the club open on the backswing, and referred to it as "pronation," an intimidating term old Scottish professionals had used to add value to their golf lessons; and he cupped his left

HIS SECRET ABSOLUTELY PREVENTED A HOOK, THE ONE SHOT A NATION OF SLICERS DEVOUTLY WISHED TO HIT. IT WAS FOOL'S GOLD.

wrist inward at the top of the backswing. That was it. The punch line: Hogan acknowledged that his technique was less than worthless for most of the people reading about it. "I doubt if it will be worth a doggone to the weekend duffer and it will ruin a bad golfer," he wrote in the second-to-last paragraph. His Secret absolutely prevented a hook, the one shot a nation of slicers devoutly wished to hit. It was fool's gold.

The consensus among the pros was that Hogan hadn't revealed much and he had taken *Life* for a ride. They shouldn't have blamed him, however. How often did Hogan have to demonstrate that practice, strategy, and emotional control transcended cupping the left wrist? The idea that he was holding something back persisted. Hogan was party to the continuing intrigue, because his mechanical keys changed from time to time and varied in importance. When friends asked for the "Secret," they didn't all get the same revelation from his mental storehouse. He moved Don Cherry's right hand so it was more on top of the club—"Now, leave it there," he said—and gave the lesson added weight by implying that this was the real Secret. He changed Tommy Bolt's left-hand grip, and to Tommy, that was the secret. Demaret disagreed: Hogan's hand position at the start of his downswing was the real "Secret."

In a roundabout way, the Secret became a book. A new Time-Life, Inc., magazine, *Sports Illustrated*, published some drawings it had taken from the *Life* piece. Hogan hadn't given his permission and called to tell *Life* sports editor Marshall Smith, "I'm gonna sue you for every nickel you're worth." Partly to avoid a lawsuit, and partly because

Time-Life founder Henry Luce smelled an opportunity, the company paid Hogan ten thousand dollars and offered another twenty thousand if he would write an instructional book. Hogan accepted.

Luce sensed a Hogan book would work because of the amazing amount of interest in the two "Hogan's Secret" issues. However, Time-Life, Inc., published magazines, not books. No problem: Luce, a big thinker with a flair (and the money) for the dramatic, bought A. S. Barnes and Company, a fairly large book publisher.

A lively in-house competition ensued between *Life* and *SI* for the Hogan project. *SI* won: its staff would produce the words and pictures, and it would have the honor of serializing the book. *SI* managing editor Sidney James gave the words part of the job to his golf writer, Herbert Warren Wind. For the artwork, he hired medical illustrator Anthony Ravielli.

The Hogan-Wind-Ravielli collaboration, entitled *Five Lessons: The Modern Fundamentals of Golf*, would become the best-selling golf instruction book of all time.

"Tony Ravielli and I first went to Fort Worth in June 1956 and met with Hogan in his office," Wind recalls. "He and I had always gotten along, because I treated him as a man of some importance, which he was. He can be an SOB, as you know, but he was as nice as can be and went out of his way to make things work. He took us out to dinner. I was surprised at his grasp of the English language, and at the rather nice way he presented his criticisms or questions."

During that first four- to five-day meeting, Wind taped Hogan's responses to the questions he had prepared, while Ravielli took photographs of Hogan in his office and at Colonial. When they reconvened in the fall, Hogan's enthusiasm for the project actually increased.

"Ravielli was really the key player," Wind says. "Hogan looked at Tony's roughs—which he did in pencil—

and said, 'My God, Tony, I've never seen anything like this. We've really got something here.' He became much looser. . . . I began writing so fast."

In his drawings of Hogan, Ravielli used an extremely difficult technique called eye lashing. By varying the pressure on his crow quill—a steel ink pen with a fine point—he created beautifully graphic three-dimensional effects.

Wind had to work 115 consecutive days, but he and Ravielli hit their deadline. "Ben Hogan Says: You Can Play in the 70s!" headlined the March 11, 1957, *SI*. Wind called Hogan at Seminole for his reaction. "I haven't really seen it yet, Herb," Hogan said. "I admit I wasn't prepared to see the members of the club here on the practice tee, holding up the magazine."

With its specificity and detail, and with Ravielli's medical illustration-style drawings, *Five Lessons* became the *Gray's Anatomy* of golf. At last the sport's instructors had a manual, and teach-yourselfers had a road map. As with any textbook, each page required time to absorb. Those who expected a page-turner didn't like it. A more fundamental criticism held that the absorption of very fine detail—such as the correct way to waggle the club, the proper location of calluses on the hands, and the feeling you should have on the inside muscles of the legs—was not worth the effort. These textbook haters argued that dissection was not knowledge, that breaking a thing into pieces and giving each piece a name was the busywork of academicians. As a guide for the 30 percent of golf most golfers focus on, however, *Five Lessons* was a masterpiece.

Interestingly, the Secret wasn't mentioned in Hogan's text. And that revelation he had had in 1946? Turns out it didn't have anything to do with mechanics:

In 1946 my attitude suddenly changed. . . . I
would guess what lay behind my new

confidence was this: I had stopped trying to do a great many things perfectly because it had become clear in my mind that this ambitious overthoroughness was neither possible nor advisable, nor even necessary. . . . ALL THAT IS REALLY REQUIRED TO PLAY GOOD GOLF IS TO EXECUTE PROPERLY A RELATIVELY SMALL NUMBER OF TRUE FUNDAMENTAL MOVEMENTS.

The capital letters were Hogan's.

"Hogan and I are starting a company to build golf clubs," Pollard Simon said, "and we need a factory. You got anything?" It was 10:00 A.M. in Fort Worth, a few days after Hogan's return from the ticker-tape parade in New York.

Dan Greenwood held the phone and pondered the question. "No," he said. "No, wait a minute, I do know of a place. Warren McKeever owns it, a big warehouse south of University. It's never been occupied, and it's got a good-looking front end for offices." Greenwood, Hogan, and Simon met at the single-story, pale brick building at 2912 West Pafford Street an hour later.

"How much?" Simon asked.

"Fifty thousand dollars."

Nods between Hogan and Simon.

"Yeah, we'll take it," Simon said, and took out his checkbook.

Hogan oversaw the purchase and installation of club-making equipment, and he hired and trained the people to forge, grind, sand, whip, shape, finish, shaft, grip, and polish. As his secretary he hired Claribel Kelly, a woman with whom he had gone to elementary school back in Dublin. She called him Ben, and they related to each other like brother and sister. He moved very deliberately while setting up the factory, trying not to make any mistakes. The first production run of Ben Hogan golf clubs came down the line in the summer of '54, almost a full year after they had bought the building. Hogan examined the gleaming new Hogan irons—and hated them. "Scrap 'em," he said. Scrap 'em? Simon was aghast. That's one hundred thousand dollars' worth of clubs! Hogan quickly recognized that his own purity—or rigidity—about this new enterprise made him and Simon a bad match. He went to the bank, borrowed $450,000, and bought his partner out. Marvin Leonard, the company's second-largest investor, later put together a group—which included singer Bing Crosby—who took Hogan's name off the note.

With the company up and running, a union organizer came to the Ben Hogan Company plant. When the workers called an organizing meeting, Hogan spoke first. Gardner Dickinson, Hogan's former assistant at Tamarisk, was on hand. This is his recollection of Hogan's "Sermon on the Factory Floor":

> I understand that all of you fellows want to organize my business here and join a union. Well, that is certainly your privilege. If you'd like to pay a nice portion of your salaries to a union, be my guest. You obviously think that by organizing you're going to make a lot more money, and, in effect, tell me, the boss, what you're going to do. Before you vote, let me tell you just one thing: I've already started over once, and I can and will do so again, if necessary. So far, neither I nor my investors have made one damned cent. When we do make some money, I'll see to it that you make some, too. Until that happens, you're not

going to make one damn cent more than I can afford to pay you. And if any of you don't like those terms, you can go straight to the pay window and draw your severance pay, because in thirty minutes this plant will be operating full-blast again. Period!

The workers did not join the union.

Within a couple years, Hogan clubs began to sell. The first commandment of golf club sales—consumers buy what the best professionals use—benefited the Hogan Company greatly. Snead used Wilsons, didn't he? But what did Mangrum play with? And who were Mr. Spalding and Mr. MacGregor, anyway? But Hogan and Hogan golf sticks merged in the popular mind, so that buying the clubs was an act of identifying with the man. The company extended the fantasy by concentrating its marketing and advertising on "the better player." Good idea; who wasn't, or didn't intend to be, a "better player"? The other guys made clubs for every skill level and bank balance and filled their advertising with hard-to-believe, exclamation-point-filled puffery. Hogan purveyed only premium. Wilson's salesmen wore golf clothing, but Hogan's men wore coats and ties. "Do you want to sell something, or do you want to look like you want a starting time?" Hogan asked his men rhetorically. The company's ads always referred to the founder's "demanding standards of quality." Hogan gave his company its culture and its image, commodities a business can do without, but not very well.

Hogan delegated. Even before American Machine and Foundry (AMF) bought the company in July 1960, he had attained perfection in his business life—the two-hour day. He parked his (usually black) Cadillac by the back door to his office each morning at exactly 10:00, and entered his square, brown-paneled, brown-carpeted office dressed in a suit and tie in the same muted color range as his car and his decor. A flattering photograph of Valerie sat on the table behind his desk. An inscribed picture of Eisenhower hung on the wall to his right. He left his office at twelve, and it didn't matter who was killing time with Claribel in the outer office, waiting to see the Man. One day Ike called a little too close to noon.

"Mr. Hogan, the president's on line two," Claribel said.

"I'm not playing golf with that goddamn hack," Hogan muttered. Then he picked up the phone.

His brief appearances at the office might give the impression that Hogan was a mere figurehead in his company, but he wasn't. He stayed close with vice president of sales Lion Price and his department, and very close with a humorous, skinny, ex-navy man named Gene Sheeley. Sheeley's title was master model maker. He built custom and prototype clubs.

"Hogan's driver was forty-two and seven-eighths inches long and stiff as a goddamn pole," Sheeley recalls. "Very big block, heavy. Eleven degrees bulge, twelve degrees roll. He went to a forty-four-inch driver after 1967."

Sheeley made clubs for Hogan's own use, clubs for him to test and approve or disapprove for production, and he custom ground clubs for God-knows-how-many finicky touring pros. Sheeley tells story after story about his thirty-year relationship with "Mr. Hogan," most of them ending with some perfect but profane Hogan one-liner. But Sheeley is apprehensive about quoting his friend's saying a naughty word.

The club-maker's protectiveness and loyalty is the common thread running between Hogan and his employees from the glory days. Hogan Company veterans, particularly sales reps who were welcome to drop into his office for a long chat anytime they were in town, cannot understand their old boss's image as a cold, impersonal man. At the annual sales meeting in August, Hogan introduced the new clubs he and Sheeley had come up with and explained why and how they were the best on the market. He played in the postmeeting golf tournament, and his playing partners were the winners of a lottery among the top sellers from the previous year. Once he wore a cheap blond wig for his talk to the sales force to make a point about the competition's cheap equipment.

"Any time any of you fellas need to talk to me, just call," Hogan always told the meeting. "Just ask for Hennie Bogan."

So where did he go every day at noon? First to lunch at a reserved table at Colonial or, after 1959, to the Men's Grill at Shady Oaks Country Club, the new course Leonard had built in Fort Worth. After that, Hogan practiced or played with the same single-mindedness that had always been his trademark. He was still what he had been since age seventeen—a professional golfer.

Hogan was a professional golfer with a split personality. Every round he played was a fight between Abel and Cain: Could his virtuous striking overcome the evil of his putting? Most of the time, unfortunately, Cain kicked Abel's butt.

His putting failures frustrated him terribly. As his episodes of apparent catatonia increased, so too did mailed-in putting tips from helpful strangers. "We were playing a practice round at Wykagyl, in New York," pro golfer Freddie Hawkins recalls. "On one hole, I hit it in the trees on the right, [Billy] Casper's in the trees on the left. Then I miss the green to the left. Casper misses it to the right. We both make our par putts from farther away than his birdie putt. Hogan misses, of course, and says, 'If you guys ever lose that putting stroke, I'll be buying a hot dog from you.'

"After another practice round, he says, 'What did you shoot? Fifty-what? Anyone who putts like you must shoot in the 50s.'"

A stickler for comportment and proper attire,
Hogan strikes a pose on the grounds of one of his
favorite courses, Fort Worth's Colonial. (Colonial
Country Club)

The '54 Masters clearly illustrated the inevitable failure of the bad putter. That year it was the Billy Joe Patton
Masters. Patton, a likable good ol' boy lumber salesman
from Morganton, North Carolina, shocked everyone by
laughing his way into the lead with nine holes left. A final-
round hole-in-one on the sixth hole helped him get there.
Hogan, playing three holes behind the loose-as-a-goose amateur, heard the thunder from the gallery when Patton holed
out and decided he would need to take some chances to
catch up.

Hogan tells reporters how he shot a third-round 69 to take the lead in the '54 Masters. (AP/Wide World)

In an attempt to make a birdie it turned out he didn't need—Patton would hit balls into the water on thirteen and fifteen, and take a seven and a six, respectively—Hogan broke his own rule by firing his three-iron second shot right at the flagstick on the eleventh. The ball hooked only slightly, but enough to fall into the lake. He made a double-bogey six, shot 75, and tied Snead for first. Their 289 was the highest score ever to lead the Masters.

Snead took a one-shot lead in the eighteen-hole play-off with a two-putt birdie on the thirteenth. "On fifteen, he [Hogan] used a putter from thirty feet short of the green, and

I couldn't believe it," Snead recalls. "He's gonna leave it short of the green or hit it in the lake on the other side. But he damn near holed it. I almost shit my pants." Hogan followed that brilliant putt with two horrible ones on the next green.

Snead putted first. Although Snead was sure he had hit it much too hard, his ball went only a foot past. Par. Even after Sam had demonstrated it for him, Hogan failed to read the slowness of the green and left his putt to tie the match three feet short. Then he jerked the little one, and Snead had won the Masters playoff, 70-71.

Again and again similar scenarios played out. Sometimes Hogan's putter turned to stone at a single dramatic juncture, as, for example, at the 1956 U.S. Open when he yipped a thirty-inch putt on the seventy-first hole and lost by one to Middlecoff. Other times his putting failures piled up like debris against a dam. At the Masters in '55 he missed from close in throughout the final round when a couple of early makes might have shaken Middlecoff, the nervous front-runner. An inconsistent putter could not hide at Augusta National. Hogan never contended there for four rounds again.

U.S. Open golf courses, on the other hand, de-emphasized putting. High rough near greens eliminated chip-and-putt artists. Narrow fairways waylaid wild drivers. Twice more, Hogan almost had enough left to win golf's biggest tournament. His defeats at the Olympic Club in San Francisco in 1955 and at Cherry Hills, near Denver, in 1960, were the bookends on the final phase of Hogan's career as a champion golfer.

The wonderful or terrible irony of the '55 Open at Olympic was that it was the first tournament won with Hogan clubs. Jack Fleck, who had followed Hogan's progress in the newspapers as a teenager in Davenport, Iowa, told Hogan he would like to try his new clubs. A new club company ordinarily shoots for endorsers with bigger names than the obscure Fleck. But at that point in early '55, the factory had produced exactly one set of clubs that were up to Hogan's standards—the set he used. "Sure, Jack," Hogan said, "just give us your specs."

When the tour came to Colonial in May, Fleck shot 69-72 with his old sticks, then caused a stir when he announced to the press, "I'm switching to Hogans tomorrow." Fleck's wedges weren't ready, so Hogan promised to deliver them himself at the Open.

Fleck couldn't break 80 during the practice rounds at par-70 Olympic. Hogan played better than that, but the hilly, lush course exhausted him. As at Oakland Hills, Robert Trent Jones had been hired to narrow the fairways, add bunkers, and generally make the course impossible. He succeeded: the field averaged a human hair below 80 in the first round.

Hogan looked haggard. He limped from tee to fairway to green, but he avoided the giant eucalyptus trees, the looming cypress trees, the bunkers, and the rain forest rough better than any of his fellows. After two-putting for a par on the final hole for a 287 (72-73-72-70), Hogan held his arms aloft, not in triumph, but to get the crowd to stand still and be quiet while his playing partner, Bob Harris, putted out. That done, the thousands watching in the half-amphitheater around the green stood and cheered. Gene Sarazen, doing the color for NBC-TV, rushed over to congratulate the first five-time U.S. Open winner. Hogan handed his golf ball to USGA official Joe Dey, for the association's museum. Then he trudged 120 weary steps to the bunting-draped clubhouse perched on a cliff fifty feet above the eighteenth green. Now Hogan had to wait for an hour, for the last man on the course with a chance to beat him—Fleck.

Unbeknownst to Hogan, an angel had visited Fleck on the fifth green the previous day. How else to explain it? Suddenly, "I had some kind of a wonderful feeling in my hands with the putter over the golf ball," Fleck recalled, an indescribable sense of sureness that came out of nowhere. He hadn't changed his stance or his grip or his posture. But somehow he knew the fairy dust or whatever it was would not allow him to miss any more putts. With the world watching, he birdied the seventy-second hole from eight feet to tie the mighty Hogan.

The next day, Hogan sat in front of his locker a little while before the two o'clock playoff. Fleck came over and shook hands. "Ben, I wanna wish you well out there," Fleck said. "I was comin' out of El Paso [in 1949] when you were comin' in on the ambulance. So good luck and play well."

Fleck also took a phone call before teeing off, from Porky Oliver. "Kick his ass," Oliver said.

A playoff was the last thing Hogan wanted. Olympic's cool humidity had penetrated his joints and walking its squishy hills had tired him to the bone. And the mental marathon of four rounds of U.S. Open pressure sapped him still further. Something else was working against him, too—a poor record in playoffs. Byron Nelson thought Ben's tunnel vision on four-round target scores left him somewhat unfocused during overtimes. At the minimum, it upset his routine. Nelson had beaten him in a playoff. So had Demaret and Snead. But Fleck?

Through seventeen holes, Hogan had taken five more putts than Fleck but trailed by just one shot. He had the honor on the final tee, Olympic's eighteenth, the best finishing hole in golf. No other final hole equaled the on-stage feeling it gave the player, who felt like a god from its elevated tee. The I-, O-, and U-shaped bunkers up by the green stood out like bull's-eyes on a dart board. The hole's modest length—345 yards—added to the intrigue. Birdies were possible if a golfer drove the ball in the fairway. But when attempting a putt on the tiny, severely sloping green, it was easy to imagine the diners and drinkers watching from the massive white clubhouse on the cliff. "Bet he misses it," one says to the other. Add several thousand spectators on the natural theater seats to

Hogan's smile went well with the Colonial National Invitation
Tournament trophy. (Colonial Country Club)

By this time, in 1959, Hogan was playing few tournaments while developing his club-manufacturing business. The plaid coat is emblematic of his fifth Colonial National Invitation victory, Hogan's last victory. Colonial president George Hill makes the presentation. (Colonial Country Club)

the left of the green and make the winner of the hole (probably) the U.S. Open champion, and golf had one of its most irresistibly dramatic moments.

BUT HOGAN SLIPPED WHEN HE SWUNG ON THE EIGHTEENTH TEE: HIS BALL FLEW DEAD LEFT INTO THE CABBAGE, AND THE DRAMA ENDED IN SHOCK, NOT TRIUMPH.

But Hogan slipped when he swung on the eighteenth tee: his ball flew dead left into the cabbage, and the drama ended in shock, not triumph. Fleck played a cautious three-wood into the fairway. Hogan found his ball and slashed at it with a sand club, just trying to get it back in play. The ball didn't move. Another slash, and the ball went three feet. Finally, Hogan reached the surface in five and made a meaningless forty-foot putt for a six. Fleck meanwhile had made a par to win, 69-72.

"I'm through with competitive golf," Hogan said at the awards presentation, his voice cracking. A hush fell over the crowd. "I came here with the idea of trying to win. I worked harder, I think, than ever before in my life. . . . From now on, I'm a weekend golfer."

The '55 Open had been a bridge too far for Hogan. Fleck was a decade younger, and he had that angel. "The wrong man always wins at Olympic," Dan Jenkins says. "Scott Simpson over Tom Watson in '87, Billy Casper over Arnold Palmer in '66, and most of all, Fleck over Hogan." The lesson of Olympic was that old chestnut: A good putter is a match for anyone. And Hogan was no longer a good putter.

But he kept trying.

At Cherry Hills near Denver five years later, a wonderfully complicated U.S. Open passion play unfolded. Although a dozen men had a chance to win until the very end, it came down to this: Hogan versus Nicklaus versus Palmer. The symbolism was inescapable. The three best players of the second half of the century each represented more than himself, more even than an era. They were time itself. The battle of past, future, and present at Cherry Hills made the 1960 U.S. Open the greatest golf tournament ever played.

Nicklaus was twenty that summer, an opinionated, confident, and strong-as-a-bull Ohio State student between his junior and senior years. With his see-through blond crew cut and a figure that said "offensive lineman," young Jack didn't look like what he was—the best amateur golfer since his hero, Bobby Jones. Yet Hogan, a man Nicklaus barely knew well enough to say hello, may actually have been more important to his development than Bobby.

"I'd first become aware of Hogan when I was ten years old, when I first took up golf," Nicklaus recalls. "Jack Grout [Nicklaus's pro at Scioto Country Club in Columbus] was the assistant pro at Glen Garden where Hogan and Nelson grew up. . . . So I knew of 'Bennie,' as Grout called him, all through those early years.

"He had a lot of influence on my left-to-right ball flight. . . . Grout talked about the problems Hogan had hooking the ball, and I worked hard as a youngster not to have the right-to-left problem. Grout and I worked very hard against the hook, and Hogan had a lot to do with that."

Palmer, then thirty-two, had electrified the game in recent months. Not only was Arnie winning tournaments— five of them by June 1960, including the Masters for the second time—and doing it on TV, but he usually won with a breathtaking last-minute run of birdies. The Palmer Charge replaced the Hogan Trance as a favorite topic for golf writers. Arnie's appealing flair made people realize what they had been missing with Hogan and with the golfers who imitated Hogan—responsiveness.

Hogan's personality and propriety did not allow him to emote at all on the golf course, at least until he won, at which point he took off his hat and smiled. When Palmer won, he threw his hat. And he grinned and grimaced, signed autographs by the hundreds, and suffered, exalted, and joked. He responded to the gallery, and they to him. Hogan did none of the above, which heightened the new king's charisma still further.

The new king? Hogan wouldn't concede the point. Although he hadn't won a major title since 1953, Hogan had recently won a good tournament, the '59 Colonial. He wasn't done yet. How could Palmer claim to be on top until he won a U.S. Open? With their clashing styles and the size of their talents—and their egos—it was no surprise these two very competitive men didn't hit it off. Hogan and Nicklaus would frequently play future practice rounds together; Hogan and Palmer, almost never.

Hogan at the midpoint of 1960 was two months shy of his forty-eighth birthday. He looked his age, or a little more: a half-a-volleyball-sized paunch at the belt line, gray hair eroded by male pattern baldness, channels running from the sides of his nose to the sides of his mouth more sharply pronounced than ever, and the appraising, blue gray eyes still frighteningly hawklike. The package suggested a successful businessman, exactly what he was. The Ben Hogan Company had performed so well that a big corporation, AMF, wanted to buy it. They had put an attractive offer on the table and wanted Hogan to remain as president. Six weeks after the Open, he would accept it.

The state of his golf game was, as usual, mixed. Despite advancing age and occasional left shoulder surgery (he has had four operations on it, the last one in 1967) Hogan could still control a golf ball as well as anyone on the planet. He had proved as much at the recent Masters, which Palmer had won, by hitting more greens in regulation than anyone else in the tournament. He had also taken the most putts. But in the Open, with its greater emphasis on tee-to-green accuracy, Hogan stood a chance.

ON THE FRONT NINE IN

THE FINAL ROUND, HOGAN

AND NICKLAUS HEARD

REPEATED SONIC BOOMS

BEHIND THEM—PALMER.

The past and future against the present.

Hogan opened poorly, with a first-round 75 that featured a duck-hooked drive off the ninth tee into a spectator's stomach. But his game returned the next day. His 67, said playing partner Dow Finsterwald, was "one of the greatest rounds of golf I ever saw."

Hogan's even-par 142 tied him with Nicklaus, seven shots behind Mike Souchak's tournament-leading 135. The Hawk and the baby Bear had the nine o'clock starting time on Open Saturday. Palmer would begin the thirty-six-hole journey at 9:12, one shot and two groups behind them.

The snowcapped Rockies stood out in the clarity of the cloudless Colorado morning when Hogan and Nicklaus teed off. While Jack concentrated in a way that recalled no one but Hogan, he couldn't help noticing how the older man played the game. "I remember Hogan playing well within himself," Nicklaus says. "He surprised me that he could hit an awful lot of right-to-left shots, very soft draws. He was very much a gentleman to play with. He couldn't have been nicer to me."

Neither man missed a shot all morning. Both shot 69 and moved in unison within three shots of Souchak's lead. Behind them, Palmer shot an erratic 72 and trailed by seven. The sun beat down through the thin mountain air and it got hot.

On the front nine in the final round, Hogan and Nicklaus heard repeated sonic booms behind them—Palmer. Arnie drove onto the fringe on the par-four first hole and made birdie, chipped in on two, and birdied three and four and six. Palmer's vocal army went nuts. Arnie responded with fists in the air and that got the gallery even more excited. But golf's greatest strategist and his pupil for the day stayed on their steady way, until, when it came down to the end, only they remained with Arnie.

Hogan took a share of the lead at the par-three fifteenth. He hit his iron shot twenty feet from the hole and made it, the first putt of any length he had holed all day. He was four under par for the day, four under for the round, and he had hit every fairway and every green. Palmer, the co-leader, might have been riding a wave of emotion. Nicklaus, just one shot behind, had strength, talent, and youth. But Hogan had perfection.

Then came a par at the sixteenth, followed by two shots to lay up short of the moat guarding the green on the par-five seventeenth. Hogan was left with just a wedge shot of forty or fifty yards. But the green was very shallow and hard near the flagstick, and there was that water.

"Go find out if anyone is more than four under," Hogan ordered his old friend from Los Angeles, Bob William.

While William ran to a nearby scoreboard, Hogan smoked and weighed his options. Go for the flag or play safe? What if he trailed by one? William ran back, exhausted from the heat, the thirty-five-hole walk, and now the one-hundred-yard dash. He answered Hogan's very specific request specifically, "No, no one is more than four under."

Almost before William could get out of his shadow, Hogan hit his punch-cut spin shot dead at the flag, a gutsy go-for-broke shot you would expect from Palmer. It was perfect. It was too perfect. The ball landed over the water, but Hogan had put so much juice on it that the ball danced backward, into the water.

Tight-lipped and obviously mad as hell, Hogan surveyed the damage. He put his shoed right foot in the water experimentally, didn't like it, removed the shoe, and stepped back in, in just the sock. Didn't like it, and tried again with a bare foot in the shoe. Finally he set and splashed the ball out

Although Hogan officially won four U.S. Open titles, he has five Open champion's medals on display at Fort Worth's Colonial Country Club. The fifth is for the 1942 Hale America Open. Although not recognized as an official Open, the Hale America had all the trappings of one, including USGA administration. (Colonial Country Club)

of the shallow water about eight feet above the hole, a wonderful shot. But he missed the putt.

After Nicklaus drove on the long uphill par-four eighteenth, Hogan stepped up. He knew a birdie was his only hope. But a little variance in the Swiss watch precision of his preshot routine betrayed his fury from the bogey on seventeen. His waggle, the normally gentle back-and-forth wave of the club before he swung, this time had the violence of a fist smacked into a palm. He ripped into the drive but hooked the ball just a little too much. It found more water. Now thoroughly deflated, he took a triple-bogey seven.

"When his ball spun back off the edge of seventeen, I think that physically took a lot out of him, and hooking it into the water on eighteen drained him," Nicklaus recalls. "But he handled himself really well, right down to the end, and he was still the same person, the same gentleman at the end as he was at the beginning. I admired that in him, and I enjoyed that."

Palmer won, and looked "almost embarrassed" afterward, according to Bob William, "like he got away with something." Nicklaus was second. With his bogey, triple-bogey finish, Hogan fell into a tie for ninth.

Perhaps it had to end that way. The present and the future must be served, while the past just fades away.

CHAPTER 8

# THE END

I DON'T LIKE THE GLAMOUR. I JUST LIKE THE GAME.
—BEN HOGAN

On a hot, Houston-humid day in May 1971, Ben Hogan played his final round of competitive golf. After consecutive par fours on Champions Golf Club's three numbingly long opening holes, Hogan stepped to the tee on the 230-yard, par-three fourth. An unkempt ravine defended the left side of the green, and the flagstick was stuck on the left front. A sucker pin, but Hogan aimed a two-iron right at it. The ball rifled toward the flag.

No one had expected to see him inside the ropes again. After playing in the 1967 U.S. Open, Hogan had undergone a fourth operation on his left shoulder, and his fifty-fifth birthday had come and gone. His return had caused a sensation: someone counted thirty-one touring pros in his gallery in Houston. They shyly asked him for bits of wisdom in the locker room or for his autograph. But Hogan had less interest in changing grips or swings than in telling those Age-of-Aquarius golf pros to dress more sensibly and to get a damn haircut.

The kind, cooperative, elder statesman's role fit him like Valerie's shoes. *Golf* magazine photographer Leonard Kamsler had been told to go to Champions and get a sequence of Hogan swinging. "That camera was too noisy to take out on the course, so every day I waited on the practice tee for Hogan, and he never showed up," Kamsler recalls. "So I went into the bag room, and one of the guys said, 'I'll tell you where he practices. Go over to the fifth fairway on the Jackrabbit course about an hour before his starting time, and you'll see him warming up.' So I did, and I saw him, and he saw me walking across the fairway, draggin' wires and batteries and everything. And he immediately put his club in his bag and walked away."

Hogan's two-iron shot reached its apogee, drifted two yards left, and fell into the hazard. His audience gasped. He teed up another, same club, same shot—and again it went into the Cypress Creek gorge. As did, stubbornly, a third two-iron and a third ball into the pit. There was silence from the crowd now, as if they had witnessed an embarrassing accident. Hogan trudged grimly down the fairway and descended into the hazard. While climbing down among the rocks, bluebonnets, and Dallis grass after his third golf ball, he twisted his left knee—the same knee he had injured in the accident twenty-two years before. He took a nine on the hole and made the turn with a 44, eight over par.

Hogan played on, his limp more pronounced with each step. It looked to be too much for him—the heat, the pain, the length of the golf course. The back nine began with par-fours of 453 and 460 yards, and twelve was another killer par-three, 213 yards. Hogan had money and fifty-eight years of age, and he had never needed applause. So what was he doing there?

He had a dozen reasons. His friends Jimmy Demaret and Jack Burke Jr. owned the place, and they made him comfortable, allowing him to develop a routine: the club manager oversaw his meals, the waiters knew his drink, and he and Valerie stayed in a cottage across the street from the club. He had his own table in the dining room -- second from the fireplace, back row—and he ate there every night at 7:00 sharp. Demaret spotted him sitting alone one night, apparently waiting for Valerie to join him. "Hey, look, you guys," Demaret said to his jolly companions. "There's Hogan sitting with all his friends." He liked the course: just the year before, he had finished tied for ninth in the Houston Champions International. Yet Hogan was kidding himself if he had begun to pretend that a tie for ninth would satisfy him.

DEMARET SPOTTED HIM SITTING ALONE ONE NIGHT, APPARENTLY WAITING FOR VALERIE TO JOIN HIM. "HEY, LOOK, YOU GUYS," DEMARET SAID TO HIS JOLLY COMPANIONS. "THERE'S HOGAN SITTING WITH ALL HIS FRIENDS."

His overriding motive for being in Houston was somewhat sad—he had nothing else to do. Other men his age were entering grandfatherhood or peaking in their business careers and making firm retirement plans. But Hogan's undiversified life had none of these things.

He parred the tenth hole. On the eleventh tee, he swung and slipped so badly he almost fell. And the self-deception ended. He had his caddie pick up the ball and said "so long" to his playing partners, Dick Lotz and Charles Coody. Then he rode back to the clubhouse in a cart, his arms crossed, his eyes down.

Later he joined a gin rummy game in Champions' big, churchlike locker room. A man insinuated himself into the ring of spectators around the table. He cleared his throat and extended his hand. "Mr. Hogan," he said, "my name is Joe Smith. You might not remember me, but we played golf together once back in about 1958."

Hogan let the man rot for a minute. He kept his hands and his eyes on his cards. "You're right," he finally said. "I don't remember you."

This was not the way Ben Hogan would have preferred to end his incredible competitive career, head down on a golf cart leaving in the middle of a round at Houston in 1971. (Photo courtesy of Burt Darden)

For every Rocky Marciano there are a hundred Muhammad Alis. Rocky retired as the undefeated heavyweight champion, while Ali fought too long and finished his career with an inglorious loss to Leon Spinks. Having fought and sacrificed to reach the mountaintop, some great athletes find the urge to admire the view almost irresistible.

Golf is not boxing, of course, and the idea of someone's winning the U.S. Open and then quitting to spend more time with the family is absurd. A golfer wins few tournaments relative to how many he plays, yet the magical feeling of winning compels him to keep trying to recapture it. But still you wish that Hogan could have ended his run in a more fitting posture than sitting on a golf cart. Perhaps a more appropriate farewell would have been the 1967 Masters, when, suddenly, inexplicably, and on television, he shot a course-record 30 on the back nine in the third round. Augusta National's endlessly repeating galleries are the most jaded in the world, filled with applause-withholding, I-saw-Mangrum-hit-it-closer-than-that-in-'59 types. But they realized they were witnessing something special on that Saturday afternoon, and they gave Hogan a standing ovation at every green.

"You talk about something running up and down your spine," Hogan recalled years later. "I think I played the best nine holes of my life on those holes. I don't think I came close to missing a shot." Everyone wanted to talk to him afterward, of course. For a final time, he had everyone's attention. "Tomorrow's my last round as a competitor," he could have told the press, but he didn't.

Later that year Hogan captained the Ryder Cup team. That, too, might have been an opportune stage from which to say farewell. Instead the '67 Ryder Cup became better known for the friction between the captain and the team's top player. Arnold Palmer innocently asked Hogan if he had brought any British-sized golf balls, which were then optional. Palmer had obviously forgotten to practice with the 1.62-inch ball. "Did you remember to bring your clubs?" Hogan snapped back. "Anyway, who says you're playing in the match?" Arnie's stock with Hogan fell still further when, on the day before the match, he took one of the British players for a ride in his jet. Showing off, he buzzed the golf course with a few low-altitude barrel rolls. Palmer rode the bench on the morning of the second day. The United States team won 23½ to 8½, and Palmer won all five of his matches.

An argument could be made that Jack Nicklaus, Bobby Jones, or assorted other greats would rate ahead of Hogan as the best golfer of the twentieth century, but few would dispute Hogan's golf swing as the classic model for millions. (Jules Alexander)

There were, however, other ways to remember Hogan. Jay Hebert recalls the drumbeat of rain on canvas, the odors of sweat and dirt, and the feeling of solitude and work. "One time at Champions the round got called off because of rain," Hebert says. "So most of the guys get on the phone and call their girlfriends or go to the movies or whatever. . . . I went back out to the course that afternoon, even though it was still raining. And I hear this whomp, whomp coming from that big tent over there. I walk over and inside is Hogan. He's rolled up one side of the tent and he's inside hitting balls out to his caddie in the rain. 'Jay,' he says, 'if you miss one day, you've got to work twice as hard the next.' "

Hal Underwood remembers Hogan as a mystical figure. Late in the afternoon the day before the 1970 Westchester Classic, Underwood and another pro stood by the tenth tee, preparing for nine more holes of practice before dark. A smoky, metallic voice behind him said, "Boys, I'm Ben Hogan. Mind if I join you?"

"I was petrified," Underwood says. "He eagled the twelfth hole—a drive and a three-wood to two feet. Then on sixteen, a par-three, he shanked it, and the ball rattled around in the TV tower behind the fifteenth green. Hogan held out his hand, his caddie put another ball in it, and he ripped it right into the center of the green. He and the caddie walked right past that first ball. I hesitated. Should I pick the ball up for him, or get it and keep it for myself? But the way he acted . . . it had me convinced that first shot never happened." Underwood didn't pick it up.

When Nick Faldo remembers meeting Hogan in November 1992, he shakes his head and laughs at the memory. They ate at Hogan's private table at Shady Oaks, the one in a nook by the window, and they got along famously. Hogan signed Faldo's dog-eared copy of *Five Lessons*. The Englishman asked what he needed to do to win the U.S. Open. "Shoot the lowest score," Hogan shot back.

231

"After lunch, I'd really appreciate it if you'd watch me hit," Faldo said.

Hogan paused.

"Nick, you're a pretty good player, aren't ya? If I tell you something, you'll forget it. You'd be better off if you figure it out for yourself." But he hadn't said no, and Faldo excused himself to go out to the practice range.

Hogan Company president David Hueber slid over into the seat next to Hogan. "Well, Ben, are you ready to go out and watch Nick hit some balls?" he asked. A cart for his use had been parked right outside the door.

"Does he play our clubs?"

"No," Hueber answered.

Hogan swirled the Chablis in his glass. "I think I'll just finish my wine," he said. He didn't watch Faldo.

The staff at *Golf Digest* recall a frustrating Hogan. One day in 1992 he let them know through Hueber that he was now ready to reveal the "real" Secret (that again), "the keys to the vault." But hours before Hogan and an interviewer were to meet, the whole thing fell apart.

"How much will this be worth to the magazine?" Hogan asked Hueber.

"Maybe seventy-five thousand dollars," Hueber answered.

"And how much to the Hogan Company?"

"Also about seventy-five thousand dollars."

"Then they ought to pay me $150,000," Hogan said. "Tell 'em."

*Golf Digest* declined.

"It wasn't greed, he was just trying to be equitable," Hueber explains. "He thought the guy providing the secret should get the same as the other parties." The same as the other parties *combined*.

A young assistant pro remembers a compassionate Ben Hogan. The pro had been asked—without warning—to

Hogan rests a knee injury at the home of Seminole Country Club president George Coleman on March 30, 1968. (AP/Wide World)

interview the same day for the head professional's job at Shady Oaks. Hogan coached him on what to say to the employment committee.

"You got a coat?" he asked.

"No, sir, I don't."

"Here," Hogan said, "take mine."

And almost every old pro on the tour had an unforgettable moment or two with the Little Man. For Doug Ford, it was sitting next to Hogan in the locker room at Riviera in 1950, Hogan's first tournament after the crash. Ford put on his shoes while trying unsuccessfully not to stare as Hogan slowly pulled those long elastic bandages onto his legs.

Shelley Mayfield once had the temerity to ask Hogan for a Hogan pitching wedge. Mayfield remembers the searching look from those ice-blue eyes at that moment; the subsequent, very formal letter acknowledging the request; a second letter announcing the club had been made; and Hogan's delivering the club himself.

Freddie Hawkins recalled *not* getting to know Hogan despite having played scores of practice rounds with him. "He was the hardest man I ever knew, emotionally," Hawkins says. "He could be gracious or he might ignore you. It was not shyness. He was too tough to be shy. It was preoccupation."

Frank Wharton also cannot forget the impossible-to-look-away-from blue eyes and the advice Hogan gave him when he joined the tour in 1963. "Don't go along with the crowd," he said. "Go your own way. There will always be a demand for a guy like that. And practice, practice. Goddamnit, practice."

"I think," Mrs. Hogan said gingerly, "that sometimes Ben has suffered from being such a perfectionist. When he wrote his [first] book, he took ten months to write it. He wouldn't stop until he thought it was right. In everything he does, he works so hard. He insisted on designing his own boxes and packages for [the Hogan Company's] clubs and golf balls. I think the price he's had to pay by being a perfectionist is that he's missed out on companionship and friends.

"Weren't there many nights," she asked him, as if the question had preyed on her mind, "when you would rather have been out with the boys going to a football game or the movies, and instead you stayed at home working?"

He studied her words carefully.

"No," Ben Hogan said.

—*Sports Illustrated*, June 20, 1955, by Joan Flynn Dreyspool

In the sixties the Hogans sold their house on Valley Ridge, moved briefly into a two-thousand-square-foot apartment a couple of miles south, then custom built their new home near Shady Oaks. Hogan oversaw the molding of each brick, and he and Valerie selected each of the pecan boards for the floor inside. The house crouched well below street level, a five-hundred-thousand-dollar Country French bunker. A passerby could see mostly red tile roof but could not see into any windows.

A detached garage apartment stood off to the right; a married couple, the Hogans' servants, lived there. There was a pool in the back yard, and behind it a low brick wall and behind the wall a jungle of vine-hung trees. "I own that lot," Hogan told *Golf Digest* writer Nick Seitz, who was allowed to visit in 1970. "I don't want a house there. You put a two-story house in there and people are going to be looking right down on you."

Seitz asked him how he spent his time nowadays.

"I play golf with friends, but we don't play friendly golf," Hogan answered.

Do you socialize?

"Yes, but not once a week. We'll go to a couple of charity balls a year. I'm not antisocial, I just don't feel good the next day. I can't work."

What about work—any business interests outside the Hogan Company?

"I piddle around in the oil business. I fool around with the stock market quite a bit. I'm in the process of

"I PLAY GOLF WITH

FRIENDS, BUT WE DON'T

PLAY FRIENDLY GOLF,"

HOGAN ANSWERED.

finding a cattle ranch. I'll find what I want. . . . I keep hearing there's no money in it, but if that were true you couldn't buy a steak."

He never did buy a ranch.

Not surprisingly, Hogan's politics were conservative and Republican. "The trouble in this country started when I was young," he told Seitz, "when the vote was extended to people who had no property. A lot of them don't give a darn. Now, I don't know what you can do." Apparently, Hogan was referring to the Nineteenth Amendment to the Constitution, which in 1920 gave women the right to vote.

After his forced retirement from tournament golf, Hogan's daily routine became a well-worn path. Two hours in the office, from ten to noon; lunch at Shady Oaks, alone at a table for eight overlooking the ninth and eighteenth greens; golf or practice if the weather was warm enough. If it wasn't warm, he would change out of his suit and try to drive the stiffness out of his aching body with a half-dozen Tylenols and a long, hot shower. On weekends, he would come to the course in golf clothing and watch football games on television.

A small break in his predictable days occurred in the late seventies, when he called Gene Sheeley into his office.

"Gene, can you make me a putter this long? Two grips, one here, one here."

Ben Hogan, golf's symbol of traditionalism, used a high-tech long putter?

"He lasted two days with it," Sheeley says. "They made so much fun of him at Shady Oaks."

Two annual events were part of his routine: the Hogan Company sales meeting and the dinner preceding the Colonial National Invitation tournament. Hogan was the man in gray in a sea of red plaid at the Colonial dinner. He had

Hogan continued to play a few select tournaments in the sixties. Here he grants an interview between rounds of the Colonial National Invitation. (Colonial Country Club)

won the tournament five times but found the champion's coat a trifle loud. After the last speech, hundreds of people always formed a line at his table. Hogan signed the programs, smiled for the cameras, and seemed to enjoy himself.

He wouldn't travel. He hated his reduction to "ceremonial" status in the golf world, which gave other graying legends a reason to hit the road. The implications of has-beenhood kept him away from the Masters champions dinner after 1967. Byron Nelson took over as emcee at the dinner and allowed Sam Snead to tell the group just one dirty joke per year. Jack Nicklaus started a tournament, the Memorial, which each year celebrates a person "who has played golf with conspicuous honor." Naturally, Jack wanted Ben. "I thanked them for the invitation," Hogan said in 1989, "but I asked them to please put it off until I was dead. I don't want to be memorialized or whatever you call it."

The Hogan Company fell into decline. It had the wrong products, missed the boat bigtime in its marketing, and finally became confused about who or what was in charge. In 1984 corporate raider Irwin Jacobs bought AMF, Hogan's parent company, and merged it into his Minstar conglomerate. After the company lost $2.5 million the next year, it hired a new president, Jerry Austry.

"Ben, we're in trouble," Austry said in his daily meetings with Hogan. "Karsten Solheim [the president of Ping, one of the top club manufacturers] has a greater voice than you do in golf equipment, and he can't play his way out of a paper bag." Austry helped wear down Hogan's resistance to the company's first nontraditional design, a new golf club to compete against Ping. The Hogan Edge would have a big cavity in the back, like Ping's easy-to-hit hacker's clubs, but its heads would be forged metal, not that hard-as-a-rock cast stuff Ping used.

While the Edge was being developed and manufactured, Austry commissioned a market survey. Its results should have surprised no one: What everybody wanted from the Ben Hogan Company was *Ben Hogan*.

"I realized we had the greatest asset in the world over in the corner and we should have him speak for the company," Austry recalls. When he asked Hogan to consider hitting the Edge for a television commercial, he chose his words very carefully. "You always gave him options," Austry says. "If you just asked a yes-or-no question, you might not like his answer."

Hogan agreed to do it. He even assented to traveling to the West Coast for the shoot, because the winter-brown grass in Fort Worth would not look good on camera. So in March 1987, Ben and Valerie got on a plane for the first time in seven years.

They shot the spot at Riviera in four days. The resultant commercial was simple: just gauze-focused images of a seventy-four-year-old man hitting golf balls and of long-time Riviera teaching pro Arturo Rios pretending to be his caddie. The ad became one of the great successes of modern advertising. Hogan Company sales zoomed from fifty million to seventy million dollars in the twelve months after the commercials first ran.

Hogan's old friends and fans mobbed him throughout the filming. "I said to myself, 'So this is why he doesn't like to travel,' " Austry recalls. "I tried to protect him. . . . I was his valet for four days, and it was one of the greatest experiences of my life."

Hogan and Austry drank "clear ones"—vodka drinks—in the Wilshire Hotel bar at the end of each day. "He talked about everything—the story of his life, how the tour got started, how people have used him, and what he thinks of golf today," Austry says. "It was fascinating."

Marvin Leonard, the stolen wheels in Oakland, and Demaret came up, but the army, Nelson, his mother, and his brother did not. "Ben said his father taught him to stand on his own and that any job is better than no job," Austry says. "After several, *several* drinks, he said Snead was the best swinger he ever saw, and that if Sam had half a brain he would have beaten everyone."

Hogan drank his vodka and tonic or his martini and added his smoke to the smoky air. "He said marketers and logos are defacing the game," Austry recalls. "He talked about his dislike for pros who play for second or for tenth. 'Players today are not hungry,' he said. 'They're robbing the people who pay to watch them.' "

Between shots or rounds, Hogan often could be seen holding a burning cigarette, contemplating whatever was to come next. Despite doctor's orders later in his life to quit smoking, Hogan would still constantly light one up. (Jules Alexander)

A few months after the sentimental journey to Riviera, Hogan almost died. His appendix ruptured, effectively spewing poison throughout his body. He spent two months in Harris Hospital in Fort Worth and lost thirty pounds. Collectors of Hogan memorabilia found it much easier to get his signature on a photograph or a magazine cover after this very serious illness. A reporter asked him if the brush with death had changed him, "mellowed" him. "I don't think so," Hogan said. "I'm the same person I think I've always been. People may have misinterpreted on occasion. They probably did."

Although still a bit shaky from his illness and from nicotine withdrawal—his doctor's orders to quit smoking had been very firm—Hogan went to New York in 1988 for the Centennial of Golf. A golfer of the century would be named at the dinner, and those in the know said the winner would be either Hogan or Nicklaus. Every big name in golf attended. Austry and a handful of Hogan Company executives accompanied their boss.

"He walked into the cocktail party before the dinner, and I've never seen a room go quiet like that," Austry recalls. "Cameras were going off and glaring so badly you couldn't see."

Snead, Nicklaus, and Palmer were in the room, but suddenly scores of people joined the photographers encircling Hogan. Austry protectively steered Ben and Valerie to a table and stationed his lieutenants around it. Like doormen at a popular nightclub, Hogan's men let Nicklaus, Johnny Miller, and others inside the circle one at a time.

The scene was repeated at the dinner. A line of well-wishers and would-you-please-sign-this-Mr.-Hogans formed at his table. "He gets irritated with that after a while, so I went and got him," Austry says. "I took him to the men's room, and he says, 'Stay here and watch the door. I need a smoke.' He didn't want Valerie to find out."

Nicklaus won the golfer-of-the-century award, incidentally, and Hogan went back to his cigarettes.

In May 1988 Minstar sold the Hogan Company to Tokyo-based Cosmo World. Soon after the deal was completed, East met West for lunch at Hogan's table at Shady Oaks. "Does Mr. Isutani [Cosmo World's president] understand English?" Hogan asked an interpreter. "He does," the interpreter said.

Hogan spoke to the new owner of his company loudly and slowly, as people do when addressing foreigners. "Mr. Isutani," he said, "you've bought the family jewels. Don't fuck it up."

Early in his career, Hogan was considered one of the best at consistently making short putts, but later he developed a case of the yips. (Jules Alexander)

Another look at the Hogan smile although the body posture suggests a sense of weariness late in his career. (Jules Alexander)

In 1989 Cosmo World brought in a new president, David Hueber, who asked Hogan to help with a new set of commercials. No travel and no ball hitting this time, he told the chairman of the board, just you, me, and a camera in your office. And no script.

Hueber asked about the sensation of hitting a perfect shot, and Hogan talked about the feeling that goes "up the shaft, right into your hands—and into your heart."

"No one makes a golf club like we do," Hogan said, and that became the tag line for the series of commercials. Soon after the ads ran, Hogan irons jumped from fourth to second place in sales.

He played his last eighteen-hole round in 1980 at Seminole. The love of his life—hitting golf balls—left him slowly and steadily after that. Sometime near the end of the decade, Ben Hogan swung at a ball for the last time.

With the pain of osteoarthritis—and his lifelong penchant for doing things over and over—the shower at two o'clock became an hour-long, daily ritual. After he dried off, the locker room attendant rubbed Hogan's back and left shoulder with three kinds of liniment. The lunch routine seemed to change, too. Stories leaked out of Shady Oaks that Hogan was drinking too much. Most of the time he drank no more than before, but his tolerance for alcohol had diminished. Concurrent with the ill effects of booze came a fairly rapid drop-off in his memory and, occasionally, other symptoms that suggested a deterioration of his mental faculties. Finally, he became totally dependent on Valerie, a turn of events she found to be nearly overwhelming.

Old age inflicts indignities great and small on anyone lucky enough to experience it. What happened to Ben

Hogan's health was not unusual. So the decline in his mental acuity should not be his postscript. He deserves to be remembered at his best.

Even as his vigor declined, he still was a man of obvious power. You could see it on a drizzly day in January 1990, when Snead, Gene Sarazen, Chi Chi Rodriguez, Bob Toski, Billy Casper, Gene Littler, Doug Ford, and Orville Moody all joined Hogan for a photo shoot at Shady Oaks. A company in Japan had had an idea to build a golf course on Guam called the Legends and thus needed a set of golf-legend endorsers. Hogan agreed to the fifty-thousand-dollar-a-man boondoggle because he wouldn't have to travel and it would allow him to see old friends. But the old friends talked *about* him more than *with* him.

Snead and Chi Chi observed Hogan's lighting a cigarette with the butt of another.

"He's always done that," Snead said.

"And he doesn't have no emphysema?" Rodriguez asked.

"All I want is one picture with Hogan," Toski said.

Snead, whispering, added, "I bet you five dollars he never goes to Guam."

The photography proceeded at Hogan's pace. Several times the other eight were in place, the lights were right, the cameras focused, and . . . no Hogan. Then he would take his place and smile, still the most photogenic man in the room.

The next day he was back to his seat by the window, a cigarette in his left hand, a drink in the right.

What was he thinking? It was impossible to know and impossible not to wonder. Some of his thoughts would be in all caps, because he thought in absolutes: THERE IS ONE CORRECT BASIC STANCE. But what about those parts of life he couldn't correct with applied science and practice? He

A gaze from the tee down the fairway shows a thinking machine in motion, strategizing hole management. (Jules Alexander)

never gave voice to any psychological conflicts, but he hinted at a very big one whenever he was asked if he would tell a writer the story of his life. Usually, he dismissed the idea out of hand; an autobiography seemed to him like blowing your own horn. But sometimes he said if he ever did bare his soul, it would only be with a woman writer. That—and the fact that he only worked with aspiring female golfers—suggested that his father's suicide caused his son to distrust men. Valerie was his only confidante, his only real friend. Did Hogan understand how his father's self-murder could have affected him?

Whether or not Hogan recognized the possible connection between what happened to him at age nine and the man he became may never be known. But from a performance standpoint, Hogan understood himself better than any athlete ever. *That* was Hogan's Secret. It didn't become a book or a magazine series because mental toughness, self-control, focus, and the connection between mood and performance couldn't be photographed. It was difficult for him to describe and for us dilettantes to apply. He didn't think we would understand.

<blockquote>AMERICANS ARE FICKLE WITH CELEBRITIES, BUT HOGAN NEVER LOST HIS GRIP. THE CRASH, THE COMEBACK, AND THE MOVIE ESTABLISHED A PUBLIC PERSONA THAT WAS UNFORGETTABLE.</blockquote>

Yet that went both ways. Few public people ever understood the public less than did Hogan. He couldn't understand casual golfers—or casual anything—because he had been purposeful all day, every day, since he was nine. And he never comprehended the esteem so many people felt for him. Americans are fickle with celebrities, but Hogan never lost his grip. The crash, the comeback, and the movie established a public persona that was unforgettable—the Secret, *Five Lessons*, ticker tape, and reclusion cemented it.

As for his place in the small frame of golf history, a hundred tantalizing questions remain. What if the Hogan and Palmer eras had been reversed; would golf have achieved the popularity it now enjoys? What if he had missed that bus; how many more tournaments might he have won?

Yet in the bigger picture, Hogan left no doubt as to his place. He became an idea quite apart from golf. His name alone defined concentration, determination, even perfection. The Little Man had no yardage book, no golf glove, no self-congratulation, no logo, no bullshit, and no pretense.

Hogan shows the classic form sculpted from thousands of hours on the practice tee—"digging it out of the ground." (Jules Alexander)

Everything he accomplished, he dug out of the ground. Ben Hogan was an imperfect but honorable man, a champion and a gentleman.

A seven-foot bronze statue of Hogan stands on an elevated plaza by the clubhouse at Colonial Country Club (see page 250). A similar heroic-sized bronze of Byron Nelson was erected at his club just outside Dallas. The nine-foot Nelson smiles and leans on his driver, inviting you to talk. "How are you doing, Byron? What a beautiful day!" But the Hogan statue talks to *you*. He is posed in a full follow-through, head up, eyes on the horizon. "Watch this shot," the bronze Hogan says. "Watch this swing."

And stand back.

(Statue by Paul Tadlock, photo by David Wharton)

# BEN HOGAN'S
## NOTABLE ACHIEVEMENTS

| | |
|---|---|
| Player of the Year | 1948, 1950, 1951, 1953 |
| Vardon Trophy Winner | 1940, 1941, 1942, 1946, 1948 |
| Ryder Cup Team Player | 1941, 1947, 1951 (undefeated) |
| Ryder Cup Team Captain | 1947, 1949, 1967 (undefeated) |
| PGA Champion | 1946, 1948 |
| British Open Champion | 1953 |
| U.S. Open Champion | 1948, 1950, 1951, 1953 |
| Masters Champion | 1951, 1953 |
| Leading Money Winner | 1940, 1941, 1942, 1946, 1948 |

Won sixty-three PGA tournaments, third all-time behind Sam Snead and Jack Nicklaus

Out of 292 career tournaments:
  —finished in top three 139 times
  —finished in top ten 241 times

# BIBLIOGRAPHY

*The 1995 PGA Tour Media Guide.*

Barkow, Al. *The History of the PGA Tour.* New York: Doubleday, 1989.

Bolt, Tommy. *The Hole Truth.* Philadelphia: J.B. Lippincott, 1971.

Demaret, Jimmy. *My Partner Ben Hogan.* New York: McGraw-Hill, 1954.

Derr, John. *Uphill is Easier.* Pinehurst, North Carolina: Cricket Productions, 1995.

Dickinson, Gardner. *Let 'er Rip.* Marietta, Georgia: Longstreet Press, 1994.

*Golf Magazine's Encyclopedia of Golf.* New York: Harper and Row, 1970.

Hamer, Malcolm. *The Ryder Cup: The Players.* London: Kingswood Press, 1992.

Hogan, Ben. *Five Lessons.* New York: A. S. Barnes and Co., 1957.

Hogan, Ben. *Power Golf.* New York: A. S. Barnes and Co., 1948.

Johnson, Salvatore. *The Official U.S. Open Almanac.* Dallas: Taylor, 1995.

McCormack, Mark. *The Wonderful World of Professional Golf.* New York: Atheneum, 1973.

Nelson, Byron. *How I Played the Game.* Dallas: Taylor, 1993.

Neziroglue Fugen, and Jose A. Yaryua-Tobias. *Over and Over Again.* New York: Lexington Books, 1991.

Sampson, Curt. *The Eternal Summer.* Dallas: Taylor, 1992.

Sommers, Robert. *The U.S. Open.* New York: Atheneum, 1987.

Stowers, Carlton. *Men in Blue.* Dallas: Dallas Police Press, 1983.

# INDEX